SOCIETY A

Chewong family

SOCIETY AND COSMOS

Chewong of Peninsular Malaysia

With a New Preface

SIGNE HOWELL

Foreword by
RODNEY NEEDHAM

THE UNIVERSITY OF CHICAGO PRESS
Chicago and London

The University of Chicago Press, Chicago 60637
The University of Chicago Press, Ltd., London

© 1984 by Oxford University Press
© 1989 by Signe Howell
All rights reserved. Originally published 1984
University of Chicago Press edition 1989
Printed in the United States of America

98 97 96 95 94 93 92 91 90 89   5 4 3 2 1

Library of Congress Cataloging in Publication Data

Howell, Signe.
  Society and cosmos : Chewong of Peninsular Malaysia, with a new
preface / Signe Howell : foreword by Rodney Needham.
      p.   cm.
  Reprint. Originally published: Singapore; New York : Oxford
University Press, 1984.
  Bibliography: p.
  Includes index.
  1. Chewong (Malaysian people) I. Title.
DS595.2.C47H68   1989
959.5′1004992—dc20   89-34995
ISBN 0-226-35505-5 (alk. paper)   CIP

Contents

Tables

Maps

Figure

Plates

Orthography

IN the spelling system used in this book each symbol represents one phoneme. The following list gives the nearest English equivalent to the letter and symbols used.

a	pronounced like 'a' in 'flask'
æ	pronounced like 'a' in 'gas'
ai	pronounced like 'y' in 'my'
e	pronounced like 'e' in 'bed'
i	pronounced like 'ie' in 'piece'
kh	pronounced like 'ch' in German 'ach' or Scottish 'loch'
o	pronounced like 'o' in 'woman'
ò	pronounced like 'o' in 'hot'
u	pronounced like 'o' in 'who'
ö	pronounced like 'ö' in German 'öffnen'
ch	pronounced like 'ch' in 'chop'

An apostrophe after a vowel indicates a glottal stop. An acute accent over an 'e' indicates a stress on the syllable, and one over a final 'i' indicates a stress on this letter.

Foreword

LICHTENBERG once commented that forewords could be called lightning-conductors. There is no call for that kind of precaution in the case of this engrossing study of the Chewong. The construction is unusually sound, and its foundations are as steady as suitable preparations could make them. Dr Howell has fashioned a repository of knowledge that has every chance of enduring, and of withstanding critical irruptions. She has comprehensively recorded for posterity, including the descendants of the Chewong themselves, the intriguing singularity of a minor but intricate form of civilization, and she has presented the comparative science of social facts with an analytical exercise that offers a distinct technical interest and the promise of theoretical consequence.

The division of her exposition among the three main aspects of relations, consciousness, and rules, which she progressively conjoins into a perspicuous synthesis, makes for an account that procures analytical conviction and at the same time conveys a sense of the integrity of Chewong conceptions of themselves and the hidden or transformed beings that throng their world. The result is an important and professionally admirable contribution to Malaysian ethnography, and one that was certainly not foreseen when the grounds for the enterprise were first plotted.

It was at the instance of Charles Ogilvie, the pioneer ethnographer of the Chewong, that two of them entered the service of the Game Department. These were Beng and his younger brother Patong, who will both be met in Dr Howell's pages. For my part, I encountered them nearly thirty years ago, when I was afforded the opportunity to make an ethnographic excursion on the slopes of Gunong Benom, and they were attached to me as guides and trackers. At the end of the reconnaissance I took the occasion to put to them, mainly to Beng as the senior and the more experienced, some routine questions about their society. The main part of the notes that I took, during brief sessions on two successive days, were to be incorporated into an article;[1] and when, twenty-two years later, Signe Howell asked my advice about field research it was this that I gave her. Thanks to the sympathetic co-operation and fore-sight of the Jabatan Orang Asli of Malaysia, she was in due course permitted to live with the Chewong, and the outcome is the present monograph. It marks for me the culmination to a memorable acquaintance with the Chewong and, regrettably, the termination of five years of collaboration at Oxford as the author's supervisor. This work is her masterpiece, and, as will be appreciated, it is to me a source and token of much satisfaction, both personal and professional.

The book itself can be left to speak for itself, and it requires no explication or critical assessment here. What I should like merely to mention, however, is the special interest of Dr Howell's accounts of a new instance of non-hierarchical classification, the regulated management of emotion, the ingenious idea of the Chewong that each species of being has its own distinct vision of things, and, from a more analytical point of view, the governing operation of opposition, reversal, and metamorphosis as organizing principles in Chewong metaphysics. A particular credit to Dr Howell's report, also, is that it persuasively enables the reader to participate imaginatively in Chewong modes of coming to terms with their experience, and to comprehend how apposite and sufficient are the explanations provided by their tradition in the control of their natural environment and the interpretation of the quandaries of human life.

All Souls College, Oxford   RODNEY NEEDHAM
Trinity Term, 1983

---

[1] Rodney Needham, 'Ethnographic Notes on the Siwang of central Malaya', *Journal of the Malayan Branch of the Royal Asiatic Society* 29 (1956), pp. 49–69; cf. 'Some Ethnographic Notes on Semelai in Northern Pahang'. *J.M.B.R.A.S.* 47 (1974), pp. 123–9; 'Minor Reports concerning Negritos in Northern Pahang', *J.M.B.R.A.S.* 49 (1976), pp. 184–93. An application that proved especially valuable on a theoretical score was the analysis of my notes in connexion with the significance of a relative age; see the section on the 'Siwang' in 'Age, Category, and Descent', *Bijdragen tot de Taal-, Land- en Volkenkunde* 122 (1966), pp. 1–35 (at pp. 10–15); reprinted in my *Remarks and Inventions: Skeptical Essays about Kinship* (London: Tavistock Publication, 1974), chap. 2 (Siwang at pp. 82–8).

Preface, 1989

THIS book first appeared in 1984, published by Oxford University Press, and went out of print two years later. It now reemerges in paperback. There are three main reasons for my submitting it afresh. First, there is an increasing scholarly interest in the aboriginal peoples of Peninsular Malaysia, and the ready availability of comparative ethnographies is therefore important. Second, the socioeconomic condition of the aboriginals is undergoing rapid change; detailed expositions of their beliefs and practices may assist the peoples themselves in thinking about and protecting their identities, or in informing members of the dominant cultures of the country about Malaysia's minority populations. Third, a new edition in a modestly priced paperback makes the book accessible to a larger audience.

Anthropologically, the Malaysian aboriginal societies deserve close scrutiny on several counts. As our knowledge about various groups increases, the case for regarding this as a culture area becomes a strong one. Permutations and variations on similar themes appear again and again among different groups, presenting challenging theoretical problems in cross-cultural comparison. Aboriginal mythology, rituals, and practical activities all display a predominant hunting-gathering ideology—even where shifting cultivation is regularly practiced. They thus challenge "purist" definitions of hunter-gatherers. Moreover, the focus of most research so far differs importantly from that of other hunter-gatherer studies in which economic practices, settlement patterns, and ecological adaptations have been elaborated. The studies by anthropologists with fieldwork experience from the aboriginal peoples of Malaysia have—almost without exception—examined their religious ideas and practices, not their economic ones. In many cases this was forced upon the anthropologists by the empirical situations they encountered, where ideology constructed and encompassed practice. A related point is that many who write about these societies are notably preoccupied with psychological issues. A major reason for this is, I think, the phenomenon, puzzling to the Western observer, of an apparently thoroughgoing cultural commitment to peaceful interaction. This has led several anthropologists of the region (myself included) to investigate indigenous psychological categories and explanations, linking these to indigenous conceptions of personhood and human nature.

It would appear, therefore, that Malaysian aboriginal societies are prime examples of ethnographic reality dictating the theoretical concerns of the ethnographers—sometimes to the extent that they have been forced radically to change their research plans.

Rapid and serious changes affecting the lives of the aboriginals are occurring in present-day Malaysia, mainly precipitated by large-scale logging, but also by government policies. I have not been back to the Chewong since autumn 1981. None was literate and I had no means of staying in contact. However, I have recently had news of them; news that I find disturbing. During my stay they repeatedly told me how much they love the forest and have no desire to leave it in order to become settled farmers: "It is not our way to live in the same place all the time. We like to move all the time, to follow the game and the fruit. There is no point in giving us crops that need regular tending, we have no desire to care for crops. Everything we need for our life we can obtain in the forest." These and similar sentiments were regularly expressed to me—provoked mostly by efforts, no doubt well-intentioned, by agents of the government to turn them into farmers. It is therefore with profound disquiet that I hear that most of the Chewong are now living in a government-supported village near Gandah, that a major road has been built right up to the village, enabling motorized transport to penetrate into their territory, that a school has been built, that hunting is becoming rare, and that a money-based economy is rapidly becoming the norm. Since they do not have the resources, know-how, or experience to take advantage of a capitalist market economy, they will probably be placed at the bottom of the Malaysian socioeconomic ladder. In short, all they did not want appears to have occurred.

Mine are not the naive expressions of a sentimental outsider, advocating the artificial preservation of the "noble savage." I recognize that it is unlikely that the Malaysian aboriginal peoples could have continued their relatively undisturbed way of life. What is difficult to accept is that they have such minimal control over their lives and future; that they have no legal rights to their land; that they have virtually no means—financial, institutional, or legal—at their disposal for fighting for their rights; and that, unlike most other Fourth World peoples, their exposure to the dominant cultures surrounding them is of such recent and sudden origin that there have been few opportunities for them to understand what is happening and hence to formulate effective countermeasures. Aboriginal consciousness is in its infancy; it is to be hoped that it will develop in time to be effective. Because their philosophy is based on a perception of human nature (that is, aboriginal human nature, not that of outsiders) as peaceful and timid, the Chewong are particulary ill-equipped to withstand outside pressures and violations.

In the preface to the original edition of this book, I expressed the hope that one day my work would prove of interest to literate Chewong as a record of their past. Today, less than ten years since I lived amongst them, it seems that such a time may be much closer than I anticipated. Rereading the book in the light of recent ideas and research, there are sections whose interpretations and emphases I might wish to change. However, insofar as any ethnographic description is necessarily subjective, alterations in the text would be made for theoretical anthropological reasons, not in order to give a truer picture of Chewong ideology and practices. As my interpretation of what I saw and heard, I feel that the book can serve the purpose of informing young and future members of the society of their cultural heritage. I also hope that this new printing will be read by their compatriots: Malays, Chinese and Indians, and that they will come to understand that aboriginal theologies and practices are alternatives no less coherent than their own.

University of Oslo   SIGNE HOWELL
March 1989

Preface

THE research for this book was undertaken during two separate field-trips to the Chewong of Central Pahang in the Malay Peninsula. My attention was first drawn to the Malay aborigines by Professor Rodney Needham, my supervisor at Oxford University, who suggested that the Chewong in particular would prove interesting, since very little was known about them. Before going to the field, I wrote an M.Litt. thesis based on all written material available on the aboriginals, and made a comparative study of their religious systems (Howell, 1977). Between September 1977 and June 1979 I spent a total of seventeen months with the Chewong. The first twelve months were interrupted only by brief trips outside to renew my permit to live in the Krau Game Reserve. At the end of this period I returned to England for three months. This allowed me to write up and review my notes, and to identify specific lacunae in my data, and areas which would merit further investigation. My findings were presented as a doctoral thesis, submitted to the University of Oxford at the end of 1980. In the autumn of 1981, I returned for three months to the Chewong. This book is a revision of the thesis, and, whenever relevant, includes material obtained on the return visit.

The Chewong consist of two separate groups, each numbering about one hundred and thirty individuals. They practise hunting, gathering, and shifting cultivation. Although each group knows about the other, they have virtually no contact. Most of my time was spent with those who live in the east, deep in the tropical rain forest of the Krau Game Reserve. At the time of my first visit they lived in five different settlements. After two months I began to live as a member of a family at the settlement of Gambir, but visited the other four settlements fairly frequently. One month towards the end of my field-work was spent with the second branch of the Chewong, who live in three settlements near Raub. Upon my return in 1981, all my time was spent with the Eastern Chewong.

The Chewong had not been subjected to an anthropological study before I went to live with them. A British game warden who first contacted them in 1938 wrote three articles about their way of life (Ogilvie, 1940, 1948, 1949). Needham met two members of the group outside their own territory and wrote two articles based on conversations within the space of two days (Needham, 1956, 1974). Ogilvie also included a word list of the Chewong language and I took with me a copy of this. Unfortunately, however, I found it of limited use as Ogilvie's rendering (he did not speak the language) often made my attempts at pronunciation incomprehensible to the Chewong; and as I began to learn the language a number of faults emerged. I therefore soon abandoned any reference to it.

I had learnt a little Malay before entering the field and with this knowledge, supplemented by a Malay dictionary, I began to pick up vocabulary. Although most older men spoke fairly fluent Malay, their vocabulary was rather basic. They did not understand the Malay for more abstract concepts, and I had to work out the Chewong words for myself. After I had been about six months with them I understood enough to make sense out of a myth that I was told, and by the time I left I had collected about eighty myths. Some of these are included in Appendix 1. Only those which are referred to in the main text are rendered in full, but I am preparing for publication a complete collection (Howell, 1982). Despite being able to record myths and songs and participate in ordinary conversation, I can by no means claim a fluency in their language. However, I never worked with an interpreter and soon stopped using Malay.

The original research, including field-work expenses, was financed by the Social Science Research Council. I would like to take this opportunity to thank them for this assistance. I also wish to thank my college, Lady Margaret Hall, Oxford, for partial exemption from fees for my last term after the S.S.R.C. grant had expired, and for financial aid towards the preparation of the thesis. My return visit was financed from two sources. I was elected to the Susette Taylor Travelling Fellowship 1981/2, awarded by Lady Margaret Hall, Oxford University. I also received a grant from Equipe de la Recherche d'Anthropologie Sociale: Morphologie, Echanges (RCP 436 Centre National de la Recherche Scientifique) in Paris. I am grateful to both these organizations for enabling me to undertake the trip.

I am indebted to a great number of institutions and individuals in Malaysia, but can name only a few here. The Department for Aboriginal Affairs, *Jabatan Orang Asli* (abbreviated to J.O.A. whenever mentioned), supported my application to carry out research with the Chewong and gave me much help throughout my stay. I particularly wish to thank Dr Baharon Azhar Raffie'i (the Director-General) who put his resources at my disposal. The medical staff at Gombak, the hospital for Orang Asli outside Kuala Lumpur, generously kept me supplied with medicines both for my own purposes as well as for dispensing among the Chewong. Staff at the regional J.O.A. offices at Raub and Temerloh facilitated my initial visits to the Chewong in these two areas. Hassan bin Hussein, the Director of the Pahang Game Department, made every effort to ensure speedy renewals of my permit to enter the Krau Game Reserve, and the police at Temerloh similarly gave their co-operation.

Dr Hood Mohamad Salleh and his wife Maherani Mohamad Ishak were most generous and kind when I first arrived in Malaysia and helped me to obtain my research application. I am extremely grateful to them both and wish to thank them for their generosity. I benefited from their experiences of having lived with Orang Asli both from a practical as well as an intellectual point of view. Nick Hornsby allowed me to use his flat whenever I was in Kuala Lumpur. Dato Howard Biles, former Protector of Aborigines in Pahang, found time to receive me in Kota Bharu. Dr Kirk Endicott gave me much useful information about conditions in Malaysia before I embarked upon my field-work.

I am more indebted than I can ever possibly express to the Chewong, who came to accept me and treat me as one of themselves. They put up with my clumsiness and inadequacies and did everything they could to protect me from accidents and misadventure of all kinds. Among them I wish to single out Modn, who appointed herself my mother and who patiently repeated her extensive knowledge again and again so that I began to understand their concepts and ideas. I also wish to thank her husband Beng, her daughter Nyom, her son Laneg, her son-in-law Kwe, all of whom answered my questions, which no doubt they often found foolish. They began to take an interest in, and even derive pleasure from, my quest for knowledge about their customs and beliefs. Patong, Taloi, Lah, Sabod, Mod and all the children at Gambir also receive my thanks. The Chewong of Kampong Yol, and Kampong Sungai Riong are also remembered with gratitude. I hope that this work may one day prove of interest to literate generations of Chewong as a record of their past.

The computer analysis discussed in Chapter 9 was undertaken by the M.R.C. Service for Analysing Repertory Grids, Oxford University, under Dr P. Slater. I am grateful to Dr Peter Collett for his aid in setting up the programme and in analysing the results.

Rodney Needham, who initially encouraged me to carry out ethnographical research among the Chewong, was a constant support while I was in the field and later when writing the thesis. His comments were always pertinent and stimulating. My intellectual debt to him will be apparent in these pages. I was given the opportunity to spend four months in Paris during the spring of 1981 as Visiting Research Fellow with the Equipe de la Recherche d'Anthropologie Sociale: Morphologie, Echanges at Ecole des Hautes Etudes en Sciences Sociales, under the direction of Louis Dumont and Daniel de Coppet. I gave a series of seminars on the Chewong concept of the person, and I benefited enormously from the discussions. I wish to take this opportunity to thank the Equipe as a whole for the active interest that they took in my Chewong material. In particular I wish to express my gratitude to Daniel de Coppet whose enthusiasm and insight led my attention to several unexplored areas in my interpretation.

Finally, I wish to thank Desmond McNeill for the many discussions on methodology which helped me to clarify my ideas, and for his unfailing emotional support throughout.

SIGNE HOWELL

INTRODUCTION

THIS is a study of the principles which govern the way the Chewong act, based on their understanding of themselves, each other, their environment, and the supernatural. I was forced to approach my theme in a slightly unusual way because Chewong society lacks the structural features that anthropologists usually focus upon in their discussions of the collective representations of a group of people. Thus there are no lineages, no alliances, no social hierarchies or other political organization, and few elaborate rituals and ceremonies. This meant that I had to look elsewhere for 'pegs' upon which to hang my analysis and interpretation.

The absence of features commonly adduced by anthropologists in their ethnographies caused me some despondency, firstly in the field and again during the initial stages of organizing my material. But I decided that the absence of these features was in itself extraordinary and worthy of study, and began to regard this as a positive and significant feature of the society.

As writing proceeded, I came to realize that although an understanding of Chewong modes of thought could not be achieved via traditional anthropological methods, this did not mean that principles could not be found, or that the Chewong were lacking in complexity. As will become apparent, Chewong cosmology is extremely rich, their relationship with the supernatural world remarkably complex, and the degree of detail contained in their traditional knowledge, which provides the meaning to most of their actions, is considerable. From the point of view of analysis and interpretation, the Chewong material therefore raises questions of methodological as well as theoretical interest.

The Chewong are extremely shy of strangers and are unusually reserved in their dealings with one another. This did not facilitate my investigations. Since there is so little ceremony and ritual, an understanding of their values and beliefs had to be reached more from talking than from observing. Once I understood something of their modes of thought, actual practices could be seen in a new light. This meant that every activity which appeared 'normal' had to be acutely observed and questioned. It was soon apparent that Chewong behaviour was far from devoid of ritual, but symbolic significance had to be looked for in the mundane activities of cooking and eating, in their attitude to, and treatment of, animals and plants, as well as their daily behaviour in the forest. I found that there were few actions which were not in some way prescribed, with accompanying notions of repercussions from transgressions; so that in order to understand Chewong modes of thought, one must focus upon the way they act in their everyday tasks.

Only by living in very close contact with the Chewong could one discern what the prescriptions were and how they fitted in with Chewong notions about themselves, the cosmology, and the super-human beings. When I eventually lived in a house as a member of a family, doing my full share of the daily chores and, as a result, being given my equal share of all food, I was able to understand how these seemingly unimportant activities in fact constituted the main manifestation of the complex set of beliefs which govern the Chewong. By constantly being questioned about ways of doing the most ordinary task, the Chewong with whom I lived came to be aware of what they took for granted, and eventually began to take pleasure in pointing out to me how and why they did something which I had not as yet witnessed. This does not mean that I found people who could provide native exegesis of their own acts and practices. Far from it; exegesis was rarely forthcoming. But a few people began to focus upon their own practices in a new way. Throughout my stay I was acutely aware of the danger of imposing my own theoretical ideas on practices and utterances, and I tried to keep an open mind, and not to make interpretations prematurely or without asking the Chewong themselves. What one 'hears' may not always be the same as what is 'said', and it may well be that my attempts to conquer this problem did not always succeed.

Although to a certain extent what I shall be presenting represents an amalgam of what I was told by numerous different people, it should be stressed that there was a remarkable conformity in the answers that different people gave to the same questions, and in the way they explained their actions. In such small groups where every-one knows everyone else, and there is a lack of social stratification, knowledge is freely available and constantly exchanged among all members of the group. This may explain why contradictory information was received by me much less frequently than by anthropologists in other societies. Also, because there were so few Chewong, I managed to know every individual personally and I worked alongside all of them at some time or another. Throughout this book I try to let the Chewong speak for themselves. Whenever possible I refer to their own interpretations or justifications. I am aware that in many instances a more detailed and far-reaching analysis could be attempted, and I intend to develop a number of these themes in future publications, but the major purpose of this book is to present a general ethnographic introduction to the Chewong.

In writing up, I again let the material dictate my approach. Guided by what struck me as significant about Chewong social interaction and ideas, I have chosen to present my interpretation, after a general introduction, in three main parts. Each part takes as its starting point a concept which appeared to offer a significant insight into the Chewong modes of thought: relations, consciousness, and rules. Part I is concerned with a whole range of relations: between human beings on the social level, between men and women, between humans and superhumans, and between the various kinds of superhuman beings. In discussing these different relationships, the basic tenet of my investigation is that the underlying notion in all Chewong relationships is an absence of stratification. Relative status as well as competition in achievement is absent from Chewong institutions and from their representations of the numerous superhuman beings.

I next suggest that Chewong society is co-existent with their cosmology, and that it is only by considering this wider social universe that one can interpret Chewong acts and statements. The superhuman beings are involved—via the medium of the rules—in Chewong daily life, and constitute an important theory of causality. Explanations are thus internal to the system as a whole, the limits of which include the cosmology, but external to the purely human part of it. The continued existence of this wider social universe is ensured through a process of prestations and exchanges between human beings, and between humans and the various categories of superhumans. They all act upon each other, and at one level of discourse all beings who are seen to possess consciousness are thought of as 'us'. The tendency for the Chewong to see the world in relativistic terms is also introduced, whereby they explain and even excuse the behaviour of the superhuman beings with respect to humans by equating it with the behaviour of humans with respect to other species.

In Part II, the concept of relativity is further explored by examining in some detail the Chewong notion of consciousness, how they conceive of the human self and person, and the implications of their ideas in these respects for their views of other beings, both super-human and animate non-human. In Part III the implications of the numerous rules which govern Chewong behaviour both individually and socially are investigated. Finally, I include a discussion on the principles of Chewong classification, attempting to reconcile the apparent lack of common principles among the various symbolic categories or classes in the realm of the superhuman beings, as well as the numerous objects singled out as vehicles for thought.

It became apparent as I proceeded with an interpretation of my data from the three perspectives just outlined that these were more closely interlinked theoretically than at first anticipated. The concept of relations is present in the discussion on consciousness, in which the major part of my examination is an attempt to discern Chewong attitudes towards themselves in terms of their attitudes towards the rest of nature and supernature. It is also a major consideration in the discussion of the rules, since these highlight Chewong notions of causality in their relationships with each other and the superhuman beings. Indeed, it could be said that the correspondence between the social and the metaphysical is mediated through the rules. Furthermore, the absence of a stratified social organization is found to coincide with a non-hierarchical classification.

Finally, a concept emerged which, at the level of abstraction, is found to underlie many Chewong ideas and practices. This is what I have called the principle of separation, or of keeping prescribed things apart. Incorrect mixing, or failure to separate correctly, invariably leads to conflict and mishap, in some cases even to annihilation and death. So a paradox can be found at the very centre of Chewong rationality: the essential unity suggested to exist between nature and supernature; between humans and superhumans, which moulds all actors into one extended society, can only be maintained through a continued process of adhering to the principle of separation.

1

The People

THIS is a study of a small group of aboriginal people in the Malay Peninsula known as the Chewong. However it must first be shown how they relate to the other Malay aborigines. Following current official Malaysian practice the term Orang Asli will be used for the aborigines as a whole, a designation which simply means 'original people'. The 1969 Census shows that there are 53,000 Orang Asli in the Peninsula distributed throughout all eleven states with the exception of Perlis and Penang. (See Table 1.1 and Map 1 for numbers and distribution.) The traditional way of discussing the Orang Asli in the literature has been to divide them into three main groups based on ethnic and cultural criteria. Thus we have the nomadic woolly-haired Negritos; the wavy-haired Senoi who practise shifting cultivation; and the more settled straight-haired Proto-Malays. Whereas the former two speak languages belonging to the Mon−Khmer sub-family of the Austro−Asiatic group of languages, the Proto-Malays are Austronesian speakers. It is usually thought that the Senoi and the Negritos came from the North, the Proto-Malays from the South. There are, however, many problems in this classification in that several groups appear to be hybrids. Thus there are groups which are linguistically classed under one branch whilst displaying racial or social characteristics normally associated with another linguistic branch. (See Skeat and Blagden, 1906; Wilkinson, 1910; Evans, 1923, 1927; Williams-Hunt, 1952; Carey, 1976; and Benjamin, 1976, 1980; on the problems of classification and origins.)

LANGUAGE AND PREHISTORY

In recent years advances have been made in the linguistic study of the Mon−Khmer-speaking Orang Asli.

Table 1.1
The Orang Asli Population in 1969

State	Negritos	Senoi	Proto-Malays	Total
Kedah	100	—	—	100
Perak	900	15,800	—	16,700
Kelantan	650	4,100	—	4,750
Trengganu	20	180	—	200
Pahang	150	9,000	10,350	19,500
Selangor	—	1,270	3,290	4,560
Negri Sembilan	—	—	3,120	3,120
Melaka	—	—	400	400
Johor	—	—	3,670	3,670
Total	1,820	30,370	20,830	53,000

Source: Department for Aboriginal Affairs, 1969 Census (Carey, 1976: 11).

Thus Diffloth divides them into three groups: the Jahaic branch, the Senoic branch, and the Semelaic branch (1974: 482). Benjamin in a much more detailed study, and using 'entirely newly gathered data' (1976: 43) confirms Diffloth's classification, but chooses to use the term 'Aslian for the Austro—Asiatic languages of the Malay Peninsula including the immediately related languages of the Negritos of southern Thailand' (43). The Aslian speakers are further sub-divided in the following manner: 'Northern Aslian: Kensiu, Kintaq Bong, Jehai, Mendriq, Bateg Deq, Mintil, Bateg Nong, and Che' Wong; Central Aslian: Semnan, Sabum, Lanoh Jengjeng, Lanoh Yir, Temiar, Semai I and II, and Jah Hut; Southern Aslian: Mah Meri, Semaq Beri, Semelai, and Temoq.' (Benjamin, 1976: 57.)

The Northern Aslian speakers correspond to the Negrito ethnic type, with the exception of the Che' Wong (my Chewong), and the Central and Southern Aslian speakers to the Senoi physical type, with the exception of Semnan, Sabum, Lanoh Jengjeng, and Lanoh Yir, all of whom are Negritos. Benjamin arrived at his classification scheme through a 'cognacy percentage matrix of vocabulary'. The Northern Aslian language group, of which the Che' Wong is a member, proves more recalcitrant to sub-grouping on this basis than do the Central and Southern ones, and Benjamin warns that 'only limited conclusions can be drawn from simple inspection' (60).

Benjamin is puzzled by the Che' Wong whom he finds to be more closely related to the Kensiu, who live more than 200 miles away, than they are to their immediate neighbours, and concludes that

Map 1
Malay Peninsula: Distribution of Aslian Languages (Approximate)

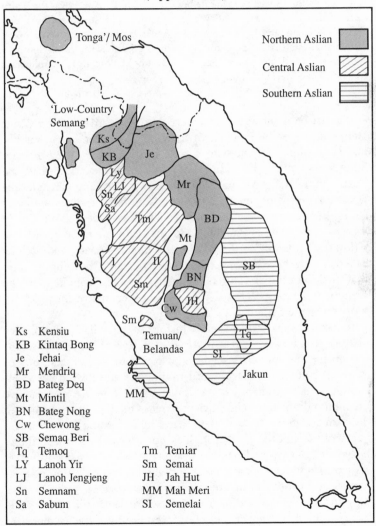

Ks	Kensiu
KB	Kintaq Bong
Je	Jehai
Mr	Mendriq
BD	Bateg Deq
Mt	Mintil
BN	Bateg Nong
Cw	Chewong
SB	Semaq Beri
Tq	Temoq
LY	Lanoh Yir
LJ	Lanoh Jengjeng
Sn	Semnam
Sa	Sabum

Tm	Temiar
Sm	Semai
JH	Jah Hut
MM	Mah Meri
SI	Semelai

close physical proximity does not necessarily result in contiguous languages (61). Later in the same paper he says:

The Che' Wong language shows a puzzling loan rate of 4% with Kensiu despite the distance which separates them. Assuming this figure to be correct, it could mean that during the early stages of Proto-Northern Aslian, Che' Wong could then have retained contact with Kensiu for long enough to cause a low but noticeable loan rate between them. Perhaps it was the return north of Jehai that spurred Che' Wong to move away eastwards. Che' Wong shows high loan rates with all Southern Aslian languages except Mah Meri, which suggests that its ancestors came into contact with Proto-Southern Aslian speakers (Semaq Beri—Semelai—Temoq) before the latter split apart but after Mah Meri had split away.

(Benjamin, 1976: 78.)

It must be mentioned, however, that the word list upon which Benjamin based his analysis of the Che' Wong language was obtained through interviewing a man by the name of Yasih from Sungei Pasu, north of Raub, Pahang, whom he met at Gombak, the hospital for Orang Asli near Kuala Lumpur. Benjamin includes the vocabulary thus obtained. This man came from a village which is some distance from the traditional Chewong habitat, and is one in which many Temuan and Jah Hut live and intermarry with the Chewong. It is one of three villages which comprise what will be called, for the sake of convenience, the Western Chewong. I found that their vocabulary differs in many respects from that of the Eastern Chewong. They have also adopted many more Malay words into their language.

Regarding the origin and early history of the Aslian peoples, very little is yet known. This is partly due to lack of historical records within the societies themselves, and partly to lack of examples of material culture. Archaeological findings in this area are few, although recent excavations on the mainland of South-East Asia have brought to light extremely ancient remains of civilization, including decorated pottery as well as bronze artefacts some five thousand years old (Diffloth, 1978: 13). It is not known who made these, however, and no archaeological artefacts have been identified as Aslian. They have been hunters and gatherers, or shifting cultivators, for centuries and are not known to have made any metal works or pottery. Their traditional utensils were, and still are in some groups, chiefly made out of organic forest produce. Even if there had been more durable goods, physical circumstances would render excavations virtually impossible. Their habitat is the primary tropical rain forest.

Failing to find any of the traditional tools used for dating the prehistory of peoples, Benjamin makes tentative suggestions regarding the chronology of the arrival and dispersal of the Aslians in the Malay Peninsula, based on glotto-chronological calculations performed on the cognacy rates. He suggests that originally all Proto-Aslians were hunters and gatherers, and that 'their language was almost certainly heterogeneous even before they entered the Peninsula' (83). He postulates that whereas the Northern Aslians remained nomads, the Central and Southern ones started practising a rudimentary form of agriculture 'sometime between 6610 and 6410 B(efore) P(resent)'; and that by 5970 B.P. northerners and southerners were speaking distinct dialects while the central people retained linguistic continuity with their neighbours both to the North and to the South (83). Finally he suggests that, as far as the Che' Wong are concerned, the 'Proto-Northern Aslians divided into blocks so that Proto-Che' Wong began to separate off to the east some time after 3900 B.P.' (84).

According to Benjamin's analysis, the Che' Wong appear to be the 'odd man out'. They are the only non-Negrito Orang Asli who speak a language belonging to the Northern Aslian branch, which (from census figures) account for the languages of 85 per cent of the total Negrito population. Maybe a more correct sample of their vocabulary would help in the analysis. Lacking qualifications to conduct a comparative linguistic analysis, I am unable to throw any light on the question, and for the moment the 'Che' Wong' must remain something of an enigma as regards their proper place on the linguistic and ethnic map of the Peninsula.

EARLIER SOURCES

Very little was known about the Chewong before I went to live with them. References were made by Schebesta and Evans to aborigines living near Gunong Benom[1] and on Sungei Lompat,[2] in Central Pahang, but neither of them managed to contact these people. It was not until Mr C. S. Ogilvie, a British game warden, went on an inspection tour of the Krau Game Reserve in 1938 that the group later known as the Che' Wông was contacted—or rather that part of

[1] *Gunong* is the Malay word for 'mountain'.
[2] *Sungei* is the Malay word for 'river'.

the Chewong speakers who live in the Krau Game Reserve, and who for present purposes will be referred to as the Eastern Chewong. The Krau Game Reserve was established by the British in 1926, and it covers the area extending, roughly, from Bukit Tapah[1] in the south to Gunong Tungku in the north, and from Gunong Benom in the west to where the Krau and Lompat rivers meet in the east. (See Map 2.) The southern half of this area is the traditional habitat of the Eastern Chewong, whereas the northern half is the habitat of the Jah Hut. The Western Chewong live in the Ulu Dong area and just north and south of Kampong Dong,[2] between Raub and Kuala Lipis. Ogilvie came to know some of the Eastern Chewong quite well over the next fifteen years and he published three brief articles about them (Ogilvie, 1940, 1948, and 1949) including a rudimentary word list. According to the Chewong who knew him best, Ogilvie never learnt their language, and always conversed with them in Malay. Because his tours of duty were necessarily brief, and he was always accompanied by Malays, Ogilvie never saw the Chewong sing and drum, nor did he witness any of their ritual acts or hear any of their myths or stories. This is clear from his articles which give virtually no information on their religious system. But he is remembered with much affection by those who had most to do with him, particularly by Beng and Patong, who are still alive today.

Needham met Beng and Patong in 1955 at Kuala Tahan on the Tembeling River where they had gone to work for Ogilvie for a couple of years, and wrote an article about Chewong society based on a two days' interview (Needham, 1956). Diffloth spent one night at Kuala Gandah, the southernmost settlement of the Game Reserve in 1968 or 1969 in order to obtain his own word list. Finally, Benjamin interviewed the man from Sungei Pasu as already described, but he never went to a Chewong settlement. These four encounters constitute the total dealings that the Chewong have had with outsiders with ethnographic interests. During the Emergency (1948–60) they had brief contacts with British soldiers and officials.

NAME OF THE GROUP

At this point a brief discussion on the group's name must be included, as this has been the subject of some uncertainty. The

[1] *Bukit* is the Malay word for 'hill'.

[2] *Kampong* is the Malay word for 'village'. I shall be using the Malay designations whenever referring to geographical locations.

matter has been discussed in detail elsewhere (Howell, 1981b) so here only a summary of the main points will be given.

The people are referred to in the literature by the following names: Maroi, Jo-Ben (also Cho-Ben, So-Ben, and Jelbeng), Kleb, Che Wông (Che' Wong, Che Wong), and Siwang. The earliest reference to them is made by Evans. On two trips made to the neighbouring Jah Hut he was told of the existence of other groups of aborigines who lived deep inside the jungle. One of these was called the Maroi, the other (a much wilder group) was known as So-Ben (Jo-Ben or Cho-Ben depending on the informant). Despite several attempts, Evans failed to contact either group (Evans, 1927: 42).

Maroi is the name of the father of Beng and Patong whom Ogilvie met before the war when he was a very old man and the group's 'leader' (Ogilvie, 1949: 12). He probably acted as spokesman whenever they emerged from the jungle to trade their produce for knives, salt, cloth, and tobacco, and the group became known as 'Maroi's people' (Orang Maroi) by the Malays and Jah Hut with whom they came into contact.

The Jelbeng, according to Ogilvie's informants as well as mine, are a totally different group of people who fled from the advances of the Malays in such haste that they took nothing with them. They fled high up on Gunong Benom where they managed to make fire by striking two stones together, but they had no knives and no clothes and they existed very precariously. They did not dare to venture forth in search of any goods, but one day Maroi met four of their kind near Ulu Lompat. He was still a young man then (c. 1880–90) and he gave them a piece of steel to make fire, two knives, and an iron digging stick. He also offered them some salt, but this they refused as they said it would cause them to swell. After this encounter the Jelbeng left for the heights of Gunong Benom and have not been seen since. Most Chewong were of the opinion that they have all been eaten by tigers; but see further implications of the Jelbeng story in Howell, 1981b.

Schebesta in his first book about the Malay Negritos mentions some groups who are separated from the main stock. These are 'the Batek, Nogn, Kleb, Temo (about 100) in central and eastern Pahang' (1974: 16). He has nothing to say about the Kleb and the Temo, never having visited either group, but on a map where he gives the locations of all the Negrito groups, we find that the Kleb are located in two separate areas: south and north-east of Raub. This is very close to where the two groups of Chewong are found today, and when we realize that the Chewong of Kampong Yol in the Ulu Dong district are referred to as Bi Kled (Kled People), it seems likely that these are the Kleb mentioned by Schebesta. The remaining Western Chewong, however, denied that they were Bi Kled, saying that Kled was an area near Gunong Pallas where the people at Yol, but not themselves, used to live a long time before. This was later confirmed by the Eastern Chewong. They were acquainted with the area known as Kled, but said that they were not Bi Kled because they had left Gunong Pallas for good. Their neighbours, the Jah Hut, refer to them by the name Jah Klet (Klet People) and do not appear to distinguish between the Eastern and the Western groups (Couillard, 1980: 5).

We now turn to the question of Che Wông versus Siwang. Ogilvie writes in his first article of 'the Che Wông, for it is such they style themselves' (1940: 22; 1949: 12). Needham disagrees with this, and relates that Beng said that the name was not 'Che Wong' and repeatedly gave it in a way that can best be rendered as 'Siwang' (Needham, 1956: 50). The Department for Aboriginal Affairs refers to them in their statistics as Che Wong. For a long time after my arrival I was unhappy about the group name, having received affirmative answers to both renderings. Finally Beng told me the following story: when Ogilvie was working for the Pahang Game Department, he was due to make his first visit to the Krau Game Reserve. At the time there was a Malay ranger living at Kuala Gandah just inside the southern boundary of the Reserve, about 6 miles north-west of Kampong Bolok (the last Malay village). Kuala Gandah was also an Orang Asli settlement. Ogilvie, knowing about the Orang Asli, asked a Malay (an employee of the Game Department at Temerloh) what the name of this group was. Apparently the man misunderstood the question, and thinking that Ogilvie wanted to know the name of the ranger, told him this was Siwang. Ogilvie, who was slightly deaf, took this to be Che Wông, and upon first meeting the Orang Asli in question referred to them as such. The people themselves, though at first puzzled, were much too polite to correct him, preferring to interpret Ogilvie's usage of 'Che Wông' as a desire on his part to avoid calling them Sakai,[1] a term that they were fully aware had derogatory connotations in common Malay usage.

---

[1] *Sakai* was the term commonly used by the Malays and the British until it was replaced by *orang asli*. It means 'slave or dependant', and in the case of the Malays was used (and in some cases still is) as a term of abuse.

At first this story seemed hard to believe, but after checking with the Game Department at Temerloh I was told that there was indeed a Siwang bin Ahmat who had worked as a ranger at Kuala Gandah before the war. Having also met his widow who still lives at Kampong Bolok, it would seem that the problem is finally solved.

Today nobody except Beng remembers the story of the origin of their name, though several of the older people said that the name was given them by 'white people' (*bi puteh*). No one could say what their original or real name is or was. 'We are forest people,' (*bi brete*) they would always reply whenever questioned further about the Chewong name. Alternatively, they would say that they were 'digging people' (*bi bai*) thus opposing themselves to the Malays who cultivate rice. Digging here could refer to wild tubers as well as to tapioca.

Whenever referring to themselves, as distinct from other Orang Asli, they would never use a name for their own group, but simply say 'us', *he*, or 'people us', *bi he*. After I had lived with them for some time and had begun to get some command of their language, adults would tell children who were frightened of me, 'but she is not *gob*, (Malay), she is one of us (*bi he*) she is a forest woman (*kòkn brete*). *Gob* is a term used by all the Orang Asli to refer either to people who are not Orang Asli, regardless of what they are, or more specifically to Malays only.

The common language and customs, together with kin relationships, form the boundary of the group, and 'us' is sufficient distinction from 'them', the outsiders. In small groups where everyone knows everyone else, and is indeed related to everyone, there is no need for a group name for the members. Outsiders, on the other hand, are of different kinds and therefore need to be named—as are individual members of the group itself. Thus Malays are known as *gob*, Chinese as *bi cina*, and all the other Orang Asli in general as *bi brete*, or *bi bai*. Each Orang Asli group other than themselves is then given an individual group name. This name is not necessarily that by which the group in question identifies itself to the outside world. The neighbouring Temuan, for instance, are known to the Chewong as *bi Nyep*, because their word for 'finished' is *nyep* and they are said to use this often.

Today, all members of the people under discussion, both those living in the Krau Game Reserve and those in the Raub District, refer to themselves as Chewong when dealing with outsiders. Since anthropologists need to fix names to different groups of people in order to be able to discuss their cultures, I am proposing to adopt the name Chewong—spelt as one word as there is no reason to make it into two. It must be stressed once more that this name is never used by the people among themselves.

A final point needs to be made in this connection. The Chewong sometimes apply blanket terms to members of their own group. This is when they refer as a whole to the people of a different settlement. Thus those from the Gambir settlement might say that the Sentao people, *bi Sentao*, have not yet started clearing a new swidden, or that the Gandah people, *bi Gandah*, sell a lot of rattan. This usage might lead the casual observer erroneously to conclude that the peoples thus referred to would not be other settlements of the same group, but totally different groups with separate linguistic and cultural identities.

PHYSICAL TYPE

The Chewong belong to the so-called Senoi physical type. The word *senoi* is taken from the Temiar language, and it merely means 'people', or 'mankind' (Carey, 1976: 17). The Senoi differ from the Negritos in so far as their skin is lighter—a warm, dark brown—and their hair wavy rather than frizzy. (See Skeat and Blagden, 1906 and Williams-Hunt, 1948 for further information.) Clearly not all members of a tribe are typical in appearance, and among the Chewong some people have virtually straight hair, others almost frizzy, but the majority have wavy, or curly hair. Their features are clear-cut and regular, with high cheekbones, and their eyes do not have the Mongoloid slit.

By Western standards they are short, the women rarely exceeding 5ft. and the men 5 ft. 4 in. They are, however, slightly taller than the Negritos (Skeat and Blagden, 1906: 35). Their bodies are slim and supple and never run to fat. In spite of their small stature they are extremely strong. Both men and women can carry heavy loads for many hours while trekking through the forest. Although they insist that they do not intermarry with the Negritos (Needham, 1956: 62), a few of the Chewong show traces of Negrito characteristics. The people at Kampong Yol said that a Batek Nong man had married one of their women and lived with them for many years until he died about ten years ago, and it is likely that the same happened to the Eastern Chewong.

LOCATION AND HABITAT

During my first stay with the Eastern Chewong, they were distributed in six different settlements. The actual numbers and locations of settlements may vary, but they appear to clear fields in the same general areas. At that time there were settlements at Ngang I, Ngang II, (Kuala) Gandah, (Kuala) Sentao, Gambir, and Pyapoz. After I had lived with the people of Gambir for about a year, they began to clear a new field at Kenem, one hour's walk away.

When I returned after an absence of two years, the Gambir and the Pyapoz settlements had been abandoned, and the inhabitants from both places had moved to Kenem. Upon my return a fission was in process as some of the Kenem people were clearing a new field at Chinless, an hour and a half's walk away to the east. Sentao had been abandoned in favour of Sempoh and Te Kayo, halfway between Sentao and Gandah. The people at Gandah had crossed the Teris River and cleared new fields there. Three families from Ngang II had moved to Henka, between Ngang and Gandah. Ngang I was abandoned, some of the families having moved to Bes, others joining the remainder of Ngang II in their move down-river. From these changes it is clear that Chewong population is in constant flux; both in terms of actual location as well as the constitution of actual membership of each settlement.

Settlements usually take their name from the nearby river, but in the case of Pyapoz it is from a species of fruit tree. There are several other areas where the Chewong had settlements in the past, and to which they may well return in the future. The most commonly mentioned are Patong, Ulu Sentao, Betong near the headwater of Sungei Pian, and another north of Pyapoz. (See Map 2 for locations of past and present settlements.)

The Western Chewong today live in three settlements in the area between Raub and Kuala Lipis, namely, Kampong Yol, Kampong Sungei Riong, and Kampong Susup (See Map 2). Those at Sungei Riong insist that this same area has been inhabited by them since a long time ago (*yamen dui*). I was unable to visit those at Kampong Susup but they are said to be an offshoot of Kampong Sungei Riong. The people at Kampong Yol, while assuring me that they had lived in the same spot for several generations, said that they used to live at Kleb on Gunong Pallas. These three settlements are today less than an hour's walk from a built-up road, and Malay farms are very close. The Western Chewong are much more mixed than the Eastern ones,

Map 2
The Chewong Area

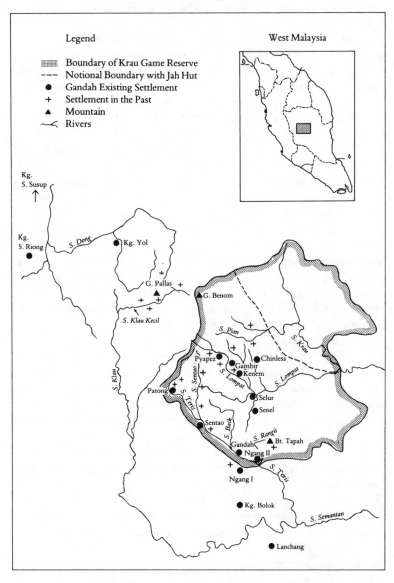

marriages having taken place with Temuan and Jah Hut for some time. The common language used by all permanent inhabitants was 'Chewong'.

The Eastern and Western groups know about each other, but whereas there is constant social intercourse among all members of each area there is virtually none between the separate areas. Beng visited the Dong people with Ogilvie just after the war and told me that the people there were 'close', i.e., related. For instance he had met a younger brother of his father, and a younger sister of his mother-in-law. Apart from Beng the only other Eastern Chewong to have visited the Western group is Al, who was married to a woman from Kampong Yol for some years. He returned alone to Sentao during my stay and had no plans ever to go back. The ex-wife had once been with her husband to Gandah, and one man from Kampong Yol had gone to Gandah and Sentao when he was still a boy. Neither group appears to want to know much about the other, and though a shortage of marriageable women exists at present in the East, the young men regard going to the Western Chewong in search of wives as no more or less desirable than marriage to the neighbouring Temuan or Jah Hut.

The Eastern Chewong, however, used to have settlements in a larger area than they do today. They cleared fields high up on Gunong Pallas and on the Kelau Kechil River. When Chinese and Malays began to make plantations in that district, however, the Chewong left. Beng was born on Gunong Pallas, and according to Ogilvie there were still Chewong there in the 1940s (Ogilvie, 1949: 16). It would appear that the split between the Eastern and Western Chewong is of fairly recent origin, and that in the not too distant past the movements of people were in this larger area. Whereas the Western Chewong were content to live in close proximity to Chinese and Malays, the Eastern ones did what the Orang Asli have generally done when more powerful outsiders encroach upon their territory—they withdrew deeper into the forest.

During the early part of the Emergency, the Eastern Chewong were moved by the newly established Department for Aboriginal Affairs to a settlement at Bukit Rumput just north of where Kampong Bolok is today. This was part of the security measures undertaken by the British in the central forest area of the Peninsula to prevent the Orang Asli from providing food to the communist insurgents hiding in the jungle. In about 1953 the Chewong were moved and were given much aid by the Department in the form of rice, tobacco, cloth, sugar, etc., and they cleared fields and planted tapioca. Despite their obvious delight at receiving all these 'presents', the Chewong were not happy living at Bukit Rumput and by about 1956 they had all returned to the deep forest. (Biles, personal communication.) They said it was frightening to live so close to *gob*, and that several families, unknown to the authorities, refused to move and continued to live in the jungle throughout this period.

Kampong Bolok is the last Malay village before the forest begins, and it is from here that one enters Chewong territory. Kampong Bolok lies about 6 miles north of Lanchang which is on the main Kuala Lumpur to Kuantan road. A dirt road was built in 1962 to Kampong Bolok and a shared 'taxi' service operates between it and Lanchang. It is at Lanchang, which consists of a few small shops along both sides of the main road, that the Chewong sell their cane (*seg*).

ECOLOGY AND ECONOMY

In June 1979 the Eastern Chewong population totalled 131 persons. (See Howell, 1981b for a detailed breakdown of this figure.) Two years later, 7 people had died and 11 babies had been born. The Western Chewong proved more difficult to count due to much intermarriage with other groups as well as to frequent movement of settlement, often to other ethnic groups, but I estimated that about 115 persons in this area may be classified as Chewong.

The Eastern Chewong live deep inside the tropical rain forest that covers north-central Malaysia. In their own parlance they are forest people (*bi brete*), and it is only once they have put a large expanse of primary forest between themselves and the rest of the world that they feel happy and secure. Because they live in a game reserve, no one may enter without a special permit from the Game Department. Logging has not affected them as it has the lives of many other Orang Asli groups. They do not seek employment in the outside world, and rely for cash exclusively upon the sale of cane and agila wood (*taba*). In the old days they also sold other forest produce to Malay peasants, such as plaited attap leaves for use as roofs, backbaskets made out of cane, and woven trays used for winnowing. They might also help in the rice harvest in return for a little rice or some plantains. Today two men, both living at Gandah, are employed as labourers by the Game Department, but this work does not take them out of the forest except for a very occasional visit to Temerloh. The Game Department maintains a hut at Gandah for their employees on their rare tours of duty. The Chewong labourers' job is to look after the hut and the surrounding land, and to act as guides. Although aware of the hospital for Orang Asli at Gombak, the Chewong are unwilling to go there. Only one woman still living has ever been, but two men apparently went there in the past. They are frightened of the outside world and do not want to leave their own kind even if it means suffering and death. Thus the Chewong carry on their traditional way of life largely untouched by outside influences. The forest and their own labour within it provides them with virtually all their necessities.

The tropical rain forest of the Malay Peninsula is characterized by enormous trees, in many cases reaching a height of 160 ft., and often with large buttresses. The tree tops form a canopy that cuts out all direct sunlight on the ground. Although the trees are so large and powerful, their roots tend to be shallow and they are easily toppled over in heavy storms. The Chewong are extremely frightened of being hit by falling trees and always take account of surrounding trees whenever they are making a camp in the forest. Existing paths frequently have to be changed owing to trees falling across them.

The undergrowth is in parts fairly dense. Numerous species of plants and creepers have spikes and thorns which make progress difficult. Paths have to be cut through the growth and continually kept open, as growth is rapid. The whole area is criss-crossed by rivers, none of which is too large to cross either by wading or by balancing on a tree trunk. Except for times when the weather has been dry for an extended period of time, the forest bed is damp and exudes a smell of decaying plant matter. Following a heavy downpour, the rivers flood, the paths become slippery, and leeches abound.

The Chewong do not usually travel on the rivers, although they know how to tie together trunks of bamboo in order to make a raft. These are mostly used for playing with, or occasionally for crossing a river. During my stay, they built rafts on two occasions to travel down the Lompat River to Kuala Lompat, and on to Kuala Krau, to ferry large quantities of unprepared canes (seg manao) which were too heavy to carry over such a distance.

Generally, however, the Chewong mode of transport is walking. The main paths between the settlements are kept clear by fairly frequent travelling. To walk from Kampong Bolok to Ngang I takes about two hours, with a further half hour to Gandah. Gandah and Ngang II are about twenty minutes apart, and visits between these two settlements take place several times a day. It takes between four and six hours to reach Sentao from Gandah. The trip to Gambir, Pyapoz, Kenem, and Chinless involves spending a night in the forest. This is always done in the same spot, where lean-tos are maintained permanently. On the way to Gambir one usually sleeps at Senel or Selur. The same applies to journeys between Pyapoz and Gandah. Pyapoz lies about half an hour's hard climb up from Gambir in the foothills of Gunong Benom. These two settlements are usually referred to as Latah Tujuh (seven waterfalls), after the large waterfall of that name in the Lompat River half an hour away. There is also a path from Latah Tujuh to Sentao which takes about six hours to traverse.

When setting out on a long trip, the Chewong always leave after breakfast at around 7 a.m. They walk until early afternoon when they stop and make camp. This means finding all materials needed to erect lean-tos: attap leaves for the roof, saplings for the main platform and roof supports, and bamboos to split and place across the floor beams. Alternatively, very large leaves may be used instead of attap for the roof, and bark instead of the split bamboo floor. Everybody takes part in the collecting and construction. Each couple builds one for themselves and· their small children, and the adolescents of each sex build for themselves. The men then go off with their blowpipes (blau) in search of the evening meal, and the women try their luck at fishing. They also gather firewood, carry water, and search for wild tubers. The camp is always made next to a river.

It rarely rains for a whole day in the forest, and showers are usually brief, occurring mainly in the afternoon. During my stay, the period from November to February—which is the main monsoon time in the Peninsula—was no wetter, or drier, than the rest of the year. In fact there is no noticeable seasonal change in the climate in this part of the forest. The Chewong do not divide the year into rainy and dry season, but they know that there is a certain time each year when the fruit trees blossom (mainly in March and April) and when the fruit is ripe (July, August and September). There is, as far as I could ascertain, no special time of the year set aside for clearing a new field or planting.

The fauna of the forest is very rich. The larger mammals are tigers, leopards, elephants, bears, tapirs, seladang, deer of various sorts, and wild pigs. Of these, only deer and pigs are hunted. There are three species of leaf monkeys, stump- and long-tailed macaques, gibbon and siamang, numerous species of squirrels, birds, bats, as well as the flying lemur, squirrel, and fox, and the binturong. All the tree dwellers are hunted by blowpipe and poisoned darts. Several species of monitor lizards, porcupines, forest rats, and tortoises are hunted with dogs and spears; as are the pigs and deer. Pigs and porcupines, both of which are attracted by the tapioca in the fields, are also killed by traps placed around the circumference of the field. These traps are made of a very hard type of bamboo which is fashioned into a sharp point, tied with cane on a spring principle, so that when released the bamboo spears the flank of the animal. String, or loop, traps are also placed in the forest for guinea-fowl.

Fishing is done by hook and line, home-made spear guns, and traps made out of cane. Apart from fish there are also large turtles in the rivers and these are dug out and killed. During my stay at Latah Tujuh some form of meat was brought to the settlement on average every three days. Hardly a day went by without some fish being caught.

Apart from hunting, the Chewong forage for numerous species of edible tubers, wild mushroom, and various varieties of vegetables, nuts, and fruit. Today they are also shifting cultivators. Tapioca (*galeh*) is the staple, and this they cultivate by the slash and burn method, moving field and habitat once every two to four years. A new small field may be cleared annually as an extension to the existing one, but once this reaches a certain size they prefer to move altogether and start afresh, rather than having to go a long distance to collect their crop. Although the main effort of cultivation goes into the planting of tapioca, which is grated and baked in bamboo cylinders into a sort of bread, the Chewong also plant plantains and bananas, sweet potatoes, papayas, sugar-cane, and chillies. When a new field is first cleared they may plant hill-rice and maize among the tapioca plants, but the yield is very small and consumed immediately upon harvesting. Tobacco is planted in clearings in the forest caused by the collapse of a large tree. According to Ogilvie, the Chewong would not survive if they did not spend a large proportion of their time in foraging, and he tells us about 'their more nomadic days' (1949: 14). This is no longer the case. The tapioca fields are large enough to support the inhabitants of the settlements, except in the case of Gandah where the people sell enough cane to enable them to eat rice as their staple. This is a very recent phenomenon, however. From the accounts of older people, the Chewong were not as sedentary, even fifty years ago, as they are now. Everybody still knows how to look for the various wild tubers. This is not an easy task as the thin stems that indicate their presence look to the outsider identical to others that can be seen everywhere. People still search for them, but more in order to have some variety in the diet than because it is needed for survival. They are, however, proud of their ability to survive from the forest alone, and I was told many times how it would not matter to them if another war should come about. During the last war the Chewong did not go to the shops for cloth, rice, and salt, and they returned to making bark cloth (Ogilvie, 1949: 13).

They told me that due to the heavy bombing of the deep forest areas both during the war and the Emergency, they had to abandon their clearings as these were prime targets. At such time they depended exclusively on hunting and gathering, taking to a nomadic way of life. 'We know how to dig and hunt, we will never die from a hungry stomach,' they kept saying, usually adding that this was not the case with their Jah Hut neighbours who 'are just like *gob*'. The Jah Hut have in fact been settled farmers for a long time, and pride themselves on this fact. (Couillard, personal communication.)

During the fruit season many people still leave their settlements in order to move closer to a large durian (*towæng*), or *payong*[1] tree; the fruit of both becoming the staple (*ratn*). Lean-tos are erected near by and they live there as long as the fruit lasts.

There are no domestic animals except dogs which are used for hunting. During my first stay they kept a few chickens originally given them by the J.O.A. These, however, were reared exclusively for selling. Upon my return, all the chickens had disappeared, and no efforts were made to acquire new ones.

In order to obtain goods from the shops, the Chewong gather and sell cane and agila wood. Money is needed to buy bush knives, axe heads, spear heads, salt, cloth, kerosene for their lamps, and, whenever some is left over, tobacco, rice, and torches.

The Western Chewong on the other hand present a very different picture. They have abandoned this traditional way of life, and have become settled, farming the same piece of land and keeping goats and cows given to them by the J.O.A. They do not go into the forest in search of fruit or tubers, and the only blowpipe I saw was com-

---

[1] The *payong* tree (*pangium edule*) bears fruit the size of a large coconut. The yellow flesh is boiled and eaten, and the twenty to thirty nuts, the size of Brazil nuts, are peeled, soaked in the river to shed the poison (see Gimlette, 1971) and eaten either grated or whole. They are often mixed in a meat stew.

pletely broken. A few of the men have guns, however, and the occasional pig and monkey or monitor lizard is shot with this. The people, and especially the women, express a deep fear of entering the jungle. Most of the children go to school at least for a few years, and the adults go out to work for local Chinese or Malays, clearing new fields, harvesting, or tapping rubber, whenever they need some cash. A large proportion of the food they eat is bought, and when I was there most of the land lay fallow. The diet of the Western Chewong was noticeably inferior to that of the Eastern ones.

DRESS, ARTEFACTS, AND HOUSING

The traditional Chewong clothing consists of loincloth, made out of the bark of the dòg tree (*Antiaris toxicaria*) which is poisonous and is also used to prepare the dart poison. The female version is called *wed* while the male one is called *ti*. The bark is hammered out on a tree-trunk with a specially made wooden club (*poal*) into a long, narrow piece. It is then soaked in the river for several days to make it supple and to remove the poison.

The women keep it in place with twisted black string, *tali gal*, which is wound several times around the hips. The bark cloth is folded over at the back, brought between the legs, under the string in front and then either pulled back over the hip along the string, or left to fall down to cover the front as an apron before being pulled back. The men do not use the strings. They tie the cloth around the waist, between the legs, and always leave the end hanging down in front. Today they do not make the barkcloth anymore, but use cotton cloth bought in the shops. The men still wear the cloth in the traditional manner (they also wear shorts), and the women use an old piece of a sarong to make the loincloth. A sarong is often worn on top of the loincloth and the strings. Barkcloth was formerly used as a sling for carrying babies in, tied either on the front or on the back of the parent; and for blankets. Nowadays, the sarong is used to carry their babies as well as to sleep in.

Women wear a long piece of cane called *sega* which is wound around their waists six to eight times and then tied together. It has several designs incised upon it representing butterflies, snakes, worms, and leaves which are used in healing rites and childbirth. It is protective against attack by non-human beings. Some people also wear rings made of a polished black fungus 'rhizomorph' around their necks and wrists (Ogilvie, 1949: 14). This is said to protect against dangers inherent in thunderstorms. Small children wear a piece of wild ginger (*bunglei*) tied to a string around their necks. The smell of this is said to be offensive to certain species of superhuman beings (*bas*) who might otherwise cause illness in small children. In the old days all adult men always wore a headband (*chin koyi*) made of plaited leaves or twined fibres; and a bandolier (*samaden*) also made of leaves, which crossed their chests and backs and was tied around their waists. These days only the shaman wears such ornaments during a healing seance (*nöpoh*). Similarly, women would always keep various kinds of leaves (*bodn*) in their loincloths, and flowers in their hair because of their sweet-smelling properties. They still do so, but not all the time. They do not tattoo themselves, but frequently they print patterns onto their face and body by covering leaves with the sap of the *pre* tree and pressing these on to the skin leaving a dark brown design. All the women, however, have pierced ears into which flowers and pieces of wood are inserted. According to Ogilvie, ear-piercing was not practised (14), but I was told that they have always done so, and old women insist that they had had their ears pierced while young. The women wear their hair in a bun (*sangol*) at the back, but the men leave it hanging loose. Unlike the Negritos, the Chewong do not make or wear combs in the hair.

Apart from the artefacts just mentioned, the Chewong make backbaskets of plaited cane (*lugn*), baskets for pressing out the moisture of the grated tapioca, also made out of cane (*kampe*), sleeping mats (*nöz*), and tobacco pouches (*sarog macau*), and other small containers of pandanus leaves. These are all plain and functional.

Bamboo cylinders were formerly used for carrying water and for cooking. These they still use when travelling, but today they have saucepans in their houses. The tapioca bread is always baked in bamboo, and on ritual occasions only bamboo may be used for all purposes. Various paraphernalia will be described later in connection with the ritual concerned, but it is interesting to note that on important or dangerous occasions, a return is made to traditional materials.

The blowpipes (*blau*) are about 8 ft. long and consist of two cylinders of bamboo, one inside the other, of about 1 in. in diameter. They may be of one piece each, or they may be spliced together. The mouthpiece is of carved wood, and the tip is reinforced by thin lengths of cane twined round it for about 4 or 5 in. and secured by melted wax. The quiver (*lug*) is a bamboo cylinder with a domed cap of woven cane. The dart (*tenlaig*) is kept in individual narrow bamboo containers inside the quiver. The darts are approximately 12 in. long, with a small notch at the pointed end which then breaks off when an animal is hit. The other end has a cone of light wood. The Chewong told me that they used to make bows and arrows (*lòdd*) and that in the old days this was the only hunting weapon, the blowpipe being of more recent origin. The arrow tips, often the sharpened bone of a lower arm of a siamang, were coated with the same poisonous solution (*dòg*) which they today apply to their dart heads. These are no longer in use.

Traditionally, Chewong houses are the lean-tos already described, although they are building more solid structures now. These stand on poles about 4 to 6 ft. off the ground, and have pointed roofs which are covered by thick thatch made out of attap leaves. Usually the roof meets the floor, but some people are beginning to make walls out of large pieces of bark. All beams and joints are tied together with cane. There is a ladder leading to the entrance which is a simple opening. The fireplace is built by heaping sand onto large leaves on the split bamboo floor, and is sometimes situated on a lower level than the main house. Some people are constantly adding to and changing their houses, whereas others are satisfied to live in simple lean-tos.

KINSHIP AND MARRIAGE

It is not my intention to discuss the Chewong kinship system in any detail. I plan to do so elsewhere at a later stage. For the moment I shall confine myself to giving an outline of the main principles involved, and start by noting that, by virtue of their small population, everyone is closely related to everyone else. Among the Chewong, kin relationships are reckoned cognatically with a bilateral classificatory terminology. This is common to all Senoi groups. (See e.g., Benjamin, 1980.) Needham confirms this, but he found that 'degrees of kinship is reckoned patrilineally in the first instance unless advantage derives otherwise' (1956: 61), and he goes on to say that,

It is recognized that alternative degrees of kinship are possible according as one reckons through the father or through the mother, and according to the individual genealogical links chosen. Which of the reckonings is adopted will depend on circumstances, but normally when a precise degree of kinship is requested and no advantages are at stake, the patrilineal status is given.

(Needham, 1956: 61.)

While agreeing with the bulk of his analysis, I could find no evidence to substantiate his claim for a preference for the patrilineal reckoning. There are often, as Needham points out, several ways of reckoning the degree of kinship, but in my experience the Chewong will always emphasize that link which is closest, regardless of it being patrilineal or matrilineal. The only time when this is not the case is when through marriage a person changes his or her status in relation to another. In these instances the affinal status is reckoned rather than the consanguinal one, but a choice is made in more distant cases. Thus they may give either consanguinal or affinal relation when reckoning beyond parent/child-in-law or brother/sister-in-law. A final point needs to be considered in this respect. When the Chewong were moved during the Emergency, they were all issued with identity cards by the British who, following Malay practice of patronyms, insisted on identifying each person by their own name plus son (daughter) of the father's name. Many Chewong are aware of this Malay practice, and whenever pressed to give their complete name, those who know of it will do so in this manner. Most will not, however, and it is likely that any patrilineal tendency discerned by Needham was due to Beng and Patong fitting their information into the known Malay model.

Despite the above, the matter is somewhat complicated by the Chewong insistence that a child is made mainly by the father. It is his continued deposit of semen in the woman's womb that slowly builds up the foetus. The mother is 'the house only'.

The implications of this on their kinship system are somewhat puzzling. There are no descent groupings of any kind among the Chewong. No patri-lineages, no patri-clans and, as already stated, an individual Chewong when asked to state the precise relationship he or she has with another will give the closest link, regardless of whether it is patrilateral or matrilateral. Although this father-link does not affect the way they think about each other in terms of kin reckoning, it does affect the marriage rules. There are no preferred or prescribed categories of marriage partners. There are, however, a few forbidden ones. Those expressly forbidden are marriage between true siblings, and between parent and child. The former is known as *jawad* and will result in the offenders being killed and eaten by a tiger. The latter is *tanko*, after the superhuman being of that name who punishes the offenders by giving them stiff joints and, if the relations are not severed, by death. Furthermore, to marry father's brother's child, or brother's child is also *tanko*. This statement reflects the male role in procreation. Such marriages would, they say, be to mix the same blood (*nai mahom*).

The concept of *tanko* is not a very rigid one, however, and can be applied to other categories if it is felt, for whatever reason, that a particular marriage ought not to take place. In all instances, the Chewong reckon according to actual genealogical distance rather than by category. Needham was told that a man might not marry 'his mother, father's sister, mother's sister, sister, sibling's daughter, or any first cousin. Marriage with a second cousin is also severely disapproved. . . . Marriage is specifically asserted to be permitted with an aunt, niece, or even granddaughter of appropriate age, so long as the relationship is at the second or more distant remove' (Needham, 1974: 87, 88). On the other hand I was told that for a man to marry his aunt would be *tanko*, but that first cousins may marry each other (and in fact frequently do) as long as it is not with father's brother's child (although this also occurs regularly). This contradiction perhaps stems from the fact that forbidden categories beyond the most basic ones, are (as are members of other symbolic classes in the Chewong thought system) dependent upon contingent circumstances. (See Chapter 9.)

Relative age (see Needham, 1974) can in practice be more important than category. Thus when a man of about fifty started to cohabit openly with a prepubescent orphaned girl (his mother's brother's daughter's daughter) the union was at first said to be *tanko* on the basis of the great difference in their ages. As neither party suffered serious disease, or died, it was later stated that it was not *tanko* after all. 'They are both still alive', I was told. However, upon my latest return the girl had died, and people had reverted to saying that the union was indeed *tanko*. This time the reason given for designating it as *tanko* was that the man had had sexual relations with the girl's mother, thus making him a classificatory father. This example demonstrates, firstly, that in assigning the marriage as *tanko*, relative age and not status was first focused upon, and secondly, that the concept of *tanko* is fluid.

During the time I spent with the Chewong all marriages were monogamous. However, polygamy may be practised. Ogilvie tells of several men with more than one wife, and the Chewong freely admitted that this is possible. It is said to happen only when there is a surplus of women, but the data obtained do not corroborate this. There would appear to be other factors involved. Similarly, it was at first said that women may not have more than one husband at any given time, but further investigations revealed that polyandry had also been practised in the not very distant past. It seems that it is less frequent than polygamy, and that its status is more ambivalent. Matrilocality is practised following a marriage. The girl is said to be very attached to her mother. Later, the couple may live with either set of parents, usually alternating their place of residence while the parents are alive.

Divorce is a common phenomenon among the Chewong, and usually seems to take place because one of the parties has found another spouse. Children may accompany either parent in the case of divorce. Normally a small child would not be separated from its mother, but older children can choose which parent they wish to live with. Whatever their choice, they are likely to spend time with both parents. Divorce is not regarded as a calamitous event though older people may try to prevent one from happening. The Chewong are normally endogamous, though marriages have sometimes taken place with members of other groups. In the case of the Eastern Chewong endogamy ideally applies to marriage among themselves, i.e., excluding the Western Chewong. Needham found the same: 'they have their own women', he was told by Beng (1956: 62). The Western Chewong take a broader view and regard their marriage group as all Orang Asli who live near by. Possibly they also exchange marriage partners with those settlements—Temuan and Jah Hut—with whom they exchange invitations for feasts.

Curiously, persistent questioning regarding ideal marriage partners, revealed that all endogamous marriages are in theory *tanko*. A 'good' marriage is one that is contracted with an outsider. Thus to marry Jah Hut, Temuan, or even *gob*, is 'better' than to marry among themselves. It is said that children are more likely to survive from such unions. However, everybody insisted that they would never in practice wish to do so.

At present there is a shortage of marriageable women among the Eastern Chewong, and this situation is not going to change in the near future. Three Chewong men have therefore married out in the last five years. They all married daughters of a Temuan man and his half-Temuan, half-Chewong wife. The remaining unmarried men were unwilling to look for wives among other Temuan families.

In-law avoidance is practised; thus it is forbidden to call one's parents-in-law and children-in-law of either sex by their real name (*chò loi*). Their nickname (*chò punlao*) has to be used in all circumstances. If someone does not have a nickname (not everybody does), then they have to be addressed or referred to as 'mother/wife/father/ husband of so-and-so'. Similarly they may not be addressed with the familiar thou (*möh*) but with the formal you (*gitn*). In these cases one refers to oneself not as I (*ing*) but as us (exclusive) (*yae*). The same rule applies to brothers and sisters of one's spouse. Not to observe these rules is to show disrespect (*tolah*) and the offender will get severe swellings of the hips and crotch. It is further disrespectful for a parent-in-law to sit close to his or her child-in-law of the opposite sex, but this does not apply when both parties are of the same sex. The affinal avoidance rule does therefore have a slight cross-sexual bias. Questions of marriage, incest, and in-law avoidance are dealt with in more detail later.

PART I
RELATIONS

INTRODUCTION

I have suggested elsewhere a redefinition of Malay aboriginal animism based on the reading of the then available literature.

If the supernatural beings are imbued with the same vital principle or essence as are disembodied spirits and the souls taking abode in objects and non-human as well as human beings, then one may extend the definition of animism—in the Malay context—into a system of belief in which there is an 'essential' unity of nature (including human beings) and supernature (including supernatural beings).

(Howell, 1977: 59.)

My field-work with the Chewong bears out this hypothesis, but I came to realize that this concept of essential unity is more pervasive, as well as more complex, than anticipated. It permeates Chewong modes of thought and is expressed in relationships at all levels.

In effect, it is suggested that Chewong society does not constitute merely the 131 human beings who form the group, but extends into the non-human and superhuman worlds, and is actually co-existent with their universe. These different worlds of 'spirits', superhuman beings of various kinds, as well as all animals, plants and inanimate objects attributed with consciousness, are not conceptually differentiated from the world of human beings. However, Chewong society is at the centre of these different worlds, which may be envisaged as surrounding the human (i.e., Chewong) world on all sides. They all act upon the human world, and the human world acts upon theirs. There is a mutual interdependence between the beings in the various worlds; manifested not only on the cosmological level of ideas, but also through a series of ongoing prestations and counter-prestations.

This larger social universe constitutes a totality in which the superhuman beings are drawn directly into the social system. The processes of exchange that are carried out between members of the various worlds ensure a constant recreation of this universe. Furthermore, human law is replaced by a system of rules governed by the retribution of the superhuman beings, and the same rules that govern human behaviour also govern that of the superhuman beings. In addition, these rules provide a theory of causality which is internal to the system as a whole, while external to the human society. The outside world, i.e., other Orang Asli groups as well as the Malays, is on the ideational level excluded from Chewong thought.

It is for the above reasons that I do not use the words supernatural world or supernatural beings here. These worlds and beings are not outside the Chewong 'natural' world, but are an integral part of it. On one level they are talked of in terms of equality, and even identity, with the human world, so that it can be said that there is no distinction between the real and the unreal. The various beings are 'our people' (*bi he*) as opposed to the outside world of Malays and other Orang Asli, who are 'different people' (*bi masign*).

On another level of discourse, differences rather than similarities are emphasized. This occurs at times of disease and death, when a contrast is drawn between human frailty and superhuman immortality and inviolability.

A further point of interest in this context is the absence of social stratification on the human as well as on the superhuman level and this, it is suggested, together with the cosmological view of society, constitute fundamental keys to the understanding of Chewong rationality. The model is therefore one of complementarity and mutual responsibility for the continued existence and recreation of the total universe, rather than one of opposition.

In order to develop my theme, I shall devote the next three chapters to a discussion of relationships of different kinds, but all between classes of beings within the Chewong larger universe. It is hoped that by focusing on each type of relationship in turn, it will emerge that not only do they constitute a whole, but also that the same principles can be found to govern each. The relationships are those between human individuals; between the sexes; and between humans and the various categories of superhuman beings.

In Chapter 2 the various values which determine the social intercourse between individuals is considered, taking as the starting point the remarkable absence of aggression and competition found to

permeate all Chewong social relations. The absence of social stratification is also discussed.

In Chapter 3, I examine the relationship between men and women
according to the model of egalitarian values, and find that it prevails
here as well. I also include a discussion on 'couvade' and suggest that
in so far as this can be said to be practised among the Chewong, it
emphasizes the complementarity of the sexes in the creative process.
In this context I introduce the concept of *ruwai* (soul or vital principle) which will be elaborated upon in subsequent chapters.

Chapter 4 discusses the superhuman beings and their relationship
with each other as well as with humans. Again I find that egalitarian
principles govern these types of relationships. Thus no individual
superhuman being, nor any class of these, is in any way envisaged as
superior to the rest. Each may have particular abilities which are part
of their identity, but these are not seen to affect their general spheres
of activities. Notions of inter-personal status and power do not enter
into Chewong conceptions about the superhuman beings any more
than they do on the strictly social level. The superhuman beings are
'people like us'. They all form part of the cosmological order in
which each class and individual play their role.

From the point of view of classification, the most striking theoretical issue arising out of the Chewong 'pantheon' is that it appears to
be few, if any, common or regular attributes and elements which
link the members of the various main categories. This issue is taken
up at the end of the chapter, to be returned to in Chapter 9.

2

Relations between Individuals

NON-VIOLENCE AND
NON-COMPETITIVENESS

BEFORE discussing the various relationships some idea of the general atmosphere of Chewong society must be given. It is sufficiently unusual to warrant elaboration. The Chewong display no aggression, nor are they competitive in matters of achievement. This peaceful way in which they live and conduct their affairs is not unique to the Chewong, but can be found among several Orang Asli groups, and has been commented upon by other anthropologists. Dentan was so struck by it that he subtitled his book 'a non-violent people of Malaya' (1968). He does not develop the theme however, but returns to it later in a paper entitled 'Childhood in a nonviolent context' (1978), in which he suggests that enculturation is the major factor in developing non-aggressive behaviour. It is a little difficult to understand from his paper exactly what he means by this, since his summary is vague enough to apply to a large number of different societies, few of which are noticeably peaceful.

The new child is the focus of much emotional, cognitive, and ritual attention, which stems from affection and concern. Its fragility is linked to its alleged timidity, epitomized by the supposed timidity of the soul. Its whims are indulged, and it is not rebuked, because, being unable to talk, 'it cannot understand'.

(Dentan, 1978: 125.)

Focusing, as I have done elsewhere (Howell, 1981a) upon the predominance of two emotions: fear and embarrassment, he suggests that there is an emphasis in Semai child-rearing practices upon avoidance rather than confrontation, and he links this with their historical and ecological situation.

Robarchek has also done field-work among the Semai, and he

discusses the non-violence in psychological terms within the 'frustration-aggression hypothesis' (1978). Apart from these two writers, none of the other anthropologists of the area has done more than comment that the Orang Asli are remarkably non-violent. It has never to my knowledge been regarded as a fundamental premise of their modes of thought, without which other manifestations of their collective representations cannot be understood.

It could be argued that to devote a whole chapter to show that certain features commonly found in human societies such as social hierarchy, status, aggression, violence, and competition, do not exist among a group of people is a gross waste of time. Two points need to be considered in this context, however. First, that the absence of these phenomena is in itself sufficiently interesting to warrant further discussion. Second, that in the Chewong situation it is not so much an absence of these phenomena as the presence of something else much more difficult to define. It is a limitation of the English language that makes the examination of what there *is* so difficult. Merely to negate the terms and talk about non-hierarchy, non-aggression, non-violence, and non-competitiveness does not give an adequate impression of a situation which is in fact a very positive one. Surely it is a reflection on us, not the Chewong, that they cannot be easily described. Though these terms are imprecise, egalitarian and peaceful will have to stand for the moment as the best description of Chewong society.

The fact that the Chewong themselves do not use words to express their particular situation in this respect does not help. But value judgements regarding situations and emotions are not verbally differentiated to any great extent among them; these are on the whole either good (*baig*) or bad (*yabud*). As shown elsewhere (Howell, 1981a), the Chewong language is poor when it comes to expressing emotional or inner states.

None of the Orang Asli has any history of warfare, either recorded by the outside world or represented in myths and legends. The Chewong language has no indigenous words for war, fight, quarrel, aggression, attack, crime, or punishment. Their reaction to encountered violence in the past has been to run away from it. When referring to the marauding Malays of the nineteenth century and earlier, they describe the attacks by using verbs which they apply in their daily life to their own activities. Thus the Malays shot (*hapud*) at them, they cut at them with knives (*chang bi wang*), they hit them (*tapad*), they took (*ankid*) the women and children, etc. When asked why they had not shot at the Malays with their poisoned darts or built traps around their homes, the Chewong always replied that it had not occurred to them. 'We were very frightened and ran away and hid', they always said, but usually added that this was stupid and they would shoot at them were they to come today. This was empty boasting, however, for I have on several occasions seen people pack up their belongings and children and flee at the approach of strangers. They live in constant fear of attack from the outside world, and stories about alleged atrocities committed against Orang Asli by Malays are always circulating. Children are brought up to fear the very word *gob*. Yet they make no preparation for counter-attack or defence. The following two incidents will serve to illustrate Chewong reaction to encountered violence.

When I first arrived there was still a settlement near Bukit Patong on the western boundary of the Krau Game Reserve. The Game Department has a hut there, and one man—Adoi—who was employed by them lived in the official hut with his wife and three children. His married son, with wife, and her father's younger brother, a widower with two children, had built a hut near by as had the parents of the son's wife and their three children. They had cleared fields together for several years and were in the process of planting a new field when a Chinese, who had banana and orange plantations near by, accused Adoi of having stolen some of his things and threatened to beat him up. The Chewong were so terrified by this (they claimed to be innocent) that all of them packed together their belongings immediately and set off on the six hours walk to Sentao in the middle of the night, never to return.

Another man, Wedn, had a confrontation with a Malay soldier near Kampong Bolok some ten years ago. The soldier threatened violence, and this so alarmed Wedn that he left Gandah where he was living at the time. He took his wife and children and went to clear fields high up on Gunong Benom. He has never been back since. He is much too frightened. During my first stay with the Chewong, some people from Sentao met him when they were on a hunting expedition. They reported that he had no salt and that his knives were worn out (note similarities with the Jelbeng myth in Chapter 1). Wedn had no intention of returning to the rest of the Chewong. He was still much too frightened of what the Malays might do to him. He went back to Gunong Benom and has not been heard of since.

One of the most striking features of Chewong life is the lack of emotional displays among adults. All the time I was there I never witnessed a quarrel, nor an outburst of anger, except among small children. In this they differ from the Semai, who indulge in serious quarrels 'in which voices are raised and threats of physical violence are at least alleged, if not actually made', and 'At least two murders have been committed between 1955 and 1977, and there is gossip about a couple of others' (Dentan, 1978: 98). The Chewong do gossip about each other's behaviour, but this is chiefly in order to keep track of what is going on, not to pass moral judgement. The only time I witnessed condemnation of someone's behaviour was the case of the old man who married the prepubescent girl. This did not lead to an open confrontation, however, since nobody actually referred to it with the man concerned. Among themselves it was discussed in terms of probable supernatural repercussions that the act would entail.

One is often told in the literature (see e.g., Coon, 1976 and Friedl, 1975) that in hunting societies the best hunters have a high status within the society and that an element of competition can be discerned among the hunters in the amount of meat they bring home. This is not the case with the Chewong. There is a total lack of inter-personal competitiveness. No value is placed on being better than the rest at something. In fact whenever someone does distinguish him- or herself in some activity this is ignored and people become uncomfortable if this is commented upon by an outsider. The ideal is that everyone is equally good at all tasks. By the time adulthood is reached all boys and girls are expected to be competent in all the duties of an adult of their own sex. The tasks of course are relatively few, and unless someone has a physical or mental handicap, everyone is able to perform satisfactorily. However, some people are clearly stronger than others, or more hard working, or more adept with the blowpipe, but whenever such superior abilities are manifested these are never commented upon, nor do they give the person in question any special status within the community.

No rivalry is thus displayed in connection with performance. Children's games have no element of competitiveness. Top-spinning, for instance, which is highly competitive among the Malays, is frequently played by Chewong children, but it never seems to occur to anyone to turn it into a competition. Neither do they race each other in any way. Women usually go together into the tapioca field to dig a basketful of tubers for making bread. They all work separately at digging and peeling, but keep asking each other how they are getting on. Usually one woman is quicker than the rest, but this never causes any resentment. As they finish they will wait for the rest to catch up and they all bring the tapioca together to the river where it is left to soak.

Although they do not compete, they do not help each other either. The ideology of non-interference that permeates Chewong life, on some levels could be described as non-involvement, a more negative way of regarding it. Individuals are expected to, and on the whole do, carry out their activities on their own. It is a rare sight to witness someone asking someone else for assistance. Similarly, offers of assistance are also rare. I have many times watched strong young men lying about all day while old, and sometimes ill, people toil with heavy work without asking for or receiving any help.

BEHAVIOUR AT MEETINGS AND PARTINGS

It should be clear by now that the Chewong are a non-demonstrative group of people. This is particularly striking to an outsider at times of meetings and departures, and the rituals involved on such occasions will be described in some detail since this will help to throw light upon the principles underlying Chewong social intercourse.

The Chewong have no words of greeting. When visitors from other settlements arrive, they walk briskly up to whichever house they are going to be sleeping in (this is dependent upon kin status), put down their blowpipes without looking left or right or acknowledging any persons present, then they enter the house and hang up their backbaskets on a beam. They sit down close together and the occupants of the house also enter. Tobacco is exchanged, all the adults in the house rolling one or two cigarettes which they give to all the visitors in turn, usually offering the senior (that is older) people first, then the adolescents, and finally the children. Children are rarely given more than one cigarette, whereas the oldest people may be given three as a mark of respect. If they do not have any leaves for rolling, a handful of loose tobacco is given instead. If the giver has very little tobacco, he may give just one cigarette to everybody, but he will excuse this by saying to each one 'it is only one' (tungal).[1] The guests then reciprocate, matching the number of

[1]Probably from the Malay tunggal, meaning sole, single, solitary. It is the Chewong name for a particular species of cane which grows singly and they referred to this when explaining the meaning of the word.

cigarettes to each individual giver. This general exchange is carried out without any conversation. The guests may take the leaf of a cigarette given and use this for rolling one to give back, but they always use their own tobacco.

Any meat, fish, or fruit obtained on the journey is then handed over to the woman of the house. She immediately starts to prepare a meal for the visitors from her own store of food. The received food will be cooked and shared out among visitors and inhabitants at a later stage. Thus raw food is given by the visitor and cooked food by the host.

Then slowly the other members of the settlement come over to see the visitors, and tobacco, information, and news are exchanged in a quiet and subdued manner. The first topic to be brought up once the itinerary of the guests' journey has been ascertained, is usually that of disease. Who has been ill, what was the cause, and what sort of cures were attempted, and how they are getting on, is reported by both sides. In any serious cases this information is immediately passed on to others as they enter the house, but no one displays worry or seems to be upset about their relatives' misfortunes.

This behaviour cannot be accounted for by lack of acquaintance. All Chewong know each other intimately from birth, most having lived together at some time. People move frequently throughout their lives, changing settlements and clearing fields with different families. Residence groups are forming and reforming constantly. Apart from actually resettling, individuals and whole families go on visits to other settlements for months on end. And yet each encounter is conducted with such reserve and formality that the casual observer would conclude that the parties had never met before.

Husbands and wives look at each other expressionlessly after a time apart; he walks straight past her and enters the house. Small children never run up to greet their father when he returns home. Members of the same settlement, and household, also go through the ritual tobacco exchange whenever they return after just one night's absence, and when neighbours drop in for a chat in the evening, they are given cigarettes by their hosts. In these cases the visitors do not reciprocate, however. The same thing is done when encountering someone while out in the jungle.

Departures on the other hand are much more demonstrative. A couple of days before visitors are due to go home, and if the journey involves spending one night or more in the jungle, tapioca is dug and made into bread for them to eat on the way. Everyone talks about the

impending departure, saying to the visitors 'you are leaving tomorrow'. On the actual morning, the whole settlement will turn out to
watch, and the visitors will say in loud voices to everyone present,
'I'm going home' (*ing weg*) to which the reply is 'I'll be seeing you'
(*endagn*). Often gifts are given by the hosts. For the women it may be
a roll of the string they use to keep their loincloths in place, and for
the men a container of dart poison. Short term visitors also call out
'*ing weg*'.

Van Gennep has suggested that arrivals and departures display the
three stages discerned by him in rites of passage in general: separation, transition, and incorporation. All crossings of boundaries or
movement from one state or category to another are marked by
people everywhere in this manner. Although the procedure is
always the same, the actual length and intricacy of each stage vary
according to different rituals and different peoples (1960: 28). The
Chewong situation just described clearly conforms to his model of
rites of passage, but an interesting point to note in the Chewong
material is that in the two events, the outstanding features in each are
inversed. A summary will make the point clear. Arrival rituals stress
the incorporation stage of the passage, and departure rituals stress
the separation stage. Arrivals are distinguished by no emotional
expressions. No acknowledgement is made by, or of, the visitors
until they are inside the house. No words are exchanged, no looks.
Once inside, however, the visitors hand over any food they may
have brought to the host, and tobacco is exchanged between all
visitors and all inhabitants. Then news is exchanged, and a meal is
offered. The visitors have now been incorporated into the group.
Departures on the other hand are animated rather than subdued.
After a last meal inside the house, gifts are given by the hosts to the
visitors, and verbal exchange rather than tobacco exchange is participated in by all present. The actual point of departure is stressed
whereas the point of arrival was ignored.

In most discussions of rites of passage in the ethnographic literature, arrivals and departures are usually ignored and concentration
focused on the so-called 'life-crises' such as birth, initiation, marriage, and death. In Chewong society, however, where so little
formalized behaviour is displayed, it is very striking to observe the
solemnity of their encounters; and this leads one to ask whether this
particular ritual has any further ramifications. It is a commonplace to
state that relationships of exchange are an integral part of any
society. To the Chewong who live so far apart from each other, and

rarely meet, the notion of society could easily disappear. By this very formal act of exchanging tobacco and food upon encounters, the individual Chewong is making a statement about the existence of a wider society. They are affirming its existence and ensuring its continuity. It is worth noting that these acts are only carried out among themselves, 'our people' (*bi he*), and are not extended to visiting members of other Orang Asli groups.

POLITICAL ORGANIZATION AND LEADERSHIP

Unlike some Orang Asli groups (see e.g., Hood, 1974 on the Semelai) but similar to others, e.g., the Negritos (see Endicott, 1975) the Chewong do not have any political hierarchy. There are no leaders or headmen, though often an older man will act as a representative in their dealings with outsiders, e.g., in the case of Maroi discussed on p. 17. He will only do so because he speaks Malay better and is less timid. He has no status within the society at any other times. This point needs some discussion since Needham was told of three political offices among them; *to menteri*, *to pelima*, and *to jinang*, 'which form a hierarchical order and supervise important agreements, legal cases, conduct divorce and marriages, and settle disputes' (Needham, 1956: 58, 64). None of these exist any more, although I was told they did in the past, having now been replaced by the J.O.A. appointed Batin, but from my observation of the workings of Chewong social order it is very doubtful whether they ever did exist except in name. The Chewong have not been living in complete isolation from the world around them. They are aware that the Malays have institutions and political offices ranging from the *raja* (prince) to the village headman. They know about police and soldiers, and the titles listed by Needham are in fact variations on Malay titles. These may have been made up to parallel Malay institutions, possibly in reaction to enquiries from outsiders. That they had no meaning in real terms can be deduced from an informant's statement that the Chewong are very different from Malays. 'They (the Malays) are very frightened of their prince (*raja*), headmen (*penghulu*), and chief of soldiers (*ketua askar*). They do whatever they tell them to do. We Chewong are not like that. We are not frightened of our own people,' they said. The officially appointed Batin does not regard himself, nor is he regarded by the rest of the community, as having any authority over the rest. They can see no reason why he should receive his annual stipend. It was the practice of the British to appoint one Batin of each Orang Asli group. They channelled their information and gifts via this person in the hope of receiving news about guerrilla activities in the forest, but the selection was often done arbitrarily. If they met an older man who seemed co-operative and intelligent, he would be appointed (Biles, personal communication).

The first Chewong Batin was Tengk, known as Raja Tengk, and three of his sons have held the position since his death. The current holder, Bak, does so because his two brothers have died and the J.O.A. assumed that the title should stay within the lineage of Tengk. None of the other brothers had sons old enough to be granted this position. Bak is very frightened of Malays and did not want to be Batin at all, but he never dared say so when the J.O.A. insisted that he took over. The shaman does not fulfil any political role within the society, as is often the case in societies with little or no specific political hierarchy, although he does exercise authority on the cosmological plane.

The Chewong, then, do not acknowledge any form of institutionalized authority among themselves. Old people, due to their wider experience and knowledge are, however, accorded a fair amount of respect, but this does not mean that they can assert any form of authority over the rest. There are certain expectations of assistance linked to specific roles, such as those of husband and wife, and that of a son-in-law, but in neither of these relationships does the notion of power or relative status enter. Retribution for failing to behave in the appropriate manner is in all cases supernatural, not human.

Needham was told by Beng about the existence of various fines for specific offences. Theft, adultery, seduction, rape, and murder are listed by him as warranting payment in various quantities of spears and plates by the offender. When checking this with Beng, Needham's informant, I was told the same, but none of the other members of the group knew anything about such a system. When asked for examples of these fines having been paid, Beng could not give any. Whenever I was told about adultery in the past (a fairly frequent occurrence) I always asked how many spears and/or plates the man had paid to the woman's husband and was always told none. 'That is not our way,' they would reply. The same applies to theft. On one occasion during my stay, it happened that someone stole some rice and tobacco. I asked if the thief had been punished and was told that he had not, but that his wife had been very angry with him. This hardly counts as a formal punishment.

Seduction occurred once. This was the case of the old man and the young girl already referred to twice. Once he realized that public opinion was against the affair—not only because it was felt that the age difference was excessive, but also because he had not notified the girl's older brother about his intentions—he took his new wife and his children from a previous marriage away from the settlement where they lived and started to clear a new field some distance away. Later it was stated by several people that this union was *tanko*, but although he was not formally told about this view, he apparently knew what was being said. However, no one made any attempts to prevent the marriage from continuing, or imposed any restrictions upon his movements, nor, as far as could be seen, did they behave towards him in any way differently from what they had before. The important point to note from these examples is that the Chewong have no legal or political machinery which comes into operation to cope with situations in which people step out of line, nor does any headman stand forward to pass judgement or impose punishment. By removing himself physically, the man in question acknowledged that he had acted in such a way as to offend accepted ideas about good behaviour. It is likely that the seriousness of an offence determines the distance a person moves. They said that if ever one member of the group were to kill another, he would move far away, being much too ashamed to continue living amongst friends and relatives.

The following account by Evans about the 'Kerau River Sakai-Jakun' (the Jah Hut) may throw some light upon the question of fines for specific trespasses:

Plates and spears are the media in which tribal fines are paid . . . the fine for murder was sixty-six spears, while incest in the worst degree is said to have been punishable by a fine of one hundred and sixty spears. Other minor fines were—for stealing crops, one spear and one plate; unfaithfulness on a woman's part, six spears and two plates. . . . Payment by a suitor to a father for the hand of a virgin daughter is sixty spears, but actually only from three to six are paid.

(Evans, 1927: 38.)

Beng knows the Jah Hut well and probably reiterated their practices when interviewed by Needham.

3

Relations between the Sexes

THE concept of status found to be lacking on a general political level is also absent from the relationship between men and women. The Chewong creation myth is interesting in this context, as it expresses their basic attitude on this question. The whole myth will be rendered and discussed at a later stage, and only a brief summary of the pertinent points will be given here.

A superhuman being, known variously as Tohan[1] or Allah Ta'Allah told his Nabi[2] to make human beings, beri. He told him to make one couple, kelamin, one man and one woman, and to fashion them out of earth. This the Nabi did, and he was given breath, njug, from Tohan in order to animate the mannikins.

These two beings married each other, but when the woman became pregnant and went into labour, neither of them knew what was happening, so the husband cut open his wife's stomach and found a baby inside. The baby lived, but the woman died. The father did not know what to do, but his wife's ghost told him in a dream to suckle the child from his elbow. When he did this milk appeared and the child survived.

The two points to be stressed here are: firstly, that both sexes were created simultaneously and in an identical manner; and secondly, that both parents shared in the child-rearing; the wife's ghost by telling her husband how he could feed the child thereby showing her concern, and the husband by actually being the source of milk. It is interesting to note how the two functions normally associated with

---

[1] *Tuhan* is the Malay word for God. In the Chewong context it is spelled as it is pronounced. *Allah Ta' Allah* is from the Arabic *Allah Taala* meaning God Most High.

[2] *Nabi* is the Malay for Prophet. It usually refers to Muhammad.

Clearly all these three names are taken directly from the Malays. I was told that the Chewong Tohan was not the same as the Malay. 'We also have a Tohan, but he is different. He only helps the forest people, not the Malays.' It is most likely that the Chewong have consciously copied Malay usage. It must not be assumed that their notions of Tohan and Nabi bear any relation to the Islamic ones.

parenthood are inversed, by which the Chewong are ascribing to the event of creation a special significance as well as placing it outside historical time. Yet although the sexual functions are inversed, the myth emphasizes the point that child-rearing is a shared responsibility.

The notions of sharing, exchange, and reciprocity play a large part in Chewong conception of marriage, as indeed they do in all their relationships, both human and superhuman. In the case of a married couple, certain activities are chiefly associated with the role of being a husband, others with that of being a wife. Although these can be seen to be complementary, the boundaries between them are not rigid, and there is nothing in their symbolic structures that prevents overlap.

An examination of Myths 1 and 2 (see Appendix 1), will illustrate the point about complementarity clearly. The theme of vagina dentana is a common one in mythology, but analogous ideas applied to men is rarely found. In Myth 1, women suffer from a man having thorns on his penis, and in Myth 2, men similarly suffer from a woman having thorns in her vagina. In both cases the word *gilé* is used to indicate thorns. Several interesting conclusions may be drawn from these myths, but here it is only suggested firstly, that among the Chewong both men and women not only tell myths, but that they also create them; and secondly, that female sexuality is no more, or less, threatening to men than is male sexuality to women.

MARRIAGE AND SEX ROLES

Marriage is primarily a co-operative union in which the husband and wife team forms a self-sufficient economic unit. Together they can accomplish all the jobs necessary for survival: clearing and planting new fields, hunting, fishing, gathering, housebuilding, cooking, and child-rearing. Even where more than one family lives in a settlement—and this is the majority of cases—the married couples each perform these tasks separately though often alongside each other. Of these, hunting is the one that most signifies the male domain, and child-rearing the female one. The men spend at least half their time in work connected with hunting or fishing. When not actually out on a hunting or fishing trip they work at home preparing darts, repairing (or more correctly servicing) their blowpipes, making poison, as well as building, repairing, and inspecting the pig and porcupine traps in the fields. Apart from hunting with the blowpipe they also go hunting with dogs and spear. Blowpipe hunting is usually a solitary occupation, but sometimes young boys accompany an older man in order to learn the craft. Once the first child is born women rarely accompany their husbands on hunting trips of just one day's duration, but when he goes on a longer one which involves spending a few nights away from the settlement the wife and children will also go.

The women give birth approximately once every eighteen months to two years. Although the infant mortality rate is about 50 per cent, women are kept busy looking after babies and infants. Babies are suckled until the next one arrives, and a mother will never leave her baby by itself and rarely with other women. This means that most of the time she has to carry out her work with a baby strapped to her front or back.

However, these activities can be, and are, participated in by both sexes. Women often make darts for their husbands and are always on the look-out for the species of bamboo used for this purpose when they are in the forest. No woman had her own blowpipe while I was there, but women often took one of their husband's and went in search of a squirrel or some other arboreal animal that had been spotted in the vicinity. They said that in the recent past several women were adept with the blowpipe and would go hunting successfully on their own. In one case a woman went hunting every day when her husband was sick for a long time. Both men and women fish and go in search of the giant turtles that inhabit the rivers. Women also inspect the traps in the fields, and whenever they come across a monitor lizard or a tortoise while out in the forest they will chase it.

Although the produce of the field is primarily a female responsibility, men often participate in planting, harvesting, and preparation of the food. If the wife is sick, heavily pregnant, or newly delivered, the husband does most of the household chores including cooking and preparing tapioca bread. The responsibility of helping is his rather than the woman's mother or other female relatives.

Clearing a new field is work shared by the couple, usually alongside other couples. The man does the heavy work such as cutting down the trees and the initial clearing of the undergrowth and fallen branches. The women clear at a later stage and help in burning it off. On the whole planting is done by women.

Two tasks can be said to symbolize maleness and femaleness respectively, and children learn how to accomplish them from older members of their own sex. The boys learn how to find good bamboo for a blowpipe and how to fashion one; while the girls learn where to look for pandanus leaves used for making mats and bags of various kinds and how to plait them. The Chewong see these two tasks as analogous and complementary. They are talked about in similar terms. Thus I was told that the men measure the correct length of a dart by holding it against their lower arm. It should reach from the elbow to the tip of the little finger. The women measure the correct length of a leaf for a mat by holding it from one extended hand across the chest to the other extended hand.

Ideally, a girl is not ready to marry until she has mastered the art of mat making, or a boy until he has proved his proficiency at blowpipe hunting. Other conditions also should be fulfilled. A girl is not old enough to be married until her breasts are fully developed, but in several cases younger girls were married. The procedure for getting a spouse is very simple. A boy will ask, through an intermediary, a man for his daughter. There is thus a bias towards male initiative. The Chewong will say that so and so 'would not give his daughter' to someone, but the same can also be said about a mother. Clearly the matter is discussed between the parents, who also consult the wishes of their daughter, and it is very doubtful that any girl would be married against her will. The Chewong acknowledge attraction between the sexes, and are willing to let that be the guiding factor. The Chewong talk about being engaged and having a fiancé (*tuneng*) and sometime during this period the girl has to make a tobacco pouch for her intended husband. She also plaits a sleeping mat which can accommodate two persons. He gives a sarong to his prospective father-in-law, via the same intermediary, and possibly a knife and some money. These (with the exception of the money) are handed over to the girl. If a wedding ceremony is to take place, it has to wait until the couple has had sexual intercourse in the forest. Once this has occurred, the intermediary decides the day. It seems likely that the practice of having a wedding (*nika*) is not an indigenous practice, but one copied from the Malays. The older people told me that they had not had one. 'In the old days there was no problem', they would say 'we just slept together.' In fact their term for marriage, or married, is just 'sleep together' (*abn nai*). This was confirmed by the older people in the Dong area where wedding ceremonies are very elaborate, due to Malay and Temuan influences. When Patong's and Taloi's daughter was engaged, everybody expected a big feast to be given because he is the richest of all the men, having worked for the Game Department for many years, and she is very energetic when it comes to collecting and selling cane. Patong himself talked about all the food he would buy and how people from all the settlements would come. Yet the event took place with no invitations being issued, so no one knew about it until afterwards, and Patong did not buy anything special. No one commented adversely upon this, however, and probably they did not really expect a feast.

The one wedding that I observed took on some aspects of a feast, but perhaps this was mainly because I had offered to buy rice, brown sugar, and flour. Only the people from Pyapoz and Gambir were present. There was, however, a small ceremony in which the couple sat next to each other for the first time. They fed each other out of the same bowl, drank out of the same cup, and shared a cigarette. They were then addressed separately by an old man and an old woman who reminded them of their duties as husband and wife. In the case of the husband, he was told by the old man not to be lazy, but to keep his wife provided with a steady supply of game (*ai*). 'You now have a wife, you must be energetic,' he was told. Similarly, the girl was told that she had to be vigilant in her cultivation and preparation of tapioca (*ratn*). 'You now have a husband. You must always have staple food ready for him.' I think that some exchange must have taken place in the old days even if the feast did not. It is said that if a man has not given his wife a sarong, he is not her 'true' husband (*teh lòi*) and he may not defend her against the Malays or any other man. It seems likely that the injunction requiring sexual intercourse in the forest before they can be regarded as husband and wife, refers to how marriages used to take place. The couple would meet secretly for brief sexual encounters in the forest over a period of time before they began publicly to cohabit.

Once two people are recognized as a couple, they live together in the girl's parents' house where they are given their own corner. They go on living here in a joint household, but with separate hearths, until the first child is born. Some time after this they will usually build their own house. It is acknowledged that their chief responsibilities are to each other and no longer to their parents.

The married couple spend much time together. The house is the focal point of activity when work does not take them away to the forest or the fields. If one of a couple is already at home, the other prefers being with him or her rather than joining another group. When they go visiting they usually do so together. This mutual reliance and co-operation manifests itself most strikingly to the outsider at the time of a birth. It is the husband who acts as midwife rather than the girl's mother or other female relatives. These may assist the husband, but he is the chief officiant.

Among the Chewong no one labour or task carries any special status.[1] Hunting is no more prestigious than is child-rearing, gathering, planting, or cooking. There is some division of labour along sexual lines whereby all men will perform those tasks better suited to their superior physical strength. But it is not *better* to be physically strong, it is just a fact of life. Another physiological fact is that only women are able to bear and suckle children, but again this does not give them any special status. The Chewong recognize the differences between men and women and their different physical and biological capabilities, but they do not apply any value judgement to these differences.

PATTERNS OF SEXUAL RELATIONS

Men and women do relate to each other in a wider social context than that of the conjugal family only. The pattern of male–female relations can be seen to fall into four distinct stages during a person's life-span.

Infants and small children of both sexes are known as *wòng*. They spend most of their time in the company of their mother, accompanying her in her daily tasks.

Although adults are very conscious of the sex of the child, often pointing playfully to the sexual organ and pronouncing its name; *leh* in the case of girls, *lah* for boys, they do not impose gender associated behaviour upon children. Boys and girls are playmates and all children play the same games and make the same toys. At night they share the sleeping mat of their parents.

Between six and eight years of age, children begin to move away from their parents and their playmates of the opposite sex, finally to join a peer group of older children of the same sex. This move is slow and intermittent, but when finally accomplished the youngsters

---

[1] After writing this whole section I was lent Karen Endicott's thesis on 'Batek Negrito Sex Roles' (1979) in which she challenges the commonly held view that 'hunting seen as a predominantly male activity, inevitably leads to higher status for men, implying that even in hunter and gatherer societies sexual asymmetry is inescapable' (171). She also claims for the Batek a complete absence of interpersonal as well as inter-sexual notions of hierarchy and status.

spend most of their time together with the peer group, sleeping with these in a special corner of the house and having virtually nothing to do with children of the opposite sex. This is also the time they start to wear loincloths, allegedly because they have become 'shy' or ashamed (*lidya*). From now until they are married the girls are referred to as 'maidens' (*kòkn ködah*) and the boys as 'bachelors' (*bujægn*).

After marriage, the focal point of social life for a couple is spouse and children. They are now 'man' (*tungkal*) and 'woman' (*kòkn*); in other words they have become adults with all the responsibilities that this entails. They are of course also 'husband' (*teh*) and 'wife' (*jeh*) but only in relation to each other. As far as the rest of the community is concerned, they are men and women. Marriage entails a virtual full-time intense relationship with one member of the opposite sex. Outside the conjugal situation, however, adult women and men tend to seek the company of members of their own sex.

Finally, when a couple become old, they cease sleeping together, and although they still fulfil their economic and social obligations to each other as well as they can, they no longer spend much time in each other's company, but prefer that of their own sex. They are now known as 'old people' (*bi badòdn*).

Although sleeping quarters within a house are delineated so that the married couple sleep in one corner, the bachelors in another, the maidens in a third, and visiting couples in a fourth, it is of no significance which corner is allocated to each group. In other words, there is no symbolic link between gender and left and right, nor with any of the four cardinal points. It is only prescriptive (*tanko*) to keep the various categories apart. How this is done is unimportant.

In ordinary daytime social intercourse the same patterning of location is repeated, but it is not prescribed. Members of opposite sex may sit next to each other (except parent- and child-in-law of the opposite sex), and they may all eat together. Furthermore, there is no order of precedence determining who is served with their food first, except when there are visitors, in which case they are always favoured. There are no activities from which either sex is excluded.

The Chewong do not have any explicit initiation rites, and as already shown, their marriage ceremony is extremely simple and may not even have taken place at all in the past. Nevertheless, I wish to suggest that there are specific categories which everybody enters and leaves at roughly the same stages of their lives. These categories correspond to the four stages discerned in the relationship between the sexes, and they may be referred to as childhood, adolescence, adulthood, and old age. Several further factors may be isolated with respect to these.

Firstly, the passage from one category to another largely depends upon the individual concerned and it does not take place suddenly and all at once. Rather, it is a sporadic and protracted process. Thus the passage from childhood to adolescence is marked by the child oscillating between parents and peer group. Similarly, that between adolescence and adulthood is also intermittent, with clandestine sexual encounters culminating in public cohabitation. The passage from adulthood to old age is less discernible. Nevertheless, it is expressed by the gradual movement away from spouse to peer group of the same sex.

Secondly, these transitions from category to category conform to what has come to be expected from a rite of passage, albeit that they are accomplished implicitly rather than explicitly.

Thirdly, the change in status is marked semantically rather than by ritual or ceremony. When an individual has been incorporated into a new group, he or she is labelled differently. Thus people earlier referred to as *wòng* become either *kòkn ködah* or *bujægn* as members of the adolescent group. *Kòkn ködah* then becomes *kòkn* and *bujægn* becomes *tungkal* when their adult status is accepted; finally, these two categories are merged as they turn into *bi badòdn*.

Fourthly, semantic differentiation based on gender only occurs in the case of two categories; those of adolescence and adulthood. There is no one word for these categories, individuals are identified as male and female, the exact term dependent upon social status. A person is a member of these two categories at that time in his or her life when they are regarded as sexually active. By contrast, children and old people who are regarded as sexually impotent are referred to by neuter terms.

SIGNIFICANCE OF CONCEPTION AND BIRTH

Only those aspects of conception and birth which highlight the relationship between husband and wife will now be discussed. Other issues connected with birth will be examined later.

The Chewong are fully aware of the link between sexual intercourse and conception. But, surprisingly, in view of the usual emphasis upon complementarity so far discerned in their ideas regarding the sexes, the Chewong believe that it is the semen which builds up (*bowad*) the foetus. Frequent and regular deposit of semen in the woman's womb right up to the time of birth contributes to the formation of the baby. First the eyes are made, then the hands, the head, the body, the thighs, and the feet. When all the parts are completed, the child 'moves' (*ohos*) and is born 'comes to earth' (*oka te*). The mother's role is described by the men as 'the child's house', or 'the child sleeps inside her'. These expressions were never used by the women, but they agree that semen makes the baby. Everybody was unanimous in stating that without men, women could not make babies and that without women, men were equally unable to procreate. The vaginal fluids also contribute, though less, to the growth of the baby.

The woman's main role is to feed the baby, both during the incubation period, and with her milk after the birth. Making and feeding can be seen as complementary in this instance. The semen and the milk are analogous; the former known as the water of the penis (*tam lah*), the latter as the water of the breast (*tam boh*). However, the chief role of the male as the maker has ramifications on their marriage rules as already discussed. In so far as one can identify an instigator, it may be claimed that whereas the initiative in marriage lies with the man, the initiative for procreation lies with the woman. Women are said to demand their husbands' penes 'morning and night' when they want to have a baby.

There is another aspect to Chewong ideas regarding conception and birth which has not yet been touched upon; namely the role of the placenta. This will be discussed in detail later; for present purposes it is sufficient to state that the placenta is regarded as the counterpart to the baby, and is referred to as its 'older sibling' (*tòh*). The Chewong say that when a woman does not have her regular periods she is pregnant and that the blood remains inside her body until the baby is born, although they do not explicitly state that the placenta is the cumulation of the menstrual blood. From this one may suggest a further complementarity between the sexes in the procreative process: the father makes the body of the child, the mother that of its counterpart, the placenta.

Throughout the pregnancy both parents are subject to dietary restrictions and these are identical for both parents. To eat any of the forbidden foods would affect the foetus detrimentally or it might lead to a difficult labour. The reason given for including the father in these prohibitions is that he 'sleeps with' his wife, a euphemism for sexual intercourse. After the birth the mother still has to observe dietary and other ritual restrictions, whereas the father no longer needs to. It is my suggestion that the father's direct participation in the creation and growth of the baby through his continued deposit of semen which is then incorporated into the foetus, is the reason for his having to avoid the foods that will damage the development of the child or lead to a difficult birth. Both parents are part of the creative process. Forbidden food eaten by either would affect the foetus. In the case of the father, by virtue of its association with the semen and the mother, by virtue of her role as container and provider of sustenance. This complementarity corresponds to ideas of mutuality discerned in their creation myth whereby both parents were responsible for the nurturing of the new-born child.

When a woman goes into labour her husband gathers the various roots and leaves required for medicine. He prepares them and gives them to his wife at the appropriate moments. Only if he is away will someone else act as midwife, usually the girl's mother or sister. He also prepares the special water which is used for washing the mother and child in. It is kept in a bamboo as no modern receptacle may be used on this occasion. If he does not know the spells required for this and for the medicines, someone who does know them will officiate.

The woman places herself next to the fireplace. She lies on her back and her husband presses her stomach at frequent intervals to aid the baby's movement. They insist that the baby cannot be delivered on its own. When the baby emerges, the husband pulls it out gently and cuts the umbilical cord with a sharpened piece of bamboo. As was the case with the water container, the cord may not be cut by a metal (or non-indigenous) knife. The navel string is tied with a piece of cane, the baby washed and handed to its mother. The rest of the umbilical cord and the placenta are carefully wrapped in an old mat or some large leaves, and the husband places it in the branches of a tree some distance away; the actual location is not specified. Having thus disposed of the afterbirth, the father covers all the blood which has fallen to the ground underneath the house with ashes.

The inclusion of the father in food restrictions raises the question of couvade. At first sight Chewong practices can be seen to conform to what has come to be regarded as couvade as found in many parts of the world. Rivière, however suggests that couvade is not a useful category which can be applied on a universal scale, and he states that 'couvade is not something in its own right, but rather an aspect of something else (it is) one among many diverse institutions that address themselves to the same problem, one of almost universal proportions, that of man's duality' (1975: 434). He is in effect proposing that the various rituals that the parents go through in connection with birth are as much to do with the child's spiritual well-being as its physical one. 'For birth to be successful, so to speak, there must be a spiritual as well as a physical creation' (431).

To make his point clear he compares couvade with the Catholic institution of *compadrazgo* which is concerned with the sponsorship of an individual's spiritual aspect. But whereas the model for the *compadrazgo* is a social one, in the couvade the model is physiological; all or part of the process of pregnancy, parturition and nurture serve as a model for the spiritual creation (433).

In the light of these suggestions, the Chewong material will now be examined, thereby introducing the fundamental concept of *ruwai* ('soul', vital principle); the relation of the *ruwai* to the body (*bi* or *bajo*); and to breath (*njug*). The Chewong claim that they do not know where the soul of a new human being comes from. They have no perception of a 'soul reservoir' from which a soul goes to a new-born child and to which it returns after its death, as is found among other Orang Asli including the Batek (Endicott, 1979: 92). They insist that it is not given by any supernatural being. In the myth related earlier, Tohan gave breath (*njug*) to the first couple, and in this context 'breath' implies 'soul' but this was a once-only act and has never been repeated by him. One might argue that once humanity had been activated, all aspects of a human being are recreated automatically once the process had been ignited. On this level there is no real split between body and soul, the two are intrinsically part of each other. When the Chewong speak of the foetus and the new-born infant they do not separate these two concepts, the child is referred to as one entity. In other contexts, however, they clearly do think of a duality. They will refer to the *ruwai* as being the 'true' person (*bi lòi*), and the body only the 'cloak' (*bajo*),[1] of the *ruwai*. Thus in dreams and shamanistic seances it is said that the *ruwai* leaves its 'cloak' and travels freely and independently about. Similarly at death, the 'cloak' becomes earth, whereas some

---

[1] The Malay word *baju* is of Persian origin and means an outer garment, a coat, jacket, or tunic (Baru, 1976). The Chewong use this word for all types of shirts, blouses, and dresses. Such garments are not indigenous to them and are not worn except when they descend to the Malay village to sell their rattan. It is likely, however, that they have observed the Malays and Chinese wearing such garments for some time. *Baju* is employed in a similar fashion by the Jah Hut, where it 'refers to the different forms in which ancestors appear to people' (Couillard, 1980: 121).

other aspect of the person becomes a ghost (*yinlugen*). The most dangerous form of disease is when an individual has lost his *ruwai*. Unless it is found and replaced in the body, the person dies.

No one could say with certainty at what point the *ruwai* is present in a baby, but most people would reply when pressed that it was not in the mother's stomach but appeared on its own after the child had been born. A stillborn child does not receive any mortuary rites, nor does one who dies within the first two days, although they are buried. It is not regarded as human yet, only when it has been sucking the milk and 'the mother has held it', i.e., held it in a true mother and child relationship of feeding, is the child a social being and its *ruwai* present. If it dies at this point all the death rituals are carried out. These examples would seem to indicate that the parents' ritual behaviour before the birth has nothing to do with the child's spiritual birth, only its physiological one. For present purposes both the parents are being classed together rather than discussing the father's role as something separate and different from that of the mother.

There are, however, indications that there is something present in the foetus which is extra to the physical being. This something may not be the fully formed *ruwai*, but as the foetus grows into a human body, so this embryo *ruwai* is also nurtured into the personage (see Chapter 5) of the human being. But whereas the physical form is complete upon birth, the child's *ruwai* is not. The concept of *ruwai* is a very complex one and will be discussed in detail later, so here it is only suggested that at some levels it is synonymous with life. According to the Chewong anything that is alive (*gòz*) has *ruwai*. In this sense *ruwai* can be said to stand for vital principle. It is this vital principle that is present in the foetus. Indeed, when a mother feels the child she is carrying move, she will say that it is alive. Since being alive implies by definition the presence of a vital principle, one must assume that this is present inside the foetus. The Chewong say that the *ruwai* is weak immediately following birth, and that until the *ruwai* is fully developed and properly fixed in the body, it is prone to attack by non-human beings and forces as well as to being lost of its own accord. From the following example it can be deduced that the *ruwai* is vulnerable while still in the womb.

A pregnant woman may not look upon a corpse. If she does so the foetus will be damaged either physically or spiritually. There were two boys both of whom were born defective. One had severe physical handicaps, but his mental faculties were normal. The other was so seriously mentally deficient that he could not really communicate in any meaningful way. I was told that in both cases their mothers had looked upon a corpse during their pregnancies, and this was why the children were born abnormal. In other words, the correct development of the foetus had somehow been stunted by the mother perceiving death while she was in the process of creating life. In the case of the mentally handicapped boy, it was his vital principle that had been affected, and his *ruwai* never developed fully. He was not regarded by the rest of the community as a full member in a social sense, although his parents loved him and cared for him; whereas the physically handicapped boy participated in social and ritual activities, there being nothing the matter with his mental faculties.

I once overheard some people talking about a woman not present at the time who was heavily pregnant, saying that she would have a difficult birth. When I enquired why, they said that she was known to 'eat alone', the cardinal 'sin' as far as the Chewong are concerned. They said that the child in the stomach could watch its mother's ungenerous behaviour and would not want to come out to be looked after by such a mean person.

Another case shows the father's mystical link with the prenatal growth of his child. Although the macaque (*bawæg*) is not prohibited food for prospective parents in general, it is in some cases a *tolæg* animal (see Chapter 4). If someone suffers from epilepsy, *òh*, it is because the *yinlugen* (ghost) of the macaque has taken the *ruwai* of the sufferer and carried it to its own land up in the clouds. These people must never eat macaque meat, or an attack will immediately follow. One man, Eh, is prone to epileptic fits. Once, however, when his wife was pregnant, he did not heed this prohibition and ate some macaque. He had a fit. His son never touches the meat, having been told about the incident. It is assumed that were he to do so, he would also have an epileptic fit.

So far, I have tried to establish the presence of a vital principle in the womb and that it (as well as the physical part of the foetus) is vulnerable and may be affected by both parents during the pregnancy. The influence may affect either the physiological or the spiritual aspect of the child, and any one act may affect either. So, although the Chewong recognize the two parts of a human being, they do not see these as necessarily independent entities. In the light of the discussion so far, it is my contention that the ritual restrictions on the part of the parents during a pregnancy are a means by which both the physiological and the spiritual aspects of the child are strengthened and developed. They signify the mystical link between parents and the growth of the child in both its aspects. The two categories *ruwai* and *bajo* are not structurally opposed. The relationship between them is analogous to that pertaining between men and women; no special value is associated with the attributes of either. Rather, they are treated in some cases as complementary: in others as interchangeable. Both empirically and symbolically complementarity and inter-dependence are emphasized rather than differences and a superordination of the one over the other.

4

Humans and Superhumans

CHEWONG religion will be discussed from the point of view that to the Chewong, religion is mainly a matter of interaction between human beings and the numerous superhuman beings who inhabit their universe. In examining the relationship of the Chewong with the supernatural I also wish to test the general thesis that a lack of relative status constitutes an underlying notion of Chewong modes of thought.

The Chewong cosmology which provides the basis for an understanding of Chewong attitudes towards the superhuman beings will be examined first. My primary concern is to discern a meaningful pattern underlying their ideas. Furthermore, the concepts of *ruwai*, *bajo*, and *njug* (soul, body, breath) already raised in the previous chapter are here interpreted in terms of their meaning within the cosmological order. They will also be taken up, in more detail, in Part II. The relationships between these concepts are central in Chewong ideas, not only regarding themselves as individuals, but also on the level of the order of the universe. Through these concepts are explained life, death, health, and food.

Each main category of superhuman being is then discussed in detail and interpreted according to how they interrelate with human beings. This is summed up in terms of an overall model of exchange.

Finally, an examination of the various superhuman beings in terms of their attributed characteristics, qualities, and actions will be made before drawing some conclusions regarding the question of classification.

COSMOLOGY

The Chewong do not have a fully consistent and complete view of the cosmos. Only those aspects that are of special interest, or are related to specific explanations and interpretations, are differentiated and highlighted. What I shall be presenting is the result of hundreds of unconnected bits of information collected throughout the period of the field-work which are then gathered together under the general heading of cosmology.

Conceptually the Chewong cosmos is centred upon Earth. It is in relation to this that all other earths and spheres are visualized and allocated their places. Earth, that is the tropical rain forest and the humans (i.e., the Chewong), the animals, trees, and plants on it, is the yardstick by which alternative worlds are described. The Chewong cosmos has much in common with those of other Orang Asli groups. It is conceived of as consisting of several layers, both above and below this Earth. Each layer is complete in itself and the underside of each forms the sky (*langit*) of the one immediately below. In the case of this earth, known as Earth Seven (Te Tujuh), its sky is the underside of Earth Six (Te Enam). It is made out of stone and touches Earth Seven at two points: where the sun rises and sets. These two points are called the sky's feet (*chan langit*). The Chewong say that the sun has a path across the sky and that it walks across this once a day. It goes below Earth at night where it forms the sun for the earth immediately below, Earth Eight (Te Lapan). When it is below, however, the sun is cool, becoming hot again upon rising on Earth Seven. Daytime on Earth Seven is night on Earth Eight and vice versa. At first sight one might accept this simply as a logical explanation. The presence or absence of the sun means light or darkness and if it is absent on this earth and present on the one below, it is fair to assume that reverse conditions prevail. This does not seem to be the full explanation, however. All the various worlds both above and below, as well as those of superhuman beings on Earth Seven itself, have night when we have day and vice versa. Rather, through employing the technique of inversion, the Chewong mark off their own world as being a different type of world from all those that cannot be perceived by the ordinary man or woman.

To name these worlds by numbers is a curious phenomenon in so far as numbers are otherwise unimportant in Chewong intellectual constructions. None can say straight off how many children he or she has without counting on the fingers. In fact only one to four are indigenous Chewong words. Beyond four they employ Malay numerals, and probably these were adopted quite recently when they began to sell cane and to handle money. This numbering of the various layers of the cosmos is likely to be due to outside influence, both from other Orang Asli groups (see e.g., Dentan, 1968 and Endicott, 1979) and the Muslim Malays where the numeral seven is of high ritual importance. In fact the Chewong do not number the rest of the earths, although one informant insisted that there are Earths One, Two, Three, Four and Five above Earth Six. He was unable to give any information about the first four, except that they are uninhabited, very small, and covered in mist. (See Figure 1 for a diagram of the Chewong cosmos.)

The first earth to be individualized is number five, known as Timoh Awan (gibbon clouds). This is the land of certain gibbon ghosts (*yinlugen timoh*) who are immortal and who take the *ruwai* of small children if they eat gibbon flesh. They take the *ruwai* up to Timoh Awan and the child becomes very sick as a result.

Earth Six, Te Enam, is more frequently referred to as Moso Awan, Sosong, or Pulao Plò (fruit island). In many ways Earth Six epitomizes the Chewong view of the ideal world. It is pleasantly cool here all the time. Their sun is cool which means that it is very good for fruit-growing. In fact the fruit trees here bear all the year round. The people who live there eat only fruit. One piece of the fruit from Earth Six is enough to satisfy a whole family. The beings are known as the original people (*bi asal*).[1] They are of both sexes, and 'people like us' (*bi he*) say the Chewong, only they have cool blood and cool eyes. They do not fall sick or die. When they become very old they metamorphose into infants. On Earth Six there is a large lake called Pulam Briyao. There is an opening in Earth Six known as Pinto Lancob, which allows access to and from Earth Seven, but nowadays several large boulders roll around the opening and it is guarded by a snake so that only great shamans are able to enter. (See also Myth 3, Appendix 1.)

As already mentioned, the underside of Earth Six forms the firmament of Earth Seven. Underneath the *langit* are clouds (*al*) and some of these—those which under certain atmospheric circumstances have a golden rim around them—are the homes of two personified superhuman beings, Tanko and his wife Ya' Subang.[2] These two make thunder and lightning on Earth.

Also between Earth Seven and the firmament is Plantor, the home

---

[1] *Asal* is from the Arabic and means origin or original. It is the root of the same word which makes *asli* in *Orang Asli*. There seems to be no explanation why it has been absorbed into the Chewong language, but it is used again and again to indicate the meaning of original. I could not discover an indigenous word for this concept.

[2] *Ya'* means grandmother. *Subang* is Malay for ear studs.

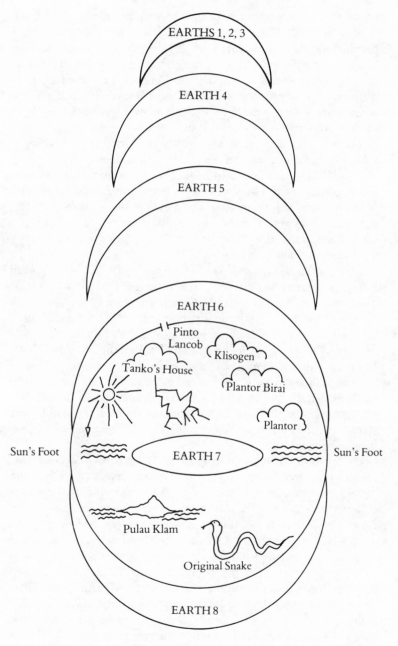

Figure 1 The Cosmos

of two other superhuman beings known as Bajægn (male) and Ponjur (female). They take the *ruwai* of those involved in accidents that include the shedding of blood. Plantor can be seen sometimes as bright red clouds at dusk. Red streaks across the sky at such times are said to be the blood of a newly dead person, or that of a pig. A different type of red clouds called Plantor Birai seen occasionally at sunrise or sunset are the homes of certain macaque ghosts (*yinlugen bawaig*) who may cause disease if someone has eaten macaque meat.

There is also another small earth in the clouds called Klisogen where a certain species of tiny frog (*britogen*) live. These frogs descend in large numbers during very heavy, prolonged downpour. They come in the rain and can be heard the following evening making a very loud humming sound as they sit on logs in, or near, the river. They return in the rain also the next day. Their arrival is seen as a sign that the particular storm is a *talaiden* storm caused by someone laughing at an animal.

Earth Seven is surrounded by ocean on all sides. All the rivers run into this ocean. The Chewong have never seen the ocean but their mythology and songs are full of references to it. Although Earth Seven is the home of ordinary humans, it also contains on it numerous other worlds invisible to the ordinary human eye. These worlds are inhabited by many different kinds of superhuman beings. In all cases the human day is their night and vice versa. Gunong Benom (Cheba Benem) the tallest mountain in the area, is particularly densely populated by various original people (*bi asal*). But river sources, waterfalls, large stones, other hills and mountains, trees, etc., may all be worlds inhabited by different species of non-human beings.

Underneath Earth Seven there are several other worlds, but these are not visualized as forming distinct separate layers. The Chewong would become confused whenever asked to pin-point where each different world was in relation to the others. These are questions of no importance to them. It is sufficient to separate each world conceptually. It is possible that they are visualized in less detail because there are no natural phenomena which can be seen below Earth and which may serve as foci for the imagination. Whatever the reason, one can distinguish three separate worlds below Earth Seven. First, there is the afterworld, Pulao Klam (fog island), also known as Pulao Nihod, Pulao Rangagn, Bapan Goleg, or Yinlugen Kael. It is situated underneath Earth Seven in the west. A corpse is always placed in the grave along an east-west axis with the head facing east.

Only the ghosts (*yinlugen*) of ordinary mortals go to Pulao Klam. The shamans (*putao*) are not buried, but are placed in a tree hut, and their *ruwai* go to live on a mountain on Earth Seven. Various personified superhuman beings also live below Earth Seven but not on Pulao Klam. The chief among these is the Original Snake (*talòden asal*) who causes the *talaiden* storms when anyone has committed *talaiden* by laughing at animals. This snake is huge, and is often referred to as *talòden naga*. It is a woman and she lives in the water underneath Earth Seven. Whenever she moves, and this she does only when someone has committed *talaiden*, water wells up and drowns all the offenders whom she then swallows. The Snake is sometimes referred to as Ya' Rud, one of Tanko's wives.

Finally there is Earth Eight (Te Lapan), where many old people (*bi badòden*) of both sexes live. These are also *bi asal*, but little is known about them apart from the myth in which they gave several important things to early mankind (see below).

All these different worlds are envisaged as separate entities with their own firmament, moon, sun, and stars as well as rivers, water, mountains, plants, etc. (See Figure 1.) Earth Seven, as human beings know it, alone among all these different worlds suffers from having a hot sun. This was even more so a long time ago. The Chewong tell the story of the sun and the moon, the chief ingredients of which are found among many of the Orang Asli groups:

Both the sun and the moon are women. They are sisters, and the sun is the elder. The stars are the moon's children. A long time ago, the sun also had children. Many little suns were in the sky during the daytime, and it was very hot on Earth Seven. One day the moon took all her children and hid them in the knot of hair that she wore at the nape of her neck. 'Where are your children?' asked the sun when she saw her. 'I have swallowed them all', replied the moon, 'why don't you eat yours as well?' she told her elder sister. So the sun did, but when the last one had been swallowed, the moon opened up her hair and let all her children fall out. The sun realised that she had been tricked. She became very angry. She quarrelled with the moon who ran away. The sun ran after her, but she could not catch up with her. She is still chasing her younger sister across the sky and below the Earth. But people were very glad, for it was no longer so very hot on this earth.

The sun is still much too hot for the Chewong's liking, however, and they blame much of their disease and misfortune on the hot sun. I was asked many times if the sun in England was a cool one. 'You have a different sun over there, do you?' they always enquired when commenting upon how rarely I became ill.

The *putao* can travel to all the different worlds during sleep or trance. The various superhuman beings cannot visit each other; they can, however, visit Earth Seven. Whenever the *putao* flies off to some other world this does not involve danger for anyone but himself. Whenever a superhuman being leaves his own world and comes to Earth Seven, on the other hand, this usually means calamity of some sort. For instance, when the Original Snake moves as a result of *talaiden*, the water from below Earth will wipe out everything and everybody on Earth. If the *bi asal* from Earth Six should decide to come to have a look at Earth Seven to see how the fruit trees that they planted long ago are faring, they descend as heavy rain and wind and this may damage people and their property. If humans inadvertently enter a *ruwai*-trap set for pigs by a *bas* (a species of harmful superhuman being) they get sick, etc. There are numerous examples to the effect that the continued equilibrium on Earth Seven is dependent upon the continued separation of the various worlds and their elements. The balance of good order is upset whenever the boundaries are crossed. The only time when this does not apply is during certain ritual situations such as the healing seance (*nöpoh*) when all the various helpers from other worlds are asked to descend.

The spatial orientation of the Chewong cosmos is simple. There is an above/below axis, and to a lesser extent, an east/west one, but these do not seem to form a nucleus for a further set of dichotomies. The neatness of this spatial orientation is somewhat brought into question by the existence of numerous worlds on Earth Seven itself which not only surround the human world, but also co-exist together with it—occupying the same space, but invisible to the ordinary human eye.

In all these different worlds—above, below, and intermingled—numerous species of superhuman beings are found. These do not, however, lend themselves to an analysis in terms of their spatial organization. In each sphere a mixture of the various attributes and characteristics is discernible. Each is represented by males and females; by helpful beings and harmful beings; by members of the different categories; and there is no significant predominance of *ruwai* being associated with one and body with another (but see discussion on death and the shaman (*putao*) in Chapter 6). Hence, despite the rather clear spatial organization which may be discerned, no similarly clear pattern emerges from an examination of the beings that are thus located in space. It follows that above and below have meaning as direction only, not as content. This question will be examined at the end of the chapter.

THE SUPERHUMAN BEINGS

The various superhuman beings will now be discussed in detail in order to determine how they are conceived of in relation to humans as well as to each other. There are several possible ways of approaching the material, all of which have advantages and disadvantages. The first point I wish to make is that unlike other writers, see e.g., Endicott and Schebesta, I have deliberately avoided the term 'god' or 'deity' and use the term 'superhuman beings' instead. Secondly, these beings are not conceptually differentiated in a way which would indicate that there is a hierarchical ordering of them.

The Chewong do, however, distinguish several categories of superhuman beings, namely 'original people' (*bi asal*); 'ghosts' (*yinlugen*); 'hidden people' (*bi inhar*); and 'disease-causing people' (*bas*). This classification will be followed. Since each category includes beings who do not display similar characteristics, and since there is a considerable overlap of these between categories; added to which Chewong attitudes to different members of each category cannot be correlated to the characteristics, this approach immediately leads one into a problem of definition, one that Endicott solved by treating each category of deity as a polythetic class of attributes. He was led to do this because of the numerous inconsistencies in the information he was given about them, and he concluded that to the Batek:

The way the deity concepts are used suggests that their main importance is as part of the conventional description of how the world works. They are the concepts in terms of which certain 'natural' processes and events are described and explained—What I am calling the deities of the Negritos are, I suggest, ideas built up out of imagined actions, corporeal images, and names—named deities normally consist of combinations of image-role sets and (that) there are more ways to combine components of a set of (more than two) elements in the set.

(Endicott, 1979: 199, 201.)

The Chewong material, however, presents different problems. The information given by the various informants about the various superhuman beings and their activities was always consistent. So although there is agreement on their attributes and characteristics, these are not easily analysed in terms of accepted notions of what constitutes a category or a class. The indigenous classification of superhuman beings therefore presents the anthropologist with several problems. There is an overlap of attributes between different sub-classes within one category, and the features of beings within one class can be diametrically opposed. For instance, within each category there are some beings who are helpful to humans and others who are harmful. Some characteristics are found scattered seemingly haphazardly throughout the categories, and it is impossible to analyse them in structural terms. (See Tables 4.1, 4.2 and 4.3 for a summary.) Despite these difficulties from the analytical point of view, I have chosen to follow the Chewong's own divisions as closely as possible, since by doing so I would maintain that most can be learnt about their modes of thought. The question of the indigenous classification will be discussed in detail in the last chapter, so here only the 'inconsistencies' in each category will be pointed out as we come across them, while discussion will mainly be concerned with the relationship between members of each category of super-human beings and between these and humanity. (The inconsistencies are, of course, only in the mind of the anthropologist and from the point of view of traditional analysis.)

BI ASAL

The original people (*bi asal*) are beings who have existed always. They were there before Earth Seven was made, before plants, animals, and humans. Some of them were instrumental in the creation and formation of human culture and can therefore best be regarded as culture heroes. Some are individualized and have specific myths attached to their names, still others are referred to collectively. Some live on earths above this one, some on earths below, and some live on Earth Seven itself, but in different worlds from that of humans. Whereas some no longer have any contact with humans, others stand in relationships of continuous exchanges between themselves and human beings. Each will be considered in turn.

Culture Heroes

The Chewong have no myths regarding the creation of the universe or that of Earth. They can offer no interpretation on how it all came about. They do, however, have a rather curious belief that every so often Earth Seven is turned upside down. Everything on it is drowned and destroyed, and the flat new surface of its earlier underside is made again into mountains, valleys, etc. New trees are planted, and new humans made. It is Tohan who causes this to happen whenever he feels it has become too dirty (*kama*) on this earth. Dirt in this context means too many people, too many deaths, too much blood from killing animals, and too much urine and faeces—all of which are said to make Earth Seven very hot and unhealthy. When this is about to happen Tohan warns all the Orang Asli who then turn into flower buds and fly up to Earth Six. The rest of mankind dies. This would seem to indicate that the *bi asal* of Earth Six are in fact 'jungle people' of earlier days, and therefore in a sense the ancestors of the Chewong, who in turn will be the ancestors of the new people to be made at a future date.

Tohan is the creator of the first humans. He is a man and he lives on Earth Seven near the sea. According to one version he also, together with the *bi asal* from Earth Six, planted all the fruit trees in the forest. They took seed from Earth Six and brought it down and sowed and planted. They planted tapioca and lived on Earth Seven for a long time. Eventually they found it too hot, and dirty (this was after the advent of human beings) so all except Tohan returned to Earth Six where they have been ever since.

The Chewong do not have any stories that account for the creation of animals. They do, however, have accounts of how the first humans were made and the sort of life they led. Ogilvie (1949: 18) was told a myth by Beng which corresponds very closely with the ones I was told by several different people on various occasions, and it is given here in full as it was told to me. An abbreviated version has already appeared earlier.

A long, long time ago there were no people on Earth Seven. Allah Ta' Allah (sometimes Tohan) told his Nabi to make people out of earth. The Nabi did not know what people were supposed to look like, so he first made the shape of an elephant. When Allah Ta' Allah saw it he said, 'That is not people (*beri*) that is an elephant (*gadjah*). Make them like us.' So the Nabi tried again and this time he made the shape of a human being. He made two shapes, one man and one woman, [in Ogilvie's version he made just one, sex unspecified] but they were not alive. So he went to Allah Ta' Allah and told him that the figures had no breath (*njug*). Allah Ta' Allah blew into his clenched fist and passed the breath into Nabi's hands. He had one breath in each hand. He started back to the two earth figures, but on the way he wanted to see what breath looked like, so he opened both fists. He could see nothing, however, and the breath disappeared. Nabi returned to Allah Ta' Allah who gave him two new breaths. He went to the figures without looking at the breath, and he placed his fist on the fontanelle of each figure in turn and blew through it. Then he hit their big toes. The two figures stood up. They were alive. They were the first human couple. They did not know what to do in order to have children. The Nabi did not know either. He tried putting a piece of firewood up the anus of the woman, but that was no good. The couple had sexual intercourse, but they did not know what this would lead to. They were stupid. The woman became pregnant, but they did not know, and when she began to have terrible stomach pains they did not understand that she was about to give birth. They did not know what to do, so the man cut open the woman's stomach and took out the child inside. The child lived, but the woman died. This is how the early people delivered their babies. There were no women in those days. When their first child was born their husbands cut open their stomachs and the women died. The husband did not know what to do with the child, but his wife's ghost (*yinlugen*) came to him in a dream and told him to let the child suck at his elbow. The man did this, and milk appeared which the child drank. This was how all babies were kept alive after their mothers had died.

This creation myth has much in common with the Batek one (see Endicott, 1979: 83), and may in some respects be influenced by them. The details about the lack of knowledge concerning sexual intercourse and childbirth, however, appear to be unique to the Chewong. There are several myths about these early days, when people were 'stupid' (*panir*) and did not know how to behave as proper human beings should. The following story about *maro*, the rule that forbids eating alone, an act which today is the primary 'sin' to the Chewong, again stresses the state of ignorance and the role of the *bi asal* as culture heroes.

In the old, old days people did not know about *maro*: that one may not eat alone but always be generous and share one's food. One day Bujægn Yed went hunting. He shot a binturong. He prepared it and cooked it in the jungle on his own. In those days people lived by the maxim 'whatever I catch I eat, whatever you catch you eat'. That was how it was in the old days. While Bujægn Yed was eating his catch of the day, Yinlugen Bud (ghost of tree trunk) came by. He is an original 'ghost' who was around before the first humans. Bud asked Yed what he was doing. 'I am eating my binturong,' replied Yed. 'If you eat alone and don't share, you *maro* [putting oneself in a state of ritual danger that can lead to death]. You must always share your food with others. Human beings must never eat alone,' Bud told him. When he heard this Yed took his binturong meat and went home. He gave the meat to his wife who was pregnant. She ate and was no longer hungry. She was about to give birth. She had bad pains in her stomach. Yed took out his knife and prepared to cut open her stomach. Yinlugen Bud who had followed Yed back to his house asked him what he was doing. 'I am going to cut open my wife's stomach so that the child can get out,' said Yed. 'No, no,' said Bud. 'Don't do that. There is an opening.' He showed Yed how to press on the stomach of the pregnant woman, and when the baby came out, Bud showed Yed how to cut the navel string with a piece of bamboo and tie it with a piece of cane. Then he showed him how to wrap the afterbirth in leaves and place it in a tree, and how to cover the blood with ashes. Yed then started to feed the child from his elbow, which was how the men used to feed their babies after their wives had died from having their stomach cut open. 'What are you doing?' asked Bud, 'there is milk in the mother's breasts.' Then Bud taught the birth spells, and the various leaves to be used for medicines after the birth. He showed him which species of tree fibres to boil and give the mother to drink, and which leaves to warm up and put on her stomach. He also told him all the *pantang* (rules) connected with birth: the woman must sleep next to the fire, she cannot go out except to relieve herself, nor can she eat meat until all bleeding has ceased. Having taught Yed all practices connected with childbirth, Yinlugen Bud returned to his own land. From then on women did not die in childbirth and people did not eat alone any more, but always brought back their game and shared it with everybody.

This myth is known by every adult Chewong. They take much pleasure in telling it, commenting continually upon the stupidity of those early people. It is always told as one story, the theme of eating alone leading into the faulty childbirth procedures, with Yinlugen Bud putting them right in both cases. Yinlugen Bud never appears in any other myths. He is known by all, but only as the culture hero in these two instances. He is still alive, but 'has returned to his own land.' As will be seen later, food, and the symbolism in connection with the handling and sharing of it, form a major part in Chewong collective representations. It is used as an important idiom for ordering their social life as well as their universe. It is therefore of interest to note that one of the first things the early humans were taught, even before they had learnt how to procreate properly, was to share their food. Man is by definition a social being, but in the Chewong case food, not marriage, is the idiom for stating this.

This myth is also of considerable significance for another reason, which may best be introduced by addressing the question why two such apparently diverse themes—the sharing of food and correct birth practices—are both contained within the same narrative.

I believe that the link between these two themes is also an important key to the understanding of Chewong ideas as a whole. What underlies them, I suggest is the abstract concept of separation—a concept which is of crucial importance in Chewong ideas and practices. In the case of food, the myth stresses that it must be divided and shared; in the case of birth procedures, the myth both identifies the correct way in which the division between mother and baby should take place, and it also specifies the need for the baby and its placenta (referred to today as the child's older sibling, *tòh*) to be separated, the latter being placed in a tree outside the swidden.

The argument can be taken one step further in each case, showing how each act of separation contributes to the formation and maintenance of society. Implicit in the myth is the absence of society as it is known today. In order to transcend the main focus from the individual to the social, permanent and reciprocal chains of relationships have to be established. Until Yinlugen Bud gave them the rule of *maro*, by which the emphasis on individuality rather than shared sociability was expelled at pain of death, society cannot be said to have existed. Secondly, by separating the child from its mother correctly the death of the mother is avoided, thereby allowing the formation of a complete family consisting of mother, father, and child—the minimum social unit of Chewong society. Thirdly, the separation of the baby from its placenta (or younger from older—another prerequisite for social life) signifies the beginning of the individual's life-span. The older sibling is said to go to the afterworld to reappear on the person's death. The life-span lasts only until such time when the two are reunited. At that point the person enters the next world, the world of *yinlugen*.

The crucial importance of the concept of separation is perhaps indicated most forcefully by the third of these, since in this case the explicit association is between separation and life on the one hand, and reunification and death on the other. The validity of this argument is most graphically supported when the method of infanticide practised by the Chewong upon unwanted babies is examined. Immediately following the birth, the parents do not cut the umbilical cord, but place it together with the placenta over the baby's nose thus suffocating him. By this act they ensure that the younger and the older are not separated at all, but remain together—thereby negating the birth. It is as if the child was never born. It is by stopping breath (*njug*), the prerequisite for life, that this is achieved.

Similarly, a stillborn baby is not separated from its placenta. In both these instances, the baby and the placenta are buried together.

The act of cutting flesh can also be discerned in these three instances. Firstly, the cutting open of the woman; secondly, the cutting of the navel string; and thirdly, the cutting up of meat to be shared. The first of these instances, which occurred before the intercession of Yinlugen Bud, was incorrect. As a result of Yinlugen Bud, however, the correct way of cutting was initiated—both with regard to parturition, and the partition of food to be shared. Finally, I would suggest that the incest rules, breach of which is death, are founded on this similar need for separation; in this instance the separation, or sharing out, of semen. Marry away from your own kind or die is the message that is conveyed here.

A series of transformations can be discerned in these instances. Each instance is different from the rest, but the underlying reason is always the same; namely the need for proper separation.

Attention should be drawn to the fact that in this myth regarding the first humans, two rules are given them, namely *maro* and *pantang*. I shall be returning to the place of rules in Chewong life in Chapter 8.

To continue the discussion on the *bi asal* as culture heroes, the following is a myth about how the Chewong learnt other practices, the knowledge of which places them firmly in the realm of culture as opposed to that of nature. In this case they are taught by *bi asal* from the earth below.

A long, long time ago there was no night on this earth—Earth Seven. The people slept during the day. They did not have fire either. If they wanted to cook tapioca they just put it on the ground. The moon was just another star. One day a boy lost his knife through a hole in the ground. He followed after it and fell down on Earth Eight which was very close to Earth Seven in those days. Very old people lived down there. Ya' Rud was there and other people who are still alive today. They gave him some food to eat. Then it became very dark and the boy was frightened. 'What is this?' he wanted to know. 'This is night,' they told him. 'We do not have night in my world,' said the boy. The people then lighted resin torches. 'What is that?' asked the boy. 'Those are resin torches,' they told him. The people on Earth Eight had fire and they made a big one. The boy was very frightened. 'What is that?' he asked. 'That is fire,' they explained. 'We do not have fire in my world,' the boy said. The people told the boy that if there was no night all the tubers would die, so they gave him night. They put night in a bamboo for him to take with him to Earth Seven. They also gave him fire, resin torches, and tobacco, and showed him how to cook food. The boy returned to this earth. When he poured out night from the bamboo and it became dark the people here became very frightened. The boy explained to them that it was night and that if they did not have night their tubers would die. He then gave them the resin torches and the fire so that they could cook their food. When he smoked the tobacco and the people saw the smoke coming out of his mouth they became very frightened, but the boy told them that it tasted good.

Two of the objects given, tobacco and fire, are of course the two items which feature in exchanges which today take place upon meetings. Tobacco is exchanged, and fire is used both to light the cigarettes and to cook the food which is also exchanged. This exchange between individual Chewong can therefore be said to take on a wider significance, drawing it into the cosmology. Whereas the tobacco exchange is explicit, the use of fire is less so. However, the Chewong acknowledge the vital role of fire, 'if we did not have fire (ɔz) we would die,' they say. A recognition of this fact, and the realization that they and fire stand in a special relationship to one another, is manifested in their statement that fire has *ruwai*, and that it is necessary to reciprocate the service it renders to mankind. This is done by giving it its 'food' which is the fur of killed animals, particularly that of monkeys. This accounts for the Chewong practice of always throwing an animal on to the fire and burning off all its fur (*pasa ai*) before cutting it up and disposing of the intestines, etc. The fur is the gift to the fire. If no meat has been caught for a while then they give it some peel from a tuber, or a certain species of leaf. There is therefore a continuous chain of exchange between humans and fire.

In this context it is interesting to note that humans also repay monkeys for shooting them and that hair is again used as the medium for payment. This is done on Pulao Klam when the *yinlugen* of the dead hunter pulls out his head hair to give to the *yinlugen* of the monkey. One hair for each monkey shot is the rule, and if there are not enough hairs on the head, the hunter takes them from his body, from his armpits, and finally, from his pubic hair.

Hair is also used as a medium to appease Tanko and the Original Snake following a *talaiden* offence. It is taken from the body, put on a burning ember and thrown on the ground.

The *bi asal* on Earth Eight no longer have any contact with the Chewong. They are still there, but do not impinge upon their life. The *putao* do not visit Earth Eight during seances, and there appear to be no references to them in the songs. They do not become spirit-guides. They are therefore of less importance than those of Earth Six who are still responsible for giving the seasonal fruits. They do not come to visit Earth Seven on any occasion. They display similar characteristics to the *bi asal* of Earth Six in so far as they have cool blood and are therefore immortal. Their sun is also cool.

Bi Asal of Earth Six

The people who live above on Earth Six are also referred to as *bi asal*, or in general conversation just as 'them' (*gödn*) accompanied by a head movement pointing upwards. Although they gave the first fruit trees to humanity and can in this respect be regarded as culture heroes, they are different from the ones just discussed in so far as there is still a continuing relationship between them and human beings. In the early days, after the creation, they lived on Earth Seven as well as on Earth Six. At that time ordinary humans could also travel between the two earths. Eventually the *bi asal* found Earth Seven too hot for their liking and they returned to Earth Six where they have lived ever since.

They rarely visit Earth Seven these days. They are frightened of the heat and the dirt. Very occasionally, however, they decide to have a look at how things are going down here, what the people are up to and how the fruit trees are doing. Then they travel down through Pinto Lancob on strong winds and rains. Some people told me that the *bi asal* actually were the rain and the wind, others that these were their paths. The Chewong are extremely frightened by heavy storms. Ordinary wind and rain that occur almost daily is not commented upon, but strong and heavy rain and wind always signify superhuman activity of some sort. One interpretation of a storm is the descent of *bi asal* from Earth Six or from Gunong Benom. Such storms can cause havoc to settlements and forest alike, destroying houses and killing people. If *bi asal* is thought to be the cause, a person, usually a man with some esoteric knowledge, will run out into the rain and shout to them to go away. 'It is we who are here, your grandchildren. We are very shy/timid (*lidya*). Don't come so close!' they shout upwards into the storm. Others will be busily preparing a special pot of incense for blowing smoke in several directions away from themselves. The smoke forms alternative paths for the *bi asal* to travel along. But although the Chewong are very frightened by the sudden advent of the *bi asal* they do not attribute to them any malevolent intentions. Rather, the *bi asal* do not seem to realize their own powers of destruction. They come quite peacefully wanting only to look, but because they are so strong and powerful, they may destroy people in the process. It is because of this that they are told not to come too close.

The following story about Earth Six and the inhabitants there was related by a man at Dong. The various elements in it were also known by the Krau Chewong, but they did not present these in one sequence.

The people who live on Earth Six above do not defecate or urinate. Their children are metamorphosed flowers. [One man said children are born from

the forehead on Earth Six above, and from the calf[1] on Earth Six below.]
Above Earth Six is Timoh Maro, where gibbon (*timoh*) people live. Above
Timoh Maro there are no people, though there are earths. Klarei (species of
cicada) also live on Earth Six. There used to be a rope connecting Earth
Seven with Earth Six above (*tali reba*). Once a man did a *nöpoh* (singing
seance) and he started to climb the rope, but he was not *putao* (shaman) and
he fell down and broke his thigh-bone. His son-in-law was *putao*. He did a
nöpoh also and started to climb up the rope. His body climbed, not just his
ruwai as is the case with *putao* today. When he reached Earth Six he saw all the
fruit trees, and he took durian, rambutan, and other fruit and placed them all
on a straw mat and wanted to bring them back with him. The people up
there would not let him take any of the fruit away. They told him that the
earth where he came from was called Earth Seven and that it was a dirty place
because the people there defecated and urinated and shed blood. So the man
went down again empty-handed. When he reached Earth Seven, he told his
father-in-law what had happened and what he had been told by the people up
on Earth Six. The people there had also told him that they would not
descend to Earth Seven because of the dirty state it was in.

The next day the man did another *nöpoh* and again he went up to Earth Six.
This time he took just a small piece of durian, but when the people saw this
they ran after him to take it back. He ran all over the place, but they
followed, wanting to expel him. Finally he fell off and crashed down to
Earth Seven where he died from the impact. When the other people from his
settlement went to look at the corpse, they found the small piece of the
durian skin in his clenched fist. This they took and cut into very many small
pieces and planted them in various places. The pieces became durian trees,
rambutan trees and all the other fruit trees.

The rope that had linked the two earths fell into the fire and was burnt.
From then on people could not climb up to Earth Six. Only the *ruwai* of great
putao can travel there these days.

A few points in this myth need elaboration. First, that the children
on Earth Six are metamorphosed flowers. The Chewong of Krau say
that the people there become very old and then turn into babies again.
It is the *bi hali* who are metamorphosed flowers. However, it will be
remembered that every so often Tohan turns over Earth Seven, at
which point everybody dies except the jungle people. They turn into
blossoms and fly up to Earth Six. In view of this, the origin of, at least
some of the *bi asal* of Earth Six can be said to be ordinary humans

---

[1] The image of birth taking place in the calf is not unknown among other *orang
asli*. The Temiar say that in 'prehistoric times women gave birth from their left calf'
(Stewart, 1949: 65); and according to the Benua—Jakun the first human woman
conceived and gave birth from her calf (Skeat, 1906, vol. II: 185). See also Myth 1,
Appendix 1.

via a series of metamorphoses: first into flowers, then into *bi asal*.

Secondly, an alternative version is given of how fruit trees originated on Earth Seven, namely by theft. The Krau Chewong told me both versions without worrying about the inconsistency; the different myths are told in different contexts. They are, however, always very insistent that the *bi asal* guard their fruit very jealously, and there are several stories about *putao* from Earth Seven ascending to Earth Six and trying to trick the people up there to let them bring back some fruit. Today it is the sign of a great *putao* if he can not only reach Earth Six but also bring back with him a small piece of the skin of a fruit from there.

In the same way that Earth Six is the ideal world as far as the Chewong are concerned, so the *bi asal* who live there symbolize their notions about ideal beings. It is to these that they compare themselves, and through this comparison that they realize their own shortcomings. In the days when all men still had free access to Earth Six there was no disease or death. If they fell sick, they would just climb (others say fly) up there and the cool environment would ensure speedy recovery. Spells always work when it is cool enough, they say, and often a whole family with one sick member will leave the settlement where it is hot and hence the spells do not 'catch' (*chab*)[1] in order to sleep on the ground (*abn ka te*). This means building a shelter in the forest where it is cool. To be cool is to be healthy and inviolable, sadly a difficult state to achieve on Earth Seven. It is not just the environment which is cool on Earth Six, the *bi asal* have cool bodies by virtue of their cool, white blood. They are frightened of humans coming up there because of their hot blood. The culmination of a shaman's training and initiation is for him to manage to fly through the Pinto Lancob to Earth Six. By so doing he has proved himself worthy of the *bi asal* who make him one of them. They slash at his wrists and let all the hot red blood run out. Then they give him cool white blood like their own. He is now a 'dew shaman' (*putao modn*) which means that he can change himself into dew, thus facilitating his entry through Pinto Lancob. Dew also becomes his spirit-guide. His body is cool like that of the *bi asal*. In the past there were great *putao* who could hold burning embers in their hands without feeling pain, or work in the sun all day without

---

[1] The best explanation of this word is conveyed by its use in connection with a tape recorder. When I thought I had recorded some songs, I found that the batteries had run out, and the songs had not been recorded. The Chewong said that the tape had not *chab*, it had not caught, or fixed, the songs.

perspiring. Thus a big *putao* does not die like the rest of humanity, he only changes his body or 'cloak' (*bajo*), as they put it. His *ruwai* is immortal. After death it joins all the other *putao* of the past who have gone to various mountains on Earth Seven, or he may join his spirit-guide wife in the forest. Strangely enough dead *putao* do not go to join the *bi asal* on Earth Six.

Despite this, the Chewong regard the *bi asal* of Earth Six as equal to themselves. They are at the same time different and the same. Again and again it was said by someone describing them to me that they are 'our people', or 'people just like us' (*bi he*). They are not fundamentally different from the ordinary humans, only some of their attributes are. But these very attributes can be obtained by those humans who wish to acquire them. Anyone, man or woman, may become *putao* should they so wish. It is a matter of not being lazy in studying with existing *putao*. When a person has studied enough, he or she meets spirit-guides in dreams and eventually with the help of these and the acquired knowledge, the *putao* can fly up to Earth Six to become a *putao modn*.

According to the Chewong view, then, the *bi asal* of Earth Six constitute a model for an ideal state of being. There is nothing, how-ever, that prevents them from attaining the same ideal conditions for themselves. They are all potential immortal and inviolable beings, and it is up to the individual to choose to attain such a state or not.

These *bi asal* do not impinge upon daily life, they are not the creators, they never become spirit-guides, they do not cause disease nor aid in their cure, but they initiate shamans. They gave the first fruit to man, whether this was by design or through theft, and man is dependent for his annual fruit season upon their goodwill. Therefore the Chewong will conduct many singing sessions (*nöpoh*) for the sole purpose of pleasing the *bi asal* when they see that the blossom season is approaching. The *putao modn* is also known as *putao plò* (fruit *putao*) and it is likely that there is a link between fruit and water, or dew. As will be seen later, moisture is associated with life, whereas dryness is associated with death. In this context one should remember how there is said to be a lake, Pulam Briyao, on Earth Six. This is the only example of the stated presence of water in a superhuman world, a further indication of its association with fruit, dew, health, and coolness. The *putao modn*, will fly up to Earth Six bringing with him the various paraphernalia made out of leaves necessary for the *nöpoh* to give to the *bi asal*. They cherish the gifts very much, as such leaves do not grow on Earth Six, and when on Earth Six they turn into blossoms and fruit. In return the *bi asal* give an abundant fruit season. They do this by throwing down flowers from the fruit trees through Pinto Lancob. The direct exchange between humans and the *bi asal* is in this instance one of identical goods. (See Myth 3, Appendix 1, for more details.)

Fruit is the ideal form of sustenance to the Chewong. They have several stories of how in the past they lived on nothing else through the intervention of their *putao*. (See Myths 3 and 4, Appendix 1.) Here they would seem to be making a direct comparison between themselves and the *bi asal*. But today they do not have fruit all the year round, and they are forced to look elsewhere for their food. Were they to eat nothing but fruit, the Chewong would also be immortal. On the other hand, they claim that they need to eat meat and say, 'if we don't eat meat we die'. They are in fact extremely fond of meat and will start complaining if more than two or three meatless days go by. It is, however, through their own activities of killing animals and shedding their blood that their own world becomes dirty, and by eating the meat that their bodies become hot. There is therefore an inherent paradox embedded in their conceptions. On the one hand they postulate the ideal state of cleanliness and coolness with its consequent state of health, yet through their desire for meat they willingly pollute themselves, all the while bemoaning their own state of pollution.

The big *putao* are said not only to eat very little of anything, but more specifically, rarely to touch meat of any kind. The *putao* is clearly classed with the *bi asal* of above. He displays the same attributes and qualities as they do. As such he is not only a mediator between ordinary humanity and these superhuman beings, but as one of them he symbolizes the unity between the two, and the possibility of fusion.

The 'Poison Maidens'

Another class of culture heroes is a group of maidens who live on Gunong Benom. They gave the dart poison to the Chewong. One man once went higher on Benom than anyone had been before. He met a group of maidens who were completely naked. He was wearing his loincloth made of bark cloth. When they saw his loincloth they wanted to learn how to make it. He showed them how to take the bark from the *ipoh* tree (*dog*), and hammer it out with a wooden hammer until it became very soft. In return the maidens showed him how to make poison (*böl*) from the same tree and how to put it on his dart heads so that animals would die quickly. The maidens wanted to marry him, but he found that he could not have sexual intercourse with them because they were too poisonous. They are still living on Gunong Benom, and are still trying to become men's spirit-guides and marry them, but because they are so poisonous men do not want them.

This category of culture hero is slightly different from the others. First of all it is exclusively female, whereas those on Earths Six and Eight contain both sexes. Others, like Tohan, Nabi, and Yinlugen Bud are all males. Moreover, an inversion of normal practice can be discerned. Dart poison, as an integral part of blowpipe hunting, the quintessential male occupation, is originally given by women; whereas creation, knowledge about birth and food practices, the quintessential female occupations, are initiated by men.

Secondly, unlike the other culture heroes who gave existence and knowledge to humans without receiving anything in return, the 'poison maidens' exchanged the poison for clothing. Thus, in a sense, as the maidens were culture heroes to humans, so humans played the same role in their relationship with the maidens.

Thirdly, these maidens are different from the rest of the culture heroes in so far as they want to continue to have relationships with humans. In this they differ from others who once their task had been performed retired into an immobile existence with no further contact with humans. The other exceptions in this respect are the people of Earth Six, who initiate *putao* and are the source of the annual fruit production. Whereas the maidens wish to have contact with people but are unable to do so because of the contagious nature of their poisonous bodies, humans wish to have contact with the *bi asal* of Earth Six, but are prevented from achieving this because of the contagious nature of their own hot bodies.

The nature of the objects exchanged is interesting not only because they are made from the same tree, but also because they can be said to be opposites. Thus the maidens gave poison, a substance which works from the inside, whereas the man gave clothing, an external wrapping. The sap for making the poison comes from inside the tree, the bark from its outside.

Finally, the gift of poison is an ambiguous one. It enables man to provide sustenance for himself in the form of meat. However, this is achieved at the expense of killing other creatures, always a sensitive matter with the Chewong. Furthermore, by shedding blood, they make Earth Seven hot, and by eating meat they make their own bodies hot, thereby accelerating the process which ultimately leads to their own individual death.

Other Bi Asal

The fear of thunder, lightning, heavy winds, and the accompanying catastrophe of flooding is prominent among many Orang Asli groups. Intimately bound to this fear is the belief that somehow these phenomena are the results of conscious acts on the part of various superhuman beings as a direct consequence of certain human transgressions. This aspect of Orang Asli religion has caught the attention of most observers and commentators, due to the rather curious belief that laughing at animals causes these superhuman beings to send the storms, and to the blood sacrifice said by many Orang Asli to be the only way to stop these storms from annihilating the whole world. Some of the problems connected with this belief will not be discussed here; my prime consideration is the Chewong conceptions, and an attempt will be made to fit these into their general attitude towards the supernatural world.

Like the Negritos (see e.g., Schebesta, 1928; Endicott, 1979), and the Semai (Dentan, 1968), the Chewong associate certain types of thunderstorm with the transgression of certain rules. The rules and their structural implications will be discussed in detail later; here I shall concentrate upon the relationship between the superhuman beings in question and human beings. Whenever there is the sound of thunder, the Chewong say 'karei!' This word is found among the Batek (Endicott, 1979: 3), Jahai (Schebesta, 1928: 185), Kenta (Schebesta: 220), Mendriq (Evans, 1937: 157), Temiar (Benjamin, 1966: 35). In most of these cases this word is said to stand for the verb 'to thunder' as well as the name of the being who causes it. Endicott suggests that it is Negrito rather than Senoi in origin, being found also among Negritos of the Philippines, and 'that the association of that name with at least some of the features of the Malayan Negrito thunder-god is very ancient. The name 'karei' seems to be pre-Mon–Khmer in origin' (1976: 180). (For a recent discussion of the 'thunder complex' in South-East Asia, see Blunt, 1981.)

I have shown elsewhere (Howell, 1977) that the Orang Asli 'thunder-god' must not be regarded as a being with an easily defined identity, either among just one group or on a comparative level. Rather, he appears as a composite of various attributes according to context and locality. If one accepts the 'thunder-god' as a polythetic concept, the problem of identity vanishes. In accordance with this view, the Chewong concept fits in as yet another combination of attributes.

Although they associate the word *karei* with thunder, this is not a name of any being who causes the thunder to happen. It refers to the phenomenon of thunder alone. In view of this, it would seem likely that they have imported the word from their Negrito neighbours. Thunder is, however, caused by one superhuman being known as Tanko [cf., the Semai *Enku* (Dentan, 1968: 20), the 'Sakai of Behang River', *Ungku* (Evans, 1918: 195), and the Malay *Tunku, Engku, tengku*, a title of high rank, in some states a royal title more or less the same as king]. Tanko lives in his house in the clouds. He causes all types of thunder, but these fall into two separate categories. First, there is the sort of thunder that occurs almost daily at certain times of the year and is nothing to worry about. It is distant and brief, and is caused by Tanko enjoying himself by playing with a loop of cane which he sends rolling over the floor of his house. The other kind, known as *talaiden*, is very different. It is caused by someone having transgressed the *talaiden* rule of laughing at an animal and this type of thunder means that the offender stands in mortal danger. *Talaiden* thunder is the sound of Tanko's laughter at the human predicament. Similarly, there are two kinds of lightning. The ordinary lightning accompanying the harmless thunder called *kilad* (cf., Malay *kilat*, lightning) is said to be the reflections of Ya' Subang's ear-rings when she shakes her head. Ya' Subang is one of Tanko's wives. She also lives in the clouds. The lightning in a *talaiden* situation is known as Tanko's fire (*òz Tanko*) and is said to be thunderbolts thrown by Tanko down to Earth. If these hit the offender he is burnt to death. Tanko also sends his thunderbolts into the hip and knee joints of those who commit incest, known simply as *tanko*. This will cause the offenders severe pain, and if the offence is a serious one, that is if the persons concerned persist in their liaison, they will die. The Chewong can give me no explanation of Tanko's role in this matter. He is, however, closely associated with sex. He is portrayed as highly sexed and on the constant look-out for new wives. When a baby is born, he gives ordinary white rice to a new-born boy to eat, but sweet, yellow rice to new-born girls. He then starts to have sexual intercourse with the baby girl. With very little girls he does this by placing his penis between their toes. Then, as they start to grow older, he moves up their legs until at puberty he has reached the vagina (cf., Myth 2, Appendix 1). This is marked by the onset of the menses, and from then on, until a woman becomes 'too old and ugly' for him to want, Tanko has sexual intercourse regularly with all females, both human and animals. The monthly blood is said to be the blood accompanying the birth of Tanko's children, *wòng Tanko*, and this expression is in fact a euphemism for menstruation. Girls and women are unaware of this regular interference of Tanko, his children go immediately to join their father in his house in the clouds. It is likely that an association is made between the colour of the rice being given to new-born girls and the menstrual blood, especially when one considers that the Chewong do not distinguish between yellow and red, both colours being called *sowòd*. Thus birth is associated with blood—both in the case of Tanko's children and that of human children. Whereas the former birth takes place without the knowledge of the woman, and the children establish no relationship with her, manifesting their existence only through the appearance of the blood; the beginning of the growth of the human child is signified by the absence of the birth of more of Tanko's children. When menstrual blood fails to appear for a long time, a woman knows that the process of creating a child has begun. She cannot carry two different kinds of children simultaneously. While the man's semen builds the foetus, the storing of menstrual blood builds its counterpart, the placenta. The production of the human child therefore requires contribution from both sexes; while that of Tanko's children requires the male contribution only. We may recall the Chewong statement that the man makes the baby and that the woman is 'the house only'. In the case of Tanko this is true; in the case of humans it is true only with regard to the actual child, but not with respect to the older sibling, his counterpart, without whom he cannot exist.

It is Tanko's semen which makes his children. This process is not complemented by the making of a placenta. It is the man's semen that makes the human child; but this process can only be started once Tanko has had sexual intercourse with a woman, thereby paving the way for the parallel production of a placenta. In this way human beings are dependent upon Tanko for making them fertile, and hence, as the Chewong state, it is impossible for a girl to become pregnant before the onset of the menses.

It is also worth noting the spatial orientation which can be seen to exist here. Tanko's children go above; the placenta is placed in the branches of a tree. Both have a direct association with menstrual blood.

But Tanko is a rather complex character. He is not to be trusted, as the following story shows.

A long time ago everybody went to plant hill rice in a newly cleared swidden. Only a young man and his aunt, *dehe*, were at home. They were picking lice out of each other's hair. Tanko came down from his house in the sky. He went up to an old man and greeted him. He saw the aunt at a distance. 'That is a very pretty girl,' he said 'I want to have a better look at her.' He walked up to the house. 'Your aunt is very pretty,' he said to the nephew, 'I want to sleep with her.' 'Well that is up to the girl herself,' replied he. 'I don't want to,' said the girl. 'Come with me into the jungle and we'll sleep together,' insisted Tanko. But the girl refused. 'I will come back and then we will get married,' said Tanko. He went into the swidden and told the old man that he was going home but that he would return in seven days and marry the girl. Then he went up to his own house.

Seven days later Tanko sent down lightning with which he picked up the girl and her nephew. He pulled them up into his house in the sky. First he took the boy, laid him over a piece of wood, hit him over the head and threw him to his dogs, which ate him. Then he picked up the girl, laid her across a piece of wood and hit her on the head. Having done this he threw her to the dogs as well. He had lied about wanting to marry the girl. He only wanted meat for his dogs.

In this story two separate messages are given. First, we are told about Tanko's sexual appetite, and secondly, about his trickery. This myth is also told to explain about Tanko as the punisher of incest. It is *tanko* (incest) for an aunt and a nephew to marry each other, but it is also *tanko* for them to have any physical contact such as picking lice out of each other's hair—as exemplified by the myth. By extension, it is also *tanko* for parents and adult children of opposite sex to be in close physical contact.

Tanko can, and does, become a spirit-guide to a *putao*, but he is an unreliable helper. There is a song entitled 'Tanko' which is still sung by the young men. Firstly, he can never enter the house where a seance (*nöpoh*) is going on, he is too hot and has to sit on a nearby mountain top. If he were to descend fully, everything would catch fire. The association here is probably with thunderbolts, but it is interesting to notice one superhuman being associated with heat. Secondly, and more importantly, he cannot be trusted actually to help his 'father' i.e., the person whose spirit-guide he is. I was told about one old woman who was very ill, and asked her son, who had Tanko as one of his spirit-guides, to call upon him to help cure her. If Tanko does help, his aid is very powerful. So the man sang his

Tanko song, and his *ruwai* went up to meet Tanko, whom he asked to help cure his mother. Tanko said he would, but in fact he took her *ruwai* and gave it to his dogs to eat, and the woman died. The Chewong have no view of what Tanko is supposed to look like. The comparison to a siamang, commonly found among the Negritos, is not encountered among them. The notion that he is evil or malevolent (see, e.g., Benjamin and Endicott) is not one that the Chewong express. His sexual activities are always talked about with laughter. In the case of *talaiden*, the Chewong do not say that he is evil or bad (*yabud*). He never instigates the *talaiden* storms, etc. unless someone has broken the *talaiden* rule and laughed at some animal. This is very clearly understood by the Chewong. If we do not commit *talaiden*, then Tanko does not make *talaiden*, they say.

In one of his aspects, that of punisher of *talaiden* offences, Tanko is closely associated with another personified superhuman being, the Original Snake (*talòden asal*), also known as *naga*,[1] or *talòden naga*, as well as Ya' Rud. This snake is a woman and she lives below the Earth. When the Chewong talk about *talaiden* they normally emphasize the Original Snake rather than Tanko. Children are told off for laughing at animals by reference to the Snake and the accompanying threat that she will come and swallow them. The special signs to look for in identifying a particular storm as being *talaiden* is not so much the thunder and lightning, made by Tanko, as the special kind of wind that is said to blow along the ground. This is the Snake's breath when someone has committed *talaiden*. This wind will blow down houses and cause large trees to fall upon the people. Another sign is the upwelling of water from the ground. This is caused by the Snake moving, thus allowing the waters which surround the Earth to penetrate the crust and to flood everybody and everything away down to the Snake, who then gobbles up the people. They always use the verb 'swallow' (*gòd*) when they talk about the Snake. This means that she not only eats the body of the offenders, but also their *ruwai*. Because of this they suffer complete extinction, there being no *yinlugen*. Whenever the Chewong fear that a particular storm might be of this *talaiden* variety they take steps to try to placate the Snake and Tanko. They will always say that it is the Snake who has to be appeased, but when asked about Tanko, they would reply: 'it is the same thing'. They first carry out a smoke-blowing ritual similar to that when the *bi asal* are thought to be descending, but in this case it is

[1] *Naga* is Sanskrit for a dragon or snake of supernatural size and as such is part of Hindu mythology. We find references to the *naga* all over South-East Asia.

meant to appease. They blow it upwards to Tanko and downwards to the Snake. If this does not help, they will cut some hair from the temple and the armpit of the person who admits to, or is suspected of, having laughed at some animal. If the hair is taken from the right temple they take hair from the left armpit and vice versa. This they put on a piece of ember from the fireplace and throw it out on the ground shouting, 'We are ashamed (*lidya*). We have laughed at such and such an animal. We pay (*bayar*).' If a child has laughed, they will add that it was a small child who did not know about the *talaiden* rule properly. There is no prescribed way to say this. The temple hair is known as 'hair for paying Tanko' (*sòg bayar Tanko*). A more powerful hair to burn and throw is pubic hair, but this is only done in extreme cases. If this does not make the storm abate, and if they observe water starting to well up, they will cut themselves on the inside of the right lower arm, and utter the same words while holding the arm out in the rain letting the blood fall on the ground. This is supposed to go down to the Snake who then accepts the sacrifice. Unlike many other Orang Asli groups who throw the blood upwards and downwards in order to appease beings in both spheres, the Chewong only throw it, as well as the hair (but not the smoke) down on the ground. This again would seem to indicate the predominant importance of the Snake.

I never witnessed the blood sacrifice, but it was said that they do carry it out in severe cases—the last one was about fifteen years ago. I observed the hair-cutting ritual on several occasions. The significance of hair as a medium of exchange has already been noted in respect to fire and to the *yinlugen* of monkeys.

Having experienced several heavy thunderstorms it is not difficult to sympathize with the Orang Asli's fear of them. They spring up quickly with very little warning. Because the soil is very shallow, the roots of huge trees are not able to grow deeply into the earth; they are therefore easily toppled over, and following a severe storm dozens of enormous trees are scattered on the ground. About four years before my arrival, three people had been killed and three badly injured while sleeping in the forest when such a storm broke out. Their fear is therefore highly justifiable. Their interpretation of such storms is less easy to understand than their fear of them. To attribute natural catastrophes to superhuman beings is not unusual, but to specify laughing at animals as the cause is puzzling. Unlike the other Orang Asli groups, the Chewong do not single out just a few animals as members of the prohibited class *talaiden*. No animal whatsoever may be teased or laughed at. They even extend this to meat being cooked and eaten, and to the saucepans in which meat is cooked. The question of laughing at animals has a number of ramifications with regard to rules governing behaviour, symbolic classification, and to humans' relationship with animals. These will be returned to.

Tanko and the Original Snake personify environmental calamities of the highest order that can befall the Chewong. Their existence makes some sort of comprehensible order out of otherwise senseless destruction. They are symbolized by one male and one female being, one from above and one from below, one from the element of air the other from that of water. They are abstract symbols of nature *par excellence*. The forces that they represent are outside man's control in the ordinary run of things, but by linking the calamities with man's actions, indeed positing them as a direct result of transgression, humans manage to bring the phenomena within their own sphere. So neither Tanko nor the Original Snake is considered by the Chewong as evil or unpredictably capricious. They insist that *talaiden* catastrophes occur only as a direct result of their own behaviour. These two beings, therefore, cannot be said to have any special power which they can exercise willy-nilly over human beings. Neither are they superior to any other superhuman beings. Like the *bi asal*, their power is limited to the specific spheres allocated to them. The various superhuman beings do not interact with each other in any way. It would not occur to the Chewong to say, for example, that Tohan is bigger or more important than Tanko. They are simply not compared to each other, rather they fulfil a role external to the narrow confines of Chewong society, but internal to the wider social universe of humans and superhumans.

The Original Snake herself does not become the spirit-guide of humans, though her younger sisters, *Bongso talòden*, of whom there are several, often do.

Tanko and the Original Snake are of particular interest in two respects which differentiate them from other beings in the Chewong pantheon. Firstly, they are both multi-faceted. Tanko is not only the maker of thunder and lightning, manifested in *talaiden* storms, but he is also the punisher of incest offences, as well as the cause of menstruation in women. The Original Snake, the wife of Tanko, is not only the punisher of *talaiden* offences (in which she is complemented by Tanko) but also, as Ya' Rud, she is one of the culture heroes who gave fire, tobacco, and night to humanity. (It is reasonable to regard Tanko also as a culture hero, in that by introducing the Chewong to marriage rules he brought them out of their pre-cultural, pre-social stage.)

The second common feature is that the type of death inflicted by both Tanko and the Original Snake is such as to cause total annihilation. Both the body and the *ruwai* are destroyed so that no *yinlugen* comes into existence, thus preventing entry into the next world. Furthermore, in more abstract terms, a complementarity between the two can be discerned. Thus they are male and female, and one lives above whereas the other lives below. They are, however, both associated with water (rain and flooding), and with air (wind), as well as with both body and *ruwai*.

Bajægn and Ponjur are two beings who live on Plantor. Plantor lies between Earths Six and Seven and can be seen sometimes at sunset as a brilliant red cloud. When it appears, the Chewong are worried and, if at all possible, they hurry indoors and wait for it to pass. Bajægn and Ponjur are male and female respectively. They are strongly associated with blood. Like Tanko, they have a seemingly insatiable sexual appetite and are constantly on the look-out for a new spouse. Whenever someone is killed, or involved in an accident, and blood is spilled, it is one of these two beings who has caused it; Bajægn causing women to have such an accident, and Ponjur men. When blood is shed they can take the *ruwai* of the person and bring it up to Plantor where they marry it. But again, they do not cause such accidents to happen haphazardly. It is only through specific transgressions (*mali*) that they are activated and may cause the mishap. Once a person has died in such an accident, his or her *ruwai* goes on living on Plantor. It does not become a *yinlugen* as do the rest of mankind. But on Plantor the *ruwai* forgets all about his or her previous life on Earth Seven. The Chewong say that these people have 'died alive' (*kabus gòz*). By this they mean that the death was sudden, and not caused by *bas* eating the *ruwai* or the abduction by some other being. This is probably why the *ruwai* is visualized as continuing to live. In this instance only the body dies.

YINLUGEN

Another class of superhuman beings are referred to as 'ghosts', *yinlugen*. As with *bi asal* there are several sub-categories, but in this case they have very little in common beyond the fact that they cause harm to human beings. Discussion here will be confined to superhuman beings, and human ghosts will be dealt with in a later chapter on the concept of the human personage. Although the Chewong employ the word *yinlugen* which is also used to describe that aspect of the individual psyche which exists after death, and as such is best translated with the English word 'ghost', the word does not seem to cover the same meaning when they talk about *yinlugen* as a class of beings. Then it means just certain beings who cause harm to humans.

Yinlugen Asal

There are several original ghosts, and they all take the human *ruwai* if given an opportunity. The opportunity in these cases comes about when people do not observe preventive ritual measures at times when these are known to be called for. The Original Earth Ghost (*yinlugen te' asal*) is a woman who lives in the earth. Her name is said by some to be Dayong. She is particularly interested in the *ruwai* of new-born and very small babies, as well as in that of the mother. During childbirth she is attracted by the smell of blood which falls to the ground underneath the house during labour, which is why a husband must cover this with ashes immediately the baby is born. Then when the Earth Ghost arrives and sees the ashes she sees them as water and she is unable to cross it and returns to the depths of the earth. Were she to eat the blood, the association between it and the mother and child is so intimate that they would fall ill and possibly die.

Small children may not bathe in the river lest their *ruwai* be taken by the Original River Ghost (*yinlugen tam asal*) also known as Ya' Katyer. They are therefore washed in heated water inside the house. If this is ever done after dark, then some glowing embers must be thrown on to the area below the house where the water falls. The smell of the water in which the baby has been washed again attracts the Earth Ghost. The burning ember looks to her like huge boulders, and she is unable to pass these.

No one may bathe in the river when rain and sunshine occur simultaneously (*sabn tiregn*). This is a time when the River Ghost emerges. For the same reason one must not bathe after dusk and before dawn. Moreover, if a small child falls accidentally into a river, someone must throw a piece of wood into the water after it otherwise the River Ghost might think that the child is a gift for her, but when she sees the wood, she takes that instead.

These two *yinlugen asal*, like the *bi asal*, were in existence before the creation of human beings. They are intimately associated with their own elements of earth and water, and if one makes contact with these at specifically dangerous times without taking ritual precautions, they are able to attack and cause disease and possible death. Yinlugen Bud has been classed with the culture heroes (see p. 68), but he is in fact a *yinlugen asal*. As such he differs from the rest in so far as he is helpful to humans having made them into social beings. The Chewong could not offer any explanation as to why he is a *yinlugen*. His inclusion in this category is another illustration of the overlap of characteristics within one category.

Tolæg

The remaining class of *yinlugen* are not, so far as could be ascertained, *yinlugen asal*. They are mystically linked to certain specific species of animals, and in certain circumstances when the flesh of the animal concerned is eaten, the *yinlugen* will take the *ruwai* of the offender.

The word *tolæg* is applied to the animals in question, to the actual prohibition itself, and to the repercussion, which is *ruwai* loss. In ordinary parlance *tolæg* means 'to walk from one place to another'. In this case it is used metaphorically to indicate the removal of the *ruwai* to the land of the *yinlugen*. The prohibition only affects small children. It is their *ruwai* which is removed if the flesh of gibbon (*timoh*), the water monitor lizard (*geriang*), the mountain tortoise (*kokh gading*), the otter (*manang*), the slow loris (*tuwò*), and in the case of a few people only, the macaque (*baweig*) are eaten by them. The prohibition also applies to pregnant and suckling women. Their own *ruwai* are not in danger, but the foetus, or suckling baby, would be affected through the mother.

Whenever the carcass of any of these animals is brought back to the settlement, there are loud shouts of '*tolæg! tolæg!*' and the children are told to keep away. The animals should have their fur burnt off in the forest, lest the children breathe the smell.

If a child does eat the meat of any of these animals its *ruwai* is taken to the world of the respective *yinlugen*. These are all in different places. That of the gibbons is above Earth Six, and is known as Timoh Awan, gibbon clouds. The mountain tortoise brings the *ruwai* to its land on top of a very high mountain, the otter to the underground headwaters of a river, the water monitor lizard to the sea, and the macaque to its land in the clouds, known as Plantor Birai. Thus the different worlds of the *yinlugen* of the *tolæg* animals are directly associated with the abodes of the species on Earth Seven. The arboreal gibbon and macaque are envisaged to have their *yinlugen* counterparts up above Earth, whereas the riverine otter is thought to inhabit subterranean river sources. The location of the tortoise *yinlugen* world on a mountain is consistent with the particular species living on hillsides; and the lizards which are often found beside rivers take the *ruwai* to the ocean underneath Earth Seven. (All rivers are said to flow into the sea.) If we examine the worlds of these various *yinlugen* in purely spatial terms, we find that they are oriented along an above-below axis. However, this further reveals that the *ruwai* is not exclusively associated with either sphere.

Macaque is a *tolæg* animal, but it is of a slightly different order. Only some people are susceptible to having their *ruwai* taken, and the result of a macaque taking the *ruwai* is an epileptic fit (*òh*). Those that are prone to this never eat macaque meat even when they are adults, as was exemplified by the case of Eh discussed earlier. The slow loris is, as will become apparent, of a different kind from the rest.

It must be pointed out that it is not the ghost of the actual animal killed that takes the *ruwai*. Rather, there seems to be a separate group of beings called gibbon ghost (*yinlugen timoh*), lizard ghost (*yinlugen geriang*), etc. each of which could be said to be the alter ego of the ordinary gibbon, lizard, etc.

BI INHAR

The next category of superhuman beings known collectively as *bi inhar*, or possibly *bi itn har*, will now be examined. *Bi*, of course, means people, or person, but the second part of this name is more difficult to translate. When Beng first mentioned these beings, he hid an object under a piece of cloth and used the Malay word for 'to hide' (*sembunyi*) to explain it. From this one may deduce that the correct appellation would be 'hidden people'. The usual word for 'to hide', however, is *podol*, and the other possibility which might have been conveyed by Beng's action, namely that they are invisible, would have been expressed by *primon*. Needham was told that dead *putao* 'had become a hidden person, *bi edn hare* (dia jadi orang sembunyi). *Bi* means "a person, man"; *edn* means "far"; and *hare* is "hidden" ', but adds 'perhaps Beng was trying to say "invisible" and did not know the Malay' (1956: 68). My own enquiries did not produce identical replies, but the Chewong did not like to talk about these people by that name, so my probings would just meet with affirmations to whatever I asked in this connection. Whereas *idn* means 'over there', *hare* was not a word I came across in any connection, and as far as I could tell they used the one word *inhar* for these beings. But whatever their correct name, in view of the above it seems likely that 'hidden people' or something very similar is being conveyed.

As a class the *bi inhar* is rather puzzling. I was frequently given contradictory information about them all through my field-work. The term is sometimes used very loosely to cover anybody with the power to take on human shape, but also with the added quality of cool eyes, thus rendering them different from ordinary humans. At other times I was told that all *bi inhar* had at some time been human. Whereas I am certain that the latter explanation is not correct, I also disregard the former, but with less certainty. Using the term spirit-guide very loosely, it appears from my questionings and observations that *bi inhar* are all those beings who are actual or potential spirit-guides. What they all have in common is that they live somewhere on Earth Seven, but not in the world visible to ordinary human eyes. Furthermore each different type has its own world (*mona'*).

The various beings referred to as *bi inhar* display vastly different characteristics and attributes, and some are consciously helpful to man, others consciously or unconsciously harmful. They are all beings who have an intimate, and in some cases regular, relationship with humans. As such they differ from the *bi asal*. Knowledge about the *bi inhar* is revealed to an individual and then passed on to the rest of the community, whereas knowledge about the *bi asal* is received knowledge from a 'long, long time ago' from those Chewong who lived together with them on Earth Seven. The *bi asal* were there before humans, and will still be there after the total destruction envisaged to take place some time in the future. The *bi inhar*, on the other hand, come and go. As long as one particular type reveals himself or herself in a dream or trance to someone, they will in a sense exist but only as long as that individual does, or the song about them is sung after this person's death. New and different ones are constantly appearing, though in the case of the best-known spirit-guides, these tend to be passed on from one person to another. The point to be emphasized is that the *bi inhar*, with the exception of *bas* discussed below, stand in a constant relationship to one or more person and that this relationship is one of reciprocity and exchange. Those in existence at the time of my visit are described below.

Dead Putao

It has already been said that unlike the *ruwai* of ordinary human beings, the *ruwai* of the *putao* does not die when his body does. He sheds his 'cloak' (*bajo*), and goes to join the *ruwai* or other *putao* of the past or his spirit-guide wife. These great *putao*, who become *bi inhar*, are referred to by many different names in the songs, e.g., Suleyman, Malim, Balogn, Salitn, and Praman. Only the very big *putao* become *bi inhar*. Strictly speaking only those *putao* become *bi inhar* who upon death are not buried as ordinary humans are, but are placed in a specially built tree-house, *sanrug*. Ogilvie gives a description of the '*sanrug*' of Maroi, the last Chewong *putao* to be thus disposed of.

> On his death he was not buried in the earth, but placed in a *sanrung*, a *sanrung* being a house specially built for the dead. This is completely enclosed by walls having no doors and no windows. His was built about twenty feet from the ground in four conveniently growing trees. The roof was thatched with palm leaves, the walls were of 'kepong' bark, and the floor also of this bark, *katuq*, overlying timbers. With him were placed in the *sanrung* his personal belongings and some food for his spirit, *jenlung*.
>
> (Ogilvie, 1949: 12.)

Ogilvie did not see the *sanrugn* himself, but was given a description of it fairly shortly after the event. The description tallies with the ones I was given, but other details are not correct. He thinks that all old men are thus disposed of, but in fact only the great *putao* were placed in a *sanrug*. It is possible, however, that in the past all old men were *putao*, there are certainly indications that this may have been so. Due partly to the resettlement of the Chewong near Kampong Bolok during the early days of the Emergency where they were apprehensive of treating their dead *putao* in such a way, and partly to the continuing fear of Malay repercussions should they find a corpse exposed in a tree-house, the Chewong have since been burying all their dead, although Beng said that he wishes to be placed in one. Women *putao* may also be placed in a *sanrugn*.

'Tree burials' are fairly common throughout South-East Asia. As far as I know, in the Malay Peninsula, only the Negritos thus dispose of their dead.

The inversion of normal funeral practices in the case of the *putao* emphasizes the special nature of these persons. Furthermore, by placing them in the tree tops, above the ground as opposed to in the ground, they symbolically express the association of the *putao* with the *bi asal* of Earth Six. It also links them with the practice of leaving the afterbirth wrapped in a mat in the branches of a tree. Thus, unlike ordinary humans who upon burial are reunited with their 'elder sibling' of the placenta and then go to the Afterworld below, the *putao* does not die. Rather, he symbolically joins his 'elder sibling' in the tree tops. Death does not result from this joining of the two parts of the individual, and the *putao* has no *yinlugen*.

The *putao bi inhar* keep a close surveillance over the daily activities of the Chewong. 'They know everything we do and what happens to us,' I was told. 'They look after (*jaga*)[1] us.' This they do in two ways. Firstly they are always called upon in songs during healing seances (*nöpoh*). They are asked to help the *putao* in his search of the lost *ruwai*. They are also asked to descend to the house in which the *nöpoh* is taking place as this protects the people there from any invading unfriendly spirits. Their presence is seen as having a general beneficial effect. Secondly, they are in daily communication with the people through the intermediary of one or more persons who at dusk every day performs something very akin to our prayer. This will be described in detail since no other mention of similar activities has appeared in the literature on other Orang Asli groups. When I visited a Jah Hut settlement on Sungei Krau I observed that they performed a ceremony reminiscent of the Chewong one and I was told that this was in fact the same thing. Since I could not understand the Jah Hut language, nor do I know much about their religious system as very little has been published, I am in no position to say whether the Jah Hut 'prayer' is of the same order as that of the Chewong. I only watched four different people conduct it among the Chewong, three of these were residing at Gambiar, and included one woman. The rest say that they do not know how to do it. It seems that the practice is of ancient origin; old people said that their fathers and grandfathers had done it, and that it is part of their 'traditional knowledge' (*paham duidui* or *hæraten kra noh*).

When the sun has just set, a bowl of embers is placed in a corner of the room and wood chips (*òz taba*) that have a pleasant—the Chewong say 'good' (*soòben*) scent are laid on top of the smouldering embers. This is kept going all through the performance, with new incense being put on it at intervals. The *bi inhar* are said to eat this smoke. It is their staple, *ratn*. On no account must it be allowed to go out as the communication would then be interrupted. (This is the same kind of wood chips used in redirecting descending *bi asal*, or in

---

[1] *Jaga* as used in Malay is of Sanskrit derivation and means to be awake, or to be watchful. The Chewong use it as meaning to protect or watch over.

atonement to Tanko and the Original Snake. It is also used in some healing rituals, and during *nopoh*. Another name is *òz niye*.)

The person squats in front of the bowl, facing the wall. He takes some of the smoke from the incense in his right fist, puts this to his mouth, and blows it upwards in four directions. This is a similar procedure to that of redirecting descending *bi asal* or diverting thunderstorms. Then he makes a handshake movement in the four cardinal directions, by extending the right hand and clasping it just above the wrist with the left. Having done this he says '*Salam alaikom, alaikom assalam, minta maaf*', 'peace upon you, upon you peace (Arabic), excuse me' (Malay). The smoke carries the words to the *bi inhar*. The speaker then embarks upon a very fast recitation rendered in a sing-song voice. He hardly stops to breathe during the entire prayer, which lasts from forty minutes to an hour. It is very difficult to understand what is being said as many Malay words are interjected, and the general development of the prayer seems to the uninitiated to leap from unfinished topic to unfinished topic. Like their songs, so much of what is expressed is unstated. A single word often serves as a reference to quite a complex idea. The speaker and the rest of the community know the shorthand system of communication and they need no further elaboration. The Chewong are extremely reticent about these prayers, and it was not until I had been with them for many months that I witnessed the first one. Even then they were reluctant to talk about it and persistently refused permission for me to tape it, on the grounds that the cassette might fall into the hands of the Malays. Since one of the purposes of the prayer is to ask the *bi inhar* to protect them against the Malays and prevent them from entering the forest, one can understand their fear.

Having made the preparations for contact with the *bi inhar*, the speaker then goes on to disparage himself; 'I know very little, I have not studied enough' and this is repeated at regular intervals as is the listing of the people to whom he is talking. 'You my grandfathers, my grandmothers, my uncles, my aunts it is I who speak.' Then the beings are asked to protect the Chewong against the Malays (*gob*), the attacks of various superhuman beings, such as *bas* and *yinlugen*, and against communist guerrillas (*bi komunis*). The names of all settlements are mentioned several times, as are the names of all the individuals in the settlement from which the performer is speaking; but not those of other settlements. If there has been a lot of disease recently this is mentioned, as are any important ventures about to be undertaken, e.g., 'my father Beng, and his nephew Tog, and myself are going to take cane down to Lanchang tomorrow. We are sleeping at Selur and at Gandah on the way. Please look after us. Don't let *gob* attack us. My mother Baha, my sister Nyom, my brother-in-law and their children will be here at Gambir while we are gone.' Whereas the incidentals are different each night, the invocations and the regular requests and information are identical and repeated many times throughout the 'prayer'. I witnessed one young man, Lamait, starting to practise praying. He had been taught the words while he was still young by his now dead father, but since he was not yet a *putao*, though he was studying, he was very self-deprecatory. 'I have not met any of you', he would say, 'but I have been told about you by my father, Jong; I hope that one day I may meet you, my grandfathers, my grandmothers, my uncles, my aunts.' Later he did meet some of them in a vision (see discussion on 'Hot and Cool Eyes' in Chapter 7) and his prayer became much more confident. He would then refer to the meeting and request cooperation.

As already mentioned, this nightly prayer is conducted on behalf of the whole community. On any given night only one person performs it. A shortened version is also undertaken at times when the threat of a major thunderstorm or high wind is imminent. Someone who has some esoteric knowledge will make the same kind of fire in the pot, blow the smoke in four directions and ask the *putao bi inhar* to watch over the people who have not yet returned from the forest. I was shown how to do this if I were ever alone at home when a storm was brewing. This kind of 'prayer' does not have to conform to a specific verbal programme. It is much more impromptu. I was told to blow the smoke so that my words would reach the *bi inhar* and just tell them the names of all the people who were still in the forest.

In view of the above, the *putao bi inhar* may be regarded as ancestor guardian spirits. They and the living stand in a relationship of exchange and reciprocity. The incense smoke that carries the words to them is their food. They are therefore dependent upon humans conducting the nightly prayer. In return for this they give protection and help.

These *bi inhar* take an active interest in any child, usually a boy, who wants to become a great *putao*. If the boy takes his esoteric studies seriously and avoids flirting with young girls, they will visit him in dreams and slowly, over a long period, initiate him. They give him spells so that eventually a proper spirit-guide (*wòng hieng*) will come to him and become part of him. Such an apprentice may not marry until he has found his *wòng hieng*. Once the novice *putao* becomes sufficiently adept he, i.e., his *ruwai*, can visit the *putao bi inhar* who will teach him spells. After he has had his blood exchanged on Earth Six, his eyes also become cool and he becomes one of the *bi inhar*, and after his death his *ruwai* goes to live amongst them. It is in this sense that the Chewong say of a dead *putao* that he has 'gone home to the mountain' (*ka weg ka cheba*). But it must be made clear that not all those who know how to say the 'prayer' or who have even met some of the dead *putao* or other *bi inhar* in a dream are regarded as great *putao* who will go to the mountain after their death. They are only a little *putao*.

Bi Hali and Other Spirit-guides

Although the dead *putao bi inhar* take an active interest in the training of *putao* and appear at healing *nöpoh*, they do not become a person's spirit-guide. Other types of *bi inhar* take on this role. The most common ones, and most adult men have at least one such, are the leaf people (*bi hali*). These are all female and since they cement their relationship with humans through marriage it follows that women do not meet them. They appear in all the songs, and in fact they give a song to their 'husbands' (*teh*) when they meet in dreams. The rest of the community knows when a young man has got such a 'wife' (*jeh*) when he first sings his own song at a *nöpoh*.

The *bi hali* are very beautiful, say the Chewong. Their bodies are completely covered in designs made by taking certain types of leaves which when dipped in a white creamy juice from the *pre* tree and printed on to the skin leave a dark brown design. They wear head-bands (*chin koyi*) plaited of sweet-smelling leaves, and have bundles of other sweet-smelling leaves tucked into their loincloths, hanging over their hips, known as *bodn*. They also have flowers in their hair. These decorations are all used by the Chewong themselves during a *nöpoh*, or whenever they feel like it. In the past, of course, all women made the same decorations on their bodies as do the *bi hali*, and they always wore *bodn*. The headband, however, is male attire, and in the not so distant past all adult males wore headbands every day. By dressing in an identical manner to the *bi hali*, the Chewong are not only stressing the conceptual closeness between themselves and the *bi hali*, but they are also making a statement about how beautiful the *bi hali* are. The *bi hali* attire and decorations span the traditional male and female ones.

The *bi hali* women are very gay and cheerful people. They dance and sing a great deal, and whenever their 'husbands', during a *nöpoh* sing the songs learnt from them, they arrive at the house. Here they sit and swing in the *riding* (loops made out of leaves and attached to the headband and to the *tali ruwai*, the string of plaited leaves that is hung across the house from one wall to another). It is along this string that the *putao*'s *ruwai* travels when it leaves his body. When many different *bi hali* are present, the house is filled with a fragrance, and often the women cry because it is so beautiful. The scent of the *bi hali* is highly coveted, but whereas everybody can smell it, only the *putao* can see the beings themselves. They themselves say in the songs how special the scent is, and they stress that it is very difficult to find. The *putao* search for plants that give the special desirable scent because when they have it, they please the *bi hali*. One can only do so with the help of the *bi hali* wife. I was told of one man who has been looking for it for 'five years'. Another *putao*, now dead, had a large piece of a bark that was regarded as particularly potent. He would chip off small pieces and exchange it for dart poison, blow-pipes, and other goods. The association of these leaf people with scent is a direct one. They live in flowers and leaves, many of which are known to possess fragrance.

They will bring dew (*modn*) so that the patient may be bathed in this in the morning. The dew is restorative. It is cool and replenishes the moisture in the body—and as has already been said, moisture signifies life. The link between dew and the *bi hali* is no doubt based upon the dew found on leaves and flowers in the morning. The dew *putao* whose spirit-guide is dew, also brings back dew from Earth Six during a *nöpoh*.

Any species of tree or plant may reveal itself as having *ruwai*, and thus *bi hali*. They come from their plant worlds and return to these when the *nöpoh* is over: 'the lemon-grass people return to the lemon-grass, the cucumber people to the cucumber', etc. (*bi siwei weg ke siwei, bi timon weg ke timon*). The *bi hali* do not eat or drink, they do not urinate or defecate. Their food, like that of the *putao bi inhar*, is the smoke from the incense burnt during *nöpoh* as well as dew.

One song which was given by a *bi inhar*, in this case Bongso from Gunong Ninyaed, will be rendered in full. *Bongso* is Malay for the youngest, last-born child, of a series. It is used in Chewong songs and myths as a personal name to indicate the youngest child of either sex. Traditionally, according to Chewong belief, all persons who are the youngest are also *putao*. A mythical character named Bongso is therefore necessarily a *putao* and expected to accomplish extraordinary feats. All the songs follow similar patterns, but only the person whose song it is may sing it during a *nöpoh*. The songs are sometimes sung in the evening before going to sleep. During a *nöpoh* men and women sit in a group and provide the percussion accompaniment by drumming bamboo of varying lengths on pieces of wood. They have one bamboo in each hand, and the act is known as *tòl lao*. Each song has its own rhythmic pattern. The *putao* take it in turn to sing, and the chorus repeats each line. Under no circumstances must the drumming be allowed to cease for the *putao*'s *ruwai* would be lost. It follows the sound of the drumming when it wants to return. All lights are extinguished. The *bi inhar* are frightened by lights because they cannot then see anything. Only bowls of burning incense are kept going throughout. The *putao* has a whisk made out of leaves with which he claps from time to time.

I cannot guarantee the word-for-word accuracy of the translation. I recorded the songs, and then tried to transcribe from the cassette, asking all the while for explanations. The Chewong insist that only the person whose song it is knows what it is all about, but in fact I discovered, after having worked on several, that they are very similar, and that there is a considerable degree of overlap of vocabulary and construction. Many words are not used in ordinary language, and many are Malay. According to the Chewong the *bi inhar* have a different language (*klugn masign*) from humans. Many of the words are just lists of flowers and plants, but they evoke to the Chewong specific *bi inhar*, and specific actions. Despite any errors in vocabulary, I nevertheless feel confident that the general outline of what is conveyed in the song is correct. When I asked what one particular word meant I was often told the reason why the word was used, what was actually implied by it as much as what it means in itself.

I have included notes on the meaning of the song immediately following the translation in order to facilitate the reading of it.

Bongso Gunong Ninyaed

Amòi! La Bongso pralaw
Mayin löpang, nanti ingat jaga juga Bongso
Masuk balai.
Ha tatyah kaming chinor
Seremdom kotom chinor padang
Seremdom di padang kuling.
Henang henaw, kiri kanan le tog löem
Riding sabogn.

Tog löem la riding Bongso,
Ah Bongso Kampong Pinang.
Söleraw kiri kanan
Kenel la buang
Bukan la mudah.
Tapi Bongso ingat jaga dalam balai,
Söreta jadi
Jangan lönkob lönkab
Lo koyī lönkai dara chinchong.
Yolang Nonsong, yolang panai,
Berelig söreta Plantor,
Berelig Plantor Saji,
Berelig Plantor Bamang.
Bukan mudah.
Hei Bongso.
Bongso, Bongso, masuk balai
Jangan malu keming Bongso, sama kita la yaman duhulu.
Bukan lang lain.
Keming Bongso halagn kita jaga
Mabog lawar, mabog malan
Lögogn pinang lögogn
Tapi Bongso dinobog malan
Tönale letag bilang
Tönale letag yampi.
La Bongso di antar kami
Antar kami keming.
La Gunong Benem serögleg ikut papaden
Lönkob lönkab. Amòi!
Sampai la Gunong Benem.
Ah Bongso töntang kolig kirir sölenod galògn lö bom
Bukan la mudah
Baderam debo di kawan ramai
Söleraw sönon lögogn.
Amòi! La Gunong Bimar.
Söleraw sönon Nintjar.
Ah, kamul sönon la med
Chachag kenel chinur.
Serenig rinye kami mani planchor,
Salener kami mani,
Silo planchor siko
Lepas mani kami siap limai
Owangi di minyeg wangian gunong
Bresigka kenel rilan
Serupa di moni chinkoyī,
Pakai chinkoyī owangi rayang gunong.

Chachag la meming chinor di Bongso jojong Benem,
Chachag keming chinor.
Padang lompod padang
He jaga keming chinchor palinog Gunong Benem
Bresig la riam.
Bukan mudah Bongso.
Sabanya di Bongso komagn hijau
Chachag chinor diam Gunong Benem.
Jadi diam kawan ramai
Bukan la mudah.
Ba sösong kabod yaman
Sösong di kabod hijau
Sösong di kabod puteh
Bukan mudah la Bongso.
Ingat jaga sömera jadi
Ingat jaga, Bongso.
Jadi komagn baderam ba ninget,
Sampai la balai
Nijo di popadn hijau
Kita mayin söreta la boï komagn
Mayin söreta la boï jijogn
Laut boï laut
Posare boï posare.
Berelig kiri kanan
Bongso suka kenel
Suka kenel buang
Tapi bukan lamad la Bongso dalam balai.
Idang lilu akan keming lompat lingit pochog serödang gading.
Planchor pochog serödang gading,
Kirai, kirai la pochog serödang.
Bongso komagn payong palas
Tredo dilidom
Tredo dilidom serödang bayang
Dolinan serödang modn.
Sudah la lilu.
Sudah lilu dalam balai la Bongso
Sudah lilu lamad la Bongso.
Jadi Bongso lippad polang,
Komero balig Kampong Pinang.
He lippad polang.
Pralaw planchor lopang,
Pralaw planchor lamodn,
Beremodn bajo.
Amòi! ah, Bongso.
Likat Gunong Dabogn.

Translation

Bongso from Mount Ninyaed[1]

Amòi! Bongso[2] flourish the whisk, the drums are speaking.
Wait, remember to be watchful also Bongso.
Enter the house.
We[3] (wear) *chinor* flowers in the hair
Serodom buds (from the) field
Serodom (flowers), *kulig* (flowers) (from the) field
Hey ho. Left, right (goes the) *tog* (leaf) whisk
Riding of *sabogn* leaves
Tog (leaf) whisk, *riding*, Bongso
Ah, Bongso! Kampong Betelnut[4]
Söleraw (leaf) whisk, left (and) right
See the throwing off[5]
Not easy
But Bongso, remember to watch over us in the house
Follow (and) become
Don't make noise (trampling over the floor)
The head swings to and fro,[6] *chinchong* maidens
Flies to *Nonsong*,[7] flies nicely
Turns over, follows (to) *Plantor*[8]
Turns over (towards) *Plantor* white
Turns over (towards) *Plantor* red
Not easy
We two Bongso
Bongso, Bongso enter the house.
Don't be shy of me, Bongso, (be) together with us from a long time ago[9]
Not now different
I, Bongso, now look after us.
Poisoned, eyes are rolling, poisoned, dizzy
Lögogn (leaves), betelnut, *lögogn* (leaves)[10]
But Bongso removes the dizziness
(He) washes the eyes with magical water
(He) washes the eyes with potent water
Bongso heals us.
He is among us.
From Mount Benom a ladder path, followed by a tree bridge.
Noise of walking feet. Amòi!
(They) arrive from Mount Benom[11]
'Ah, Bongso!' (they) see (to the) left a path obstructed by people[12]
Not easy.
All the *ramaei* (fruit) friends go
Söleraw (whisk), *söno* (leaves) (from) Nintjar[13]
Ah, mist (like) *söno* (leaves) in the eyes

Chachag (flowers on the body), see the *chinur* (flowers in the hair)[14]
We bathe under the waterfall, bathe under the spray
We bathe under the waterfall.
Walk about in the spray, walk about.
When we have bathed we put on our 'flying cloaks'
Scent of oil, scent from the mountain is carried by the wind.
See the *samaden*[15]
All like the scent of the headbands,
wearing headbands, dizzying scent from the mountain.
Chachag (flowers on the body), *chinor* (flowers in the hair), from Bongso
  of Mount Benom
Chachag (flowers on the body), *chinor* (flowers in the hair) (The) field,
  lompod (flowers) (from the) field
We guard *chinor* and *palinog* (trees) (on) Mount Benom
Samaden from far away.
Not easy, Bongso
Many green Bongso bumblebees[16]
Chachag (and) *chinor* (flowers), and *diam* (leaves) from Mount Benom
(The) *ramaei* (fruit) friends become *diam*
Not easy
Mist[17] from long ago (descends) from Sösong[18]
Green mist (descends) from Sösong
White mist (descends) from Sösong
Not easy, Bongso.
Remember to protect us from the mist that has become
(He) becomes bumblebee. They all[19] go to the tree top
Arrive from the house
Green *popadn* leaves.
We play the drums, the bumblebee follows (the sound) to the waves.
The sound of the drums follow the sound of the waves
Ocean waves, ocean
Whirlpool waves, whirlpool.
Turns over (to the) right (and) left
Bongso likes to watch[20]
Likes to watch the throwing.
But not late, Bongso, in the house
Not yet finished. I jump to the tree top, the buds of the *serödang* (tree) are
  (like) spikes
Shoots (of the) *serödang* tree top are (like) spikes
Fly, fly from the *serödang* tree top.
Bongso bumblebee, *payong* (and) *palas* (trees).
Cool mist makes it dark.
Cool mist (in the) shadow (of the) *serödang* tree
Hiding (the) *serödang* (tree) dew[21]
Already finished in the house, Bongso

Already finished late, Bongso
Bongso rolls up, wraps up, goes home
(The) wind returns to Kampong Betelnut.
We roll up, wrap up.
(When the) whisk is flourished (there is) spray of water,
Flourished, sprays of water (and) dew
Dew cloak
Amòi! Ah, Bongso
Back to Mount Dabogn[22]

Notes on the Song

1. A mountain on Earth Seven where many *bi inhar* live.
2. Bongso here means the particular *bi inhar* in question. This is an invocation on the part of the singer to make the *bi inhar* enter the house.
3. The *bi hali* are speaking.
4. This is the name of the world of some other *bi inhar*.
5. This refers to the *putao*'s *ruwai* leaving his body to travel.
6. The *putao* is in a trance, i.e., his *ruwai* has left his body.
7. The *bi hali* fly to Earth Six.
8. The *putao* always goes to Plantor during a seance. They look for the *ruwai* of the ill person there.
9. This is the *putao bi inhar* speaking. The dead shamans.
10. The poison which causes the sickness is from the *lögogn* leaf.
11. Various *bi asal* or *bi inhar*.
12. Malays. When they see them the *bi asal* do not want to proceed.
13. Mount Benom.
14. *Bi hali* are speaking again. They describe what they are wearing and what they are doing. Water symbolizes their cool (healing) properties.
15. Bandolier worn by the *putao*. When the beings who have taken the *ruwai* see this they become frightened and give it up.
16. The *putao* often turns himself into a bumblebee.
17. This means that *bas* are on their way.
18. The land of some *bas*.
19. The *putao* and the *bi inhar*.
20. The *bi inhar* laugh when they see the *ruwai* of the sick person being tossed about in the foam.
21. They hide the dew (which heals) from the *bas*.
22. Mount Benom.

Not only *bi hali* become spirit-guides; animals often do. In fact any animate or inanimate being or object may reveal itself as a spirit-guide. This was brought home to me when I heard a reference to 'Japanese aeroplane' (*kapal yapodn*) in one of the songs. I enquired about the meaning of this, and was told that one man had met in a dream the *ruwai* of a Japanese aeroplane. It became the man's spirit-guide and gave him a song. Men and women meet *ruwai*.

The relationship between a person and his spirit-guide involves many meetings, and if the person has studied to become a *putao* the spirit-guide enters the body of the *putao* and becomes one with him. It lives in his chest and is known as *wòng hieng*. *Wòng* means child; I do not know what *hieng* means. A really big *putao* has one or more *wòng hieng*, and he will never eat the flesh of the animal whose *ruwai* has become part of his own being. Many people who have established relationships with one or more *bi hali* or another personage will say that they have a *ruwai*, but will deny that they have a *wòng hieng*. But the fact that the two words are used in ordinary conversation interchangeably makes it difficult to appreciate the conceptual difference.

The *putao* who have animal *wòng hieng* may transform themselves into these animals. That is they may put on the particular animal 'cloak'. Their *ruwai* remains the same, but their 'cloak' changes. When asked if their own body was inside the animal one, they said that this was not the case, 'The foot becomes a tiger's foot, and the head becomes a tiger's head' and so on. As among most other Orang Asli groups, the tiger is the most feared animal, and as is the case elsewhere, the *putao* who has a tiger *ruwai* or *wòng hieng* is a very powerful *putao*. Modn said that her father, Yareng, had a tiger *wòng hieng*. He was able to become a tiger at will. Such tigers are different from ordinary ones, however. They never harm human beings, and whenever they go hunting, they bring some of the meat to a settlement for the people there to eat. So even when a member of the community has changed his body into that of an animal, his social obligation not to eat alone is still valid. Furthermore, when Yareng sang during a *nöpoh* many tigers would approach the house and lie underneath it. Yareng always told the people not to leave the house while he was singing because the tigers would attack them. They only respected him. He himself would sometimes go down and talk to them during a *nöpoh*. Yareng also once wanted to initiate his son Adòi into the mysteries of how to become a tiger. It is possible for these *putao* to do so if the person approached shows no fear in the tiger's presence. One day when he lay asleep, his *ruwai* went and became a tiger. Adòi was out fishing on his own, and his father in the shape of a tiger waited for him on the path home. When Adòi saw the tiger he became terrified and ran away as fast as he could. Because he had shown his fear, he did not learn how to become a tiger.

Similarly when a *putao* has died and his body has been placed in the *sanrugn*, one of his children, preferably the oldest son, should go the next day alone to the place where his father has been placed. His father, in the shape of a tiger, will wait for him, and impart much mystical knowledge if the son is not fearful. When Maroi died, Beng was supposed to go to his *sanrugn*, but he was much too frightened and did not do it. He went with some others a few days later, but the body of Maroi had vanished, only the straw mat in which the corpse had been wrapped was left behind. Maroi had 'gone home to the mountain' and become a *bi inhar*.

BAS

There is another class of beings, known as *bas*, who under certain circumstances cause harm and disease to humans. *Bas* is a generic term for many different beings who live on Earth Seven and who cause disease. Some *bas* are also *bi inhar* but others are not, so I will treat them as a separate category. The concept itself is intimately linked to that of humanity. An examination of the following version of the creation myth, told not as part of it, but as an explanation of how *bas* came into being, will show more clearly what is meant.

Original *bas* (*bas asal*), were made by Tohan also, but by mistake. When Tohan told Nabi to fashion people (*beri*), out of earth, Nabi made two figures. He went to Tohan for breath (*njug*), Tohan placed *njug* in Nabi's fist by blowing into it, but Nabi carried it wrongly, that is he wanted to have a look at *njug*, but when he opened his fist it escaped. Nabi returned to Tohan and told him that *njug* had not reached the two figures. 'Oh, they have become *bas* then!' exclaimed Tohan. And he was right. The two earth figures became *bas*. They had different eyes, and they want to eat our (true human's) *ruwai*. So Nabi made two more figures and when Tohan gave him the *njug* he carried it correctly and brought it to the two figures who became true human beings (*beri lòi*).

This story shows that *bas* are humans *manqués*, or humans gone wrong. The fact that *bas* have different eyes means that they perceive reality differently. They cause disease to humans by either taking their *ruwai*, or by attacking their bodies. In both instances, however, the *bas* do not see human beings as such, they only see meat. This constitutes an interpretation of how it is that *bas* attack and want to eat humans, an important factor when *bas* and humans are conceptually so close. One wonders whether there are myths now forgotten which describe how all the various other beings came into existence. However that may be, *bas* are usually referred to with shudders and fear. 'They want to eat us,' the Chewong say. There are stories about the awfulness of *bas*. Many are very large and their bodies, both male and female, are covered with hair. Their eyes are at the back of their heads and they do not behave as good humans do. One man who met a couple of *bas* in a dream repeatedly tells about the encounter to equally delighted and horror-struck people. The *bas* woman suckled her baby from a breast covered with long hairs. But she soon got fed up with this and threw the child away. 'You take it,' she said to her husband. 'No, I don't want it,' replied he.

Here again there is an inversion of normal attributes in order to emphasize that the *bas* though 'like us' are really quite different as well. Otherwise it would not be possible to explain how it is that they eat human *ruwai* 'as we eat meat'.

Other myths also stress the close link between humans and *bas*; and some people insist that all *bas* were human beings at some time. Whereas the evidence does not substantiate the claim, there are several *bas* who are metamorphosed people. The most frequently quoted legend is the following:

Once a man and his father-in-law were out hunting. It began to rain while the sun was also shining, and the two men took shelter near a *tangoi* tree. After a while the rain ceased. 'It has stopped raining,' said the man to his father-in-law. There was no answer. 'It has stopped raining, we can go home now,' he said more loudly. There was still no answer. He looked around, and saw that his father-in-law had turned into *bas*. He was covered in long hairs. When he saw this, the man ran away as fast as he could.

Like the *bi asal* and *bi hali* as well as human beings, the *bas* need to eat. Their food, however, is *ruwai*, be it human or animal, and *ruwai* is meat (*ai*). In this respect their food requirements are similar to those of humans, but they are different from that of the *bi asal* and the *bi inhar* both of whom eat fruit and smoke only. This is said to be their vegetable staple (*ratn*) as tubers are the staple of humans. The preferred meat of *bas* is the pig *ruwai*, and they set spear traps all over the forest to catch them. These spear traps operate on the same principle as do those placed by people around their fields, but they are invisible to the ordinary human eye, so sometimes a human *ruwai* becomes trapped in it. The faulty vision referred to in the creation myth means two things. Firstly, a *bas* cannot tell the difference between a pig *ruwai* and a human one, so when it catches a human *ruwai* it will eat it, thinking that it is in fact that of a pig. Secondly, when *bas* look at any *ruwai* they see these as meat. There is a conceptual parallel between humans and *bas* rooted in the creation myth. They both hunt the same animal, pig, in an identical manner. The difference is that human beings eat the 'cloak' of the pig whereas the *bas* eat only their *ruwai*. As far as *bas* are concerned, however, they are also eating pig meat. So in this respect they differ from the *bi asal* and other *bi inhar*, most of whom eat not meat (*ai*) but fruit or smoke (*ratn*).

Although people are frightened of *bas*, they do not conceive of them as evil in any absolute sense. Whenever they catch a human *ruwai* they do so inadvertently and not by design. They do not set their traps near human habitation, and those areas in the forest which *bas* are known to frequent, humans will avoid. One man told me that *bas* do not want to eat human *ruwai* because to do so is dirty (*kama*). Since the reason given for not practising cannibalism is also *kama*, we have yet another piece of evidence for the perceived similarity between *bas* and humans. The following story brings out these points, it was told by Modn about her grandfather.

Modn's grandfather was a big *putao*. One day when he returned from the hunt it rained while the sun was shining (*sabn tiregn*). A *bas* had built a spear trap across the path that led back to his house. The trap was released and hit her grandfather though he did not see it. When he reached home he was sick. But since he was *putao* he realized what had happened. He told all the people present that he had been caught by a *bas*' spear trap. His *ruwai* went in search of the *bas* and when he found him, Modn's grandfather said to him angrily, 'You erected spear traps on our path, and one of them hit me.' 'Oh,' said the *bas*, 'I thought it was the path of wild pigs!' 'No, it was my path. The path of people,' said Modn's grandfather. When *bas* look at humans they see pigs. When the *bas* was told that he had made a mistake and erected traps for people he was sorry. Modn's grandfather soon recovered from his fever.

There are several other examples to show that although *bas* go hunting for *ruwai*, they do not hunt the human variety. Firstly, *bas* go about at night when people are at home and asleep. But, of course, at such times people may dream, and when they dream their *ruwai* travels, and then it may encounter *bas*. *Ruwai* are in fact frequently taken by a *bas* in a dream. Secondly, the smoke from the fire in the house informs *bas* of the presence of human beings and they therefore do not come close. The occurrence of one particular atmospheric condition, however, means that *bas* are awake and active in the day time. This is the simultaneous rain and sunshine known as *sabn tiregn* which is also regarded as dangerous by other Orang Asli as well as by the Malays. As shown by the myth about the man who turned into a *bas*, it was during such a time that the metamorphosis took place, and Modn's grandfather was caught in the trap at such a time. Whenever *sabn tiregn* occurs, all outdoor activities are abandoned and everybody runs inside the house or takes shelter. If caught by *sabn tiregn* while out in the forest, and especially if there are children present, people immediately stop and make a fire. When *bas* smell the smoke they realize that they are human, and they set their traps elsewhere. Whenever people are working or resting in the forest, they usually build a fire anyway, so that *bas* and other superhuman beings will know that people are about. Smoke, of course, also frightens away wild animals but this is never given as the rationale for the act. *Sabn tiregn* is a mixing of the two categories hot and cool, and as such does not adhere to the principle of separation or of keeping things apart.

As mentioned earlier, *bas* is a generic term for many different and individualized superhuman beings. What they all have in common is that they are potentially harmful to human beings. They may take their *ruwai* and either eat it or destroy it in some other fashion, and whenever the *ruwai* is lost the person in question becomes ill and may die if it is not retrieved. They can also cause illness, or pain in specific parts of the body, by shooting darts or stabbing spears. Most of the *bas* can only attack humans if these have transgressed specific rules, but there are some who will intentionally attack people and eat their body rather than their *ruwai*. Otherwise people are attacked by *bas* by accidentally being caught in one of their traps or by going too close to their habitat.

A description follows of all the different species of *bas* that I was told about.

1. *Eng banka*. This means 'dog (that) hits'. They are a species of supernatural dog. Some say they are the ghosts (*yinlugen*) of dead dogs, others that they are just *bas*. They tend to inhabit swampy areas, and the Chewong are very fearful whenever they have to go through such places. *Eng banka* attack indiscriminately anyone who crosses their path. They take the *ruwai* of the person and bring it to their own house in the swamp where they eat it. To be attacked by an *eng banka* is serious, and unless the *ruwai* is retrieved within a couple of days, the person will die. Cause of death is frequently attributed to *eng banka*. When someone falls ill suddenly and dies within a short

period of time the chances are that an *eng banka* is to blame. It is said that there are many of these around Kampong Ngang I as many people died there a few years ago. Only very knowledgeable *putao* are able to confront *eng banka*.

2. *Ta'[1] Jijogn* live inside large fallen trees. These often lie across a path and people have to walk underneath them in order to proceed. Unless one spits on the tree-trunk, Ta' Jijogn shoots his blowpipe at one and his dart will stick in some part of the body and cause a lot of pain. Sharp sudden pains are often attributed to Ta' Jijogn and spells are tried to get rid of the pain. If this does not work, then a *putao* who knows how to extract the dart is summoned. He rubs the patient's painful spot with some leaves. Then he places the leaf in a bowl of water, and when the leaf is examined, a fishbone or the spikes of some plant are found inside. This is the dart of Ta' Jijogn. The reason why the Chewong spit on the tree-trunk is that this is regarded as dirty (*kama*), and Ta' Jijogn inside his house will run away when confronted with such dirty behaviour.

3. *Maneden.* These are *bas* who live in wild pandanus plants. They do not inhabit cultivated pandanus. The pandanus is their 'homeland' (*mona*). The *Maneden* have only one arm and one leg—if a right arm then a left leg and vice versa, and their bodies are large, 'like that of a dog'. They attack by biting and sucking the blood until nothing is left and the person dies. They bite men at the elbow and suck the blood from there, and women are bitten on their nipples. *Maneden* can be diverted from their purpose if one cuts a liana from the *hodj* nut tree (a very oily nut) and gives it this to suck instead. *Maneden* attack only when someone cuts the pandanus leaves either at dawn, dusk, or during *sabn tiregn*.

4. *Mawes* (cf., Needham, 1956: 56). The *mawes* live high up on Gunong Benom. In the old days there were many hundreds of them, but now there are very few left. Their noses are upside down and they are frightened of rain, since this would run into their nostrils, and their feet are back to front. When it rains they take a leaf and use it as an umbrella. The bones of their lower arms are sharp like knives and whenever people meet them they run because they are frightened of being cut to pieces by these arms. When in the past the

---

[1] The word *ta'* means grandfather, but it is often prefixed to names of old men in the same way that *ya'* (grandmother) is prefixed to names of old women. The various *bas* which are thus named; Ta' Boli, Ta' Nlonòi, and Ta' Tyo' are written as if they were personal names of one being. From the way they are talked about it is difficult to judge whether there really is just one of each, or whether it is a generic name.

Chewong sometimes shot at *mawes* with blowpipes, they found that they could not use the bones as knives, for they would rot away.

According to another informant, *mawes* are not really *bas*. They are quite harmless and were human a long time ago. They are very shy and do not harm humans, but run away from them whenever they happen to meet. The people at Dong call creatures with the same attributes *brai*, and they are frightened of them.

5. *Ta' Boli* lives in trees. One may not go out after dusk to chop firewood as Ta' Boli will hear the noise and come. Children are summoned home at dusk lest Ta' Boli hears their voices which attract him to the scene. His body is covered with long hair. He has lost his elder brother (*tòh*) and is always searching for him. His food is *ruwai* and he attacks by throwing his spears (known as *pochug*) at people. He can be overpowered by spells, and his spears can be extracted from the body.

6. *Ta' Nlonòi* lives in the jungle, but not in any one part of it. One is susceptible to attack from him (he takes the *ruwai*) whenever one spends a night in the jungle. There is a bird, however, which speaks whenever Ta' Nlonòi is approaching, and then one can say spells (*tankal*) to divert him.

7. *Hablis* are frequently the cause of a particular disease. They live at the 'true headwaters of rivers' (*koyī loi tam*) usually referred to as *pinto gahogn*. The true headwaters of rivers are believed to be underneath the earth. *Hablis* also take humans' *ruwai* and eat them. When this happens, *putao* will have to go to the *pinto gahogn* (it is not clear whether there is one source for all the rivers or several different ones) and say his spells there. *Hablis* are then obliged to give up the *ruwai*. *Hablis* were human in the past but their eyes became cool, their bodies, however, remained hot, so they are not immortal.

8. *Porcupine Spikes.* When a porcupine is killed—usually in a spear trap—the long quills at the back turn into *bas*, with long hair on their bodies but otherwise looking like human beings. The quills become their darts with which they shoot at humans. In fact the Chewong always pull out these spikes when they find a porcupine, and although they claimed that this was done for convenience only, I suspect that there is some link with the belief that these turn into *bas*. Some people refuse to eat porcupine meat because of their connection with *bas*.

9. *Bas Trid* causes diarrhoea in children. He arrives in lightning, and children must therefore always run inside when this occurs. Furthermore, they must never wave lighted firewood in

the air, lest Bas Trid sees this and appears. His attacks are cured by spells.

10. *Srelogen.* This is a *bas* who causes swelling of the ankles and thighs whenever someone has been bathing at full moon. This can be cured with spells.

11. *Tika.* The Chewong are very frightened of *tika.* The word is used both for the *bas* in question as well as for the disease that is a result of their activities. *Tika* are beings with very long claw-like fingers who enter the stomach of people who have mixed certain types of food, chiefly sweet foods like fruit with meat, and claw at their stomach and intestines until the person dies. There is no remedy for *tika* and it is frequently given as the cause of death.

12. *Krabo* are a milder version of *tika.* They attack the stomach also and give severe stomach upsets and diarrhoea, but there are spells as well as herbal medicines for *krabo.* The people at Dong did not know about *tika,* but described *krabo* as having the same characteristics as the former, although they are not activated by the same behaviour.

13. *Monedn* live in the forest and are the size of slow loris. They are a kind of *bas* who attack the human body, rather than the *ruwai,* with darts. If a *monedn* is encountered in the jungle, a person must cut a piece of liana, spit on it and put it on the path between the *monedn* and oneself. This stops the *monedn* from getting close because it does not want to cross the liana as the spittle has made it dirty (*kama*).

14. *Kwakö* is a *bas* that lives in the river. People must never go to bathe or to collect water after dusk or during *sabn tiregen* otherwise they will be swallowed by *kwakö. Kwakö* swallows both the body and the *ruwai,* and no *yinlugen* comes into existence. *Kwakö* pulls at a person's legs and drags him under. It is possible to retrieve the body by confronting *kwakö* with the right spells before he has swallowed the person.

15. *Blug* are *bas* who live in early morning fog, and when fog descends *blug* may enter humans' bodies and make them ill by eating the body from the inside. Whenever there is fog or mist, the Chewong burn *òz taba* to redirect the *bas* away from themselves.

16. *Ta' Tyo'* is male *bas* who lives in the tops of *tangòi* and *badong* trees. Overcast weather and drizzle may herald his arrival. He attacks only women or children by forcing their *ruwai* to follow him to his house in the *tangòi* or *badong* tree. Whenever this happens, the person becomes mad (*gila,* cf., Malay). The *ruwai* spins and spins when it follows Ta' Tyo', and the person becomes dizzy (*todmed*) and

cannot stop crying. Once the *ruwai* has followed Ta' Tyo' the person has an attack of *gila* every night but he does not remember anything about it the next morning. To be *gila* means that one's vision is impaired. Everything looks upside down and one is constantly dizzy. The cure in this case is applied to the eyes. Rotten *hòdj* fruit can be smeared on while spells are said, or the incense smoke of the *tebogn* tree can be blown across the eyes while spells are muttered. Ta' Tyo' is frightened of the smell of the *tebogn* because it is a bad smell, and he runs away and lets the *ruwai* return.

17. *Keòi* is a slightly different type of *bas*. It is also known as flying lemur (*keo*) because of the events in Myth 9. *Keòi* are among those *bas* who eat humans, that is they eat their bodies and not their *ruwai*. The *ruwai* of a person who has been eaten by a *keòi* turns into a *keòi* also and forgets about his past as a human and tries to trick people so that he can eat them. They look just like ordinary human beings, but their eyes are different, and they see only potential meat when they look at ordinary humans; they therefore contrive to kill and eat human beings by pretending that they are not *keòi*. They particularly like the blood and the stomach content of their victims.

18. *Nlab* are similar to *keòi* in that they also look human and want to eat human flesh (see Myth 16, Appendix 1). But people who are eaten by *nlab* do not become *nlab*: they just die. Their ghost, *yinlugen*, unlike that of those eaten by *keòi*, is released and goes to Pulao Klam.

19. *Bujægn Majas* lives in areas of dense growth in the jungle. He has a blowpipe and he shoots his darts at anyone who passes by. He eats the *ruwai*, but it is possible to extract the dart from the person's body. If he has taken the *ruwai*, then a *putao* can go in search of it in a *nöpoh*. Bujægn Majas' tongue is so long that he wears it around his head like a headband.

20. *Bas Kòch* (land tortoise) bites the spleen of small children which as a result become distended and hard, 'like the hand of the tortoise'. Fever follows which is intermittent but regular. This form of illness is known as *döden pli* (spleen illness) or *döden kòch* (tortoise illness) and it is in fact malaria. This *bas* takes the *ruwai* of the child and eats it, but the *ruwai* can be retrieved through spells if this is done soon enough after the symptoms appear.

21. *Ta' Nimòi* live close to humans. They bite human bodies 'like poisonous ants', but humans cannot see these bites although the bite itches terribly. The effect of Ta' Nimòi's bite can be expelled by spells.

22. *Ta' Sampar* causes bad colds. He lives near the ocean and

travels up the rivers to their headwaters. He catches *ruwai* by throwing poison (*toba*) into the river which stuns the *ruwai* ('the way we poison fish'). It is difficult for a *putao* to locate Ta' Sampar because he tends to go up small tributaries. It is possible to put up a fish net in the house during a *nöpoh* to try and catch him that way. He is, however, extremely elusive.

23. *Sayab* live in the jungle and they consume the body so that it becomes very thin. Unless the right spells are said the patient dies.

24. *Tokò* also live in the jungle and they eat the body, but only specific parts of it. Thus one man who is said to have lost his penis was said to have been attacked by Tokò. Spells may be used to help the person recover.

25. *Bibol* are very poisonous and they bite people's feet when they are out walking. Again spells may be said to expel them.

26. *Ta' Glohul* are *bas* that live in the rivers. Sometimes when someone is bathing *Ta' Glohul* comes and pulls him under so that the person drowns. *Ta' Glohul* swallows both the body and the *ruwai* so that there is no *yinlugen*. He can be frightened away by someone present at the attack spitting wild ginger (*bunglei*), the smell of which makes him let go of his victim.

27. *Mentenæ*. This *bas* has the body of an elephant, but ordinary humans do not see him. He eats the *ruwai* by attacking the body. He lives in a swamp near the Baye River, and this is why the Chewong avoid this river despite the fact that there are lots of fish in it. *Mentenæ* makes the same sound as a real elephant, and this is audible to the human ear. The footsteps, however, are invisible so that one never knows where he has been. If one steps on his urine the body comes up in blisters 'as if one has been badly burned'. These blisters may be dispelled by spells.

The above list of various types of *bas* concludes the information I managed to obtain about them. See Tables 4.2, 4.3, 4.4 and 4.5 for an analysis of their characteristics and activities. Some people would also include Bajægn and Ponjur when asked to enumerate all the types of *bas* they knew about, but most would disagree. 'They are different,' they would say. *Bas*, like the other *bi inhar*, is not a finite group of beings or types. New ones may appear at any time. The *putao* may encounter a new type when in search of a lost *ruwai*. On the whole the Chewong are not frightened by *bas* in the abstract. Fear of them does not inhibit their daily activities. It is only when someone has become ill as a result of an attack that they preoccupy themselves with worrying about them. There are, however, a few rules, the breaking of which leads to direct repercussions in the form of an attack by *bas*, and all are scrupulous in avoiding breaches of these. They also avoid going near places which *bas* are known to frequent, and avoid placing themselves in the way of *bas* during the unusual atmospheric conditions described above, and at dawn and dusk, all of which are times when *bas* may attack. Whenever returning to an empty house or lean-to in the jungle, someone walks around it, spitting in all corners and along each wall. This frightens away the *bas* that might have arrived while it was vacant. This is a means of establishing the boundary between the human and the superhuman worlds. The piece of wild ginger (*bunglei*) mentioned earlier as worn by small children around their necks, exudes a smell which *bas* find unpleasant. This is therefore an amulet against them.

Bas is not an absolute term, however. Humans are also *bas* as far as animals are concerned. This was brought home to me one day when I was sitting outside the house with Modn and we heard a leaf-monkey calling nearby. 'He is telling his wife that there are *bas* nearby,' said Modn. When I enquired what she meant, she replied that to the leaf-monkey human beings are *bas*. 'We shoot the monkeys with our blowpipes in order to eat them,' she said, 'so to them we are *bas*. We eat their bodies, their *ruwai* we do not eat. But *bas* eat our *ruwai*, it is their meat.' This event illustrates my earlier point about *bas* not being regarded as evil. In the same way that humans have to hunt and kill in order to stay alive, so *bas* must have *ruwai*. In the case of *bas*, moreover, there is the extenuating feature that they do not as a whole want to eat the *ruwai* of humans anyway.

Leeches, mosquitoes, various other types of insects that bite, as well as a type of ringworm known as *korap*, are all said to be *bas*. (Others say that they are *yinlugen*.) 'They eat our blood, so they are *bas*,' I was told.

Although by *bas* the Chewong mean beings who can and do harm them either by taking their *ruwai*, shooting arrows into them and causing pain, or eat the actual body, *bas* can also become spirit-guides and help their 'spouse' in the same way that the *bi hali* or animal *ruwai* do. It was not until I asked for the explanations of some songs that I realized that they included references to *bas* spirit-guides. If a person meets a *bas* in a dream and manages to establish a friendly relationship with it, the *bas* offers to become his or her spirit-guide and the two marry each other. After giving his new spouse a song, the *bas* will come and help the person whenever the song is sung. It will never harm its spouse, although other types of *bas* still may do so.

SUMMARY OF EXCHANGES BETWEEN HUMANS AND SUPERHUMANS

I have been suggesting that the Chewong social universe is much larger than the total number of human beings in it, that includes numerous superhuman beings who surround the human world and who play a direct role in the way in which it operates. Humans are dependent upon the non-humans, who are in turn dependent upon human beings. The relationships are marked by a series of exchanges which can be seen to constantly renew the relationships. They have been referred to in the foregoing description, and they are now brought together in a single summary diagram (Table 4.1).

The term 'exchange' is used in its widest sense, including (as shown in the diagram) non-material as well as material objects of exchange, and the time-span over which an exchange occurs is extended; indeed from this world into the afterworld in some cases.

Exchanges between human beings only are excluded. These are described elsewhere, when I note the general prescription requiring sharing and circulation of all goods between all individuals. This may be manifested in immediate reciprocity (as in the case of the tobacco exchange upon encounters) or in delayed reciprocity (as in the case of food). I have also noted the absence of exchange between categories of people (as for instance between wife-givers and wife-takers, or between mother's brother and sister's child). In the Chewong case, everything brought into a settlement is cut up and shared out immediately to all present. It is prescribed that one shares out, it is not prescribed to which individual or category one shares. Anyone present at any given time is given their equal share of whatever is being divided.

Table 4.1 thus refers only to exchanges between humans and superhumans (or non-humans), and in this instance the exchanges are between groups, or categories of beings; with all the Chewong on the one hand, and each category of superhuman being on the other. Even when just one individual Chewong officiates, he does so not for himself only, but on behalf of the whole community.

The exchanges are numerous and varied, and involve a wide range of beings. They span the period from creation of the world, and of

Table 4.1
Exchanges between Humans and Superhumans

Name	Received from Humans	Given to Humans
Tohan	⟶	body, njug (ruwai)
Earth Eight	⟶	fire, tobacco, night, torch
Yinlugen Bud	⟶	family (correct birth practice), society (share food)
Poison Maidens	⟶	dart poison
	clothes ⟵	
Dead putao	⟶	esoteric knowledge, protection
	food (smoke), prayer ⟵	
Earth Six	⟶	fruit, esoteric knowledge, dew
	food (smoke), songs, headbands, riding ⟵	
Spirit-guides	⟶	esoteric knowledge, songs, help, protection
	food (smoke), songs, headbands ⟵	
Bi hali	⟶	dew, help, songs
	food (smoke), songs	
Animals	⟶	food (meat)
	human hair (afterworld) ⟵	
Fire	⟶	means to cook
	food (fur, leaves) ⟵	
Tanko I	⟶	fertility of women, first cooked meal
	sex, children ⟵	
Tanko II	⟶	(rules)[1] thunder, illness, death
	(—)[2] smoke, human hair, food for dogs (body + ruwai) ⟵	
Original Snake	⟶	(rules)[2] storm, death
	(—)[2] smoke, human hair, blood, knife, food (body + ruwai) ⟵	
Bajægn and Ponjur	⟶	(rules)[1] accident, death
	(—)[2] spouse (ruwai) ⟵	
Bas	⟶	(rules)[1] illness, death
	(—)[2] food (body or ruwai) ⟵	
Tolæg	⟶	(rules)[1] illness, death
	(—)[2] food (ruwai) ⟵	
Earth yinlugen	⟶	(rules)[1] illness, death
	(—)[2] food (ruwai, blood) ⟵	
Water yinlugen	⟶	(rules)[1] illness, death
	(—)[2] food (ruwai) ⟵	

[1] (rules) means that the main thing given are the rules. The other things specified are 'given' only when the rules are broken.

[2] (—) indicates that if the rule is adhered to (i.e., correct behaviour 'given' to the being in question) nothing is received by the being. What is listed is what is given when the rule is broken.

society, to the death of the individual, and beyond into the after-world. The details of these exchanges are given below, but two points with regard to the system as a whole must be made.

Firstly, the scope of the exchanges and the part they play in Chewong life can be interpreted as a dynamic process which ensures the continued existence of the whole social universe. It is thus consistent with the view that regards exchanges as 'not a means employed to achieve individual goals, but rather the *common task* on which the society as a whole rests' (de Coppet, 1981: 200).

Secondly, and related to this, it is suggested that the data presented in Table 4.1 lend further credence to the view that the Chewong social universe extends far beyond human beings alone. Thus 'the society as a whole' is not simply the Chewong, but rather the totality of beings with whom they maintain relations.

It will be noted that the first three items listed in Table 4.1 are not strictly exchanges since they are never reciprocated, and no relationship continues to exist between the superhuman beings in question and the Chewong. But until human (Chewong) society existed in the same way as it does today, no exchange processes had been instituted. These three 'gifts' from the culture heroes: the human being in both its aspects of body and breath/*ruwai*; cultural artefacts; and cultural knowledge, enabled human beings to make a society and to start the processes of exchanges henceforth required in order to maintain this society. Tobacco, the most common medium of exchange between humans was given to the Chewong by the *bi asal*; so also was fire. The social unit of the family was instituted; and the first rule (*maro*) to share one's food was taught. However, nothing was given in return to these culture heroes who, in fact, after dispersing their gifts ceased to have any further relationship with humans. In this context it must be mentioned that as society came into existence, individual immortality ceased. With the introduction of meat and cooked food (hot foods) into their diet of previously uncooked fruit (cool foods) and with the prescription upon sharing, the individual Chewong encountered death. Society, therefore, was created at the expense of the individual. Furthermore, this newly-founded society has continually to be 'fed' via the medium of exchange.

The first exchange to take place was that between humans and the Poison Maidens, but this was a once-only occurrence, and again no relationship is maintained between the two groups.

Chains of exchanges exist today between the Chewong and the *bi asal* of Earth Six, with the spirit-guides, with the *bi hali*, with the dead *putao*, with Tanko in one of his aspects, with animals who are eaten, and with fire. In most of these instances the objects exchanged are identical, that is, they are food. On several occasions I have said that to the Chewong food is the most important medium for expressing society. Here this same medium is used to express the existence of the wider society into which are drawn superhuman beings. The fact that what constitutes food differs according to the species concerned, is of no importance. What is stressed by these exchanges is the recognized need for food (or the other objects specified) and the dependence upon each other to provide them. However, dead *putao*, the various spirit-guides, and the *bi asal* of Earth Six also give help and protection. They guard against the attack of various non-human agents and they help to initiate those humans who wish to become *putao*. They give esoteric knowledge in the form of spells and songs which enable the recipients to perform cures in cases of attack from harmful beings. In return for this they are given food in the form of smoke, but some are also given various paraphernalia required in a *nöpoh*, such as headbands and bandoliers. Since these beings conduct their own *nöpoh*, but do not have access to the plants required for making such objects, they are dependent upon humans to provide them.

The remainder of the superhuman beings in Table 4.1 stand in a slightly different relationship with humans. The exchange consists in the observance by the Chewong of various rules governing their daily behaviour. These rules are given by the superhuman beings and any breach leads to specific punishment by them. The rules constitute an important part of Chewong knowledge, and are regarded by them as one of the ways in which their society is unique in respect of other human societies. It is therefore fair to say that the rules may be regarded as 'gifts' on a par with the other gifts given by the culture heroes. They help to form and maintain Chewong society, and give it meaning.

As long as the rules are adhered to, the superhuman beings are given nothing—except the act of adherence. This, however, is of extreme importance. Were the Chewong to ignore them, the superhuman beings who represent them would also be ignored—and in a sense cease to exist. This is analogous to the gift of a song from a spirit-guide: the spirit-guide needs the song to be sung as much as the human being needs to be given the song. Thus humans need the rules in order to behave correctly and maintain order, and the superhuman beings need the humans to observe the rules. The adherence to them is a public recognition of the existence of the superhuman being in question.

It is only at times of transgressions of a rule that the superhuman being is given (or takes) something. In these instances they usually take food, either in the form of the *ruwai* or the body of the transgressor or the person(s) transgressed against.

In all cases, individual death is the 'punishment' which reinforces the necessity of adhering to the rules. More importantly, however, is that deviation from prescribed behaviour threatens the very fabric of the wider social universe. By observing the rules, the individual Chewong ensures not only his own continued existence, but also the continued existence of his society. This would again seem to indicate that the concept of *bas* and other harmful beings is not basically inimical to humans. The attacks only take place when humans are careless in their behaviour.

CLASSIFICATION OF
THE SUPERHUMAN BEINGS

In this chapter we have discussed the relationship between human and superhuman beings, and the material has been arranged in conformity with the Chewong classification into four main categories of superhuman beings, namely, *bi asal*, *yinlugen*, *bi inhar*, and *bas*.

In the case of the Chewong the task is peculiarly difficult because there is a considerable overlap among the four categories. Thus, some *bas* are *bi inhar*, and some *bi inhar* are *bas*. Some *bi asal* are *bas*, and some *bas* are *bi asal*. Some *bi asal* are *yinlugen*, and some *yinlugen* are *bi asal*.

The lack of rigidity becomes even more evident when one attempts to establish sub-classes within the categories which I have done in presenting the data. It must be stressed, however, that these sub-classes are to some extent imposed by myself. The Chewong do not make such a clear-cut division as is presented in Table 4.2.

The purpose of Table 4.2 is not only to summarize the sub-classes, but also to attempt to establish patterns by classifying the sub-classes according to their main attributes. It emerges from the Table that no simple patterns can be discerned. Indeed, in many cases there is not even a one-to-one relationship between sub-class and attribute.

Table 4.2
Superhuman Attributes

Category	Sub-class	Helpful/Harmful[1]	Sex	Earth[2]	May be Spirit-guide
I Bi Asal	Culture heroes	N (ex-G)	M + F	6, 7, 8	No
	Bi asal of Earth 6	G	M + F	6	No
	Poison Maidens	N (ex-G)	F	7	No (but offered)
	Other bi asal	B, G	M + F	7+, 7–	Yes, No
II Yinlugen	Yinlugen asal	B (ex-G)	M + F	7	No
	Tolæg	B	?	5, 7+, 7	Yes
III Bi Inhar	Dead putao	G	M + F	7	Yes?
	Bi hali	G	F	7	Yes
	Other spirit-guides	G	M + F	7, 7+	Yes
	(Bas)	(G, B)	(M + F)	(7)	(Yes, No)
IV Bas		B (unless spirit-guide)	M + F	7	No, Yes

[1]G = helpful (good); B = harmful (bad); N = Neutral; ex-G = Good in the past.

[2]7+ is a separate world between Earths Seven and Six.

7– is a separate world between Earths Seven and Eight.

Thus, for example, *yinlugen* may be helpful or harmful, and culture heroes may inhabit Earths Six, Seven, or Eight.

Of the four types of attributes chosen (which appear to be common to all superhuman beings, and regarded as significant by the Chewong) perhaps the most important in a discussion of relations between humans and superhumans, is the helpful/harmful dichotomy. In Table 4.3 I have therefore presented the material according to this method of categorization. Certainly the Chewong themselves place most emphasis upon this distinction.

It is evident from Table 4.3 that there is no correlation between the attributes of helpful/harmful and the four categories of superhuman beings, or the Earth that they inhabit.

The data may be subjected to a more detailed kind of analysis to try to establish correlations between various aspects of the different superhuman beings within a single category. I have chosen *bas* primarily because they constitute the largest group and therefore offer the richest possibilities for identifying, or testing patterns. So far, twenty-seven different kinds of *bas* have been described, and this information is summarized in Table 4.4. Furthermore, all *bas* are harmful and thus share one important characteristic. For the sake of completeness, I have also compiled Table 4.5 in which the remainder

Table 4.3
Helpful/Harmful Superhumans

	Sub-class	Category[1]	Earth
Helpful	*Bi asal* of Earth 6	(I)	6
	Culture heroes	(I)	6, 7, 8
	Poison Maidens	(I)	7
	Yinlugen asal	(II)	7
	Dead *putao*	(III)	7
	Other spirit-guides	(I, III, IV)	7, 7+, 7−
	Bas	(IV)	7
Harmful	Other *bi asal*	(I)	7+, 7−
	Yinlugen asal	(II)	7−
	Tolæg	(II)	5, 7+
			7, 7−
	Bi inhar	(III)	7
	Bas	(IV)	7

[1]The Roman numerals in brackets refer to the main categories used in Table 4.2.

of the harmful superhuman beings are listed according to the same criteria in Table 4.4. These Tables not only enable one to focus on activities rather than simply on attributes, but also to test the wider validity of any conclusions which might otherwise be reached. What I want to discover is whether significant correlations can be established between any of the characteristics listed. The exposition is slightly different from that of the previous two Tables in so far as I have concentrated more on activities—both of the superhuman beings and of humans in response to these.

For every being the 'object of attack' is either the *ruwai* or the body, or, in a few instances both. Because of the importance placed on the two concepts *ruwai* and body in Chewong collective representations, I begin by testing for correlations between the object of attack and each other in turn: the method of attack, method of prevention, and method of cure. I also consider their habitat. Because of the plethora of alternative habitats, and the potential significance of an above/below dichotomy, it is important that correlations against three spatial categories be tested: above, below, and on the same level as humans.

Of the twenty-seven types of *bas*, nine attack only the *ruwai*, whereas sixteen attack only the body. There are two who are specifically said to attack both *ruwai* and body—Kwakö and Ta' Glohul—both of whom live in water and pull their victims under and swallow them whole, thereby totally extinguishing them. (In this respect they display similarities with the Original Snake and Tanko.) With these exceptions all *bas*, as well as all other harmful superhuman beings, attack either the *ruwai* or the body. This statement must, however, be qualified since the interrelation between the two aspects of an individual is such that when the *ruwai* is attacked, this affects the body, which ails; and if the body is attacked this may manifest itself as illness, in which the *ruwai* similarly ails. However, for present purposes a sharp distinction between the two will be maintained.

When looking for correlations between object of attack and method of attack, none was found. Thus, all the methods distinguished are found to be used in the attacks on both the *ruwai* and the body. When we examine whether or not a *bas* ever openly confronts humans, we find that this only happens in the case of eight of them. The courses of action open to humans on catching sight of these *bas* are too varied (five different ones) to constitute a pattern. Furthermore, their acts at such times do not correspond significantly with the acts undertaken in the cure.

Table 4.4
Bas

Name of bas	Object of attack[1]	Method of attack[2]	Sight[3]	Method of prevention[4] Sight[a]	Avoid[b]	Method of cure[5]	Habitat[6] Actual[a]	Spatial[b]
Ta' Tyo'	R	A			A	T, N	J*	A
Eng banka	R	A			H	N	W	B
Ta' Boli	R	W			A	E	J*	A
Ta' Nlonòi	R	A			T	N	J	S
Hablis	R	A			H	N	W	B
Bujægn Majas	R	W			H	N, E	J	S
Bas Kòch	R	B			O	T	J	S
Ta' Sampar	R	W			O	N	W	B
Mentenæ	R	E			H	T	W	B
Ta' Glohul	R/B	A	X	T		O	W	B
Kwakö	R/B	A			A, H	N	W	B
Blug	B	E	X	T		T	A	A
Ta' Jigogn	B	W	X	S		E	J	S
Maneden	B	E	X	A	A, H	T	J	S
Mawes	B	W	X	R		O	J*	A
Porcupine quills	B	W			O	T	J	S
Srelogen	B	B			R	T	W	B
Tika	B	E			R	O	?	?
Krabo	B	E			R	T	?	?
Moneden	B	W	X	S		T	J	S
Keòi	B	E	X	K		O	H	S
Nlab	B	E	X	K		O	H	S
Ta' Nimòi	B	B			O	T	J	S
Bas Trid	B	E			R, A	T	A	A
Tokò	B	E			O	T	J	S
Sayeb	B	E			O	T	J	S
Bibol	B	B			O	T	J	S

Explanatory notes
1. R = *ruwai*; B = body
2. A = abduction; W = weapon; E = eat;
   B = bite
3. X = actually catch sight of, i.e. can be seen by anyone.
4. a T = *tankal* (spell); S = spit; A = given an alternative object;
      R = run away; K = kill
   b A = atmospheric conditions; H = known habitat;
      T = *tankal* (spell); R = rule observation; O = none
5. T = *tankal* (spell); N = *nöpoh*; E = extraction; O = none
6. a J* = jungle above ground; J = jungle; W = water;
      A = air; H = same as humans
   b A = above; B = below; S = same level

Table 4.5
Other Harmful Superhuman Beings

Name	Object of attack	Method of attack	Method of prevention	Method of cure	Habitat Actual	Habitat Spatial
Tanko I[1]	B/R	W, E	R	O	A	A
Tanko II[2]	B	W	R, T	T	A	A
Original Snake	B/R	E	R, T	O	W	B
Bajægn and Ponjur	R	A	R	N	A	A
Yinlugen Te	R	E	R	N	E	B
Yinlugen Tam	R	E	R	N	W	B
Tolæg:						
Gibbon	R	A	R	N	W	B
Lizard	R	A	R	N	W	B
Tortoise	R	A	R	N	J*	A
Otter	R	A	R	N	W	B
Flying lemur	R	A	R	N	J*	A
Macaque	R	W	R, O	T	A	A

[1]Tanko in his aspect of *talaiden* punisher.
[2]Tanko in his aspect of incest punisher.

Analysis of preventive measures which may be taken reveals that there are no rules the observation of which prevents a *bas* from an attack on the *ruwai*. All the rules refer to attack on the body only. This finding does not, however, apply to other superhuman beings. As Table 4.5 shows, the object of attack for beings other than *bas* is in all cases the *ruwai* (with the exception of Tanko and the Original Snake, both of whom take both the body and the *ruwai*), and these attacks can all be avoided by the observation of a specific rule. Otherwise all possible combinations are found.

By comparing object of attack and method of cure it is found that most attacks on the *ruwai* are by abduction, and that these can be retrieved in a *nöpoh*, whereas no attack on the body is cured in a *nöpoh*, but always by spells or extractions. The body is never abducted (except by Kwakö, Ta' Glohul, Tanko, and the Original Snake). In addition, there is always a possibility of a cure for attacks on the *ruwai*, but not always for those on the body.

On the question of habitat no correlation at all is discernible. Each possible habitat houses beings that attack both the *ruwai* and the body—even when habitat is analysed according to an above/below/same axis.

When we compare the remaining with the method of attack, we find little of significance. I will highlight those that seem of interest: there is no abduction done on confrontation; almost all abductions are negated by a *nöpoh*; all bites are cured by spells; and no *bas* that bites lives above. With regard to human responses upon confronting a *bas*, there are too few examples, and too many types of response to establish any conclusions of significance.

Having listed all the correlations that have been established, the question arises whether these demonstrate the existence of any underlying pattern and, if so, what can be concluded from it. Some interesting points do emerge such as the fact that *ruwai* loss is almost always cured by a *nöpoh*, and no attack on just the body is cured by this method. This is consistent with the notion of loss and retrieval. The other correlations found are usually already evident from a less rigorous analysis of the data, and are remarkable mainly for their paucity. Given twenty-seven types of *bas* and twelve other harmful superhuman beings, and eight different characteristics for each, an enormous number of potential combinations are generated. In the light of this, the few that have emerged are something of a disappointment, especially since they do not, in general, appear to be of great interest in symbolic terms. There are, of course, innumerable 'near fits', where a pattern emerges with only a few exceptions. But if these also are taken into account, it would be possible to 'prove' almost anything. I have therefore necessarily restricted myself to the more rigorous approach just described.

With the few exceptions noted above, the major conclusion from this analysis is therefore that it demonstrates a notable lack of pattern in the data. This point will be dealt with in the last chapter.

PART II

CONSCIOUSNESS AND RELATIVITY

INTRODUCTION

IN Part II an examination of Chewong conceptions of being and consciousness will be made. In order to establish their ideas, I begin with a discussion of their concept of *ruwai*, a concept already referred to on several occasions. It is, however, a complex and difficult concept to understand. No one term in English can be employed which covers all the shades, and indeed differences, in meaning that this word is used to convey. It must, therefore, be examined in terms of context. Three main interpretations emerge. Firstly, *ruwai* can be broadly translated as 'vital principle'. Secondly, it may be translated as 'personage' by which I mean the manifestation of consciousness as rationality, present in certain animals and plants and inanimate objects as well as in all human and superhuman beings. Thirdly, *ruwai* refers to one type of spirit-guide.

In order to understand the role of the *ruwai* of the individual, Chapter 6 will be confined to a discussion of humans alone together with an investigation of other aspects of the personage: the body, the ghost, the smell, the liver, and the name. I begin with an examination of the body and its relationship with the *ruwai*, demonstrating that they are affectively inter-linked. The discussion is then extended into the more general area of how the Chewong separate their notions about humanity from those of other, non-human, conscious beings, and the conclusion reached is that in the final instance consciousness is species-bound.

I focus in Chapter 7 on Chewong ideas regarding perception in order to see if these confirm my thesis of species-bound consciousness. I begin with the distinction made between hot and cool eyes— the former associated with humans, the latter with superhumans.

The concept of 'different eyes', the means by which the Chewong explain the different perceptions of the various species of conscious beings is then considered. Finally I discuss how the Chewong utilize symbolically the two states of hot and cool, as well as the associated phenomena of flames and smoke.

Throughout this part an attempt will be made to throw light upon the way the Chewong conceptualize their world, their relationships with one another, and with the natural and supernatural worlds, thus highlighting the concepts introduced in the previous chapters on relationships.

I shall be using Chewong myths to validate the points that I am making. This is particularly appropriate in the Chewong context since they themselves are constantly referring to the myths for explanations of behaviour and received ideas.

5
Ruwai

THE word *ruwai* is found among many of the Orang Asli Mon–Khmer speakers, and is usually translated as 'soul'. Curiously enough, Blagden lists only the Negritos of Sungai Plus as referring to the 'soul' as *ro-wai* (Skeat and Blagden, 1906, vol. 2: 720), but many other examples can be found. Thus the Temiar word for 'head-soul' is *reway* (Benjamin, 1966: 136); the Semai word for 'soul' is *ruai* (Dentan, 1968: 82); the Jah Hut word for 'soul' is *ruai* (Couillard, 1977: 5); and one of the Mendriq words for 'soul' is *reway* (Endicott, 1979: 96). The Batek, while calling the 'life-soul' *nawa* (cf., Malay *nyawa*, soul, spirit), employ the word *reway* for a serious disease caused by breaking their rules for 'irreverent rhyming' (Endicott, 1979: 80).

The word 'soul' covers a wide variety of meanings. Two which come closest to what the writers probably had in mind when they translated *ruwai* as soul are the following: 'Soul (1) The principle of life in man or animals; animate existence. (2) The principle of thought and action in man, commonly regarded as an entity distinct from the body; the spiritual part of man in contrast to the purely physical. Also occ., an analogous principle in animals.' (*Shorter Oxford English Dictionary*, 1975.)

But the Chewong concept of *ruwai* is at the same time both narrower and wider than these definitions imply It is a concept that I struggled to understand throughout the period of my field-work, and for the sake of clarity I have decided to divide this discussion into three parts. This is artificial, since the Chewong never said that there are three kinds of *ruwai*, nor, indeed, would I; the three are but parts of the same. However, such a distinction is implicit in the way they use the word.

RUWAI AS VITAL PRINCIPLE

In its most generalized usage, *ruwai* may be interpreted to mean vital principle. Everything that lives (see below) such as plants, trees, animals, humans, and superhumans is attributed with *ruwai*. As long as a tree is growing, a fruit is ripening, an animal or human pursuing their normal activities, it is taken for granted that they are alive (*gòz*) and that they have *ruwai*. As such, it is extra to the physical entity, and its presence or absence is proof of life or death.

In the case of trees and plants, manifestation of the vital principle is seen in their sap (*tam*, which also means water). When a fallen tree has dried up, the Chewong will say that the *ruwai* is finished (*hadeitn ruwai*) and that the tree has died (*ka kabus*). When the tree in question originally fell, its *ruwai* left and moved to a seed of the same species. It removes itself slowly, however. This was explained to me by reference to tapioca cultivation. When the Chewong plant tapioca, they use the stems of existing plants by cutting these into pieces each about six inches long. These sticks are placed in the ground and new stems, as well as the tubers, grow from them. Although the original stems are cut up, *ruwai* is still sufficiently present for new growth to take place. If, on the other hand, the sticks are left for a few days they dry up (*okriden*) and to plant them would be useless as there is no more *ruwai* present in them. In our terms, there is no more vital principle.

Although *tam* may usually be translated as water, it is also used to refer to certain other types of liquids, whether as a single word (as in *tam*, sap) or as a compound (as in *tam lah*, semen). The association between *tam* and life—or the presence of vital principle—is indeed so strong as to merit elaboration with a number of examples.

With regard to conception, the Chewong believe that the semen, *tam lah* (water of the penis) also known as *aig lah* (excrement of the penis), creates, or builds, the baby. The vaginal fluids, *tam leh* (water of the vagina) also play a part, although of less importance 'because there is much less of it'. As a woman reaches menopause she is said to dry out (*okriden*) and as a result ceases to be able to bear children, whereas a man does not similarly 'dry out'. Once a baby is born, the mother feeds it with her *tam bo* (breast water). This is sometimes explicitly described by the Chewong as analogous to the *tam lah* of the father.

Major loss of blood—whether as a result of an accident, or by the *bas* called Monedn sucking the blood from the body—is known to

put life in danger. But it is the resulting dryness which is emphasized. Also of significance is the parts of the body from which
Monedn sucks the blood. In the case of a man it is done from his
elbow; and in the case of woman it is sucked from her nipple. These
are precisely the same parts referred to in the creation myth in which
the early men suckled their babies from their elbows when their
wives had died, and subsequently being shown that it was the
woman's breast which contained milk.

Rain-water is regarded as the food of the trees and plants. Fruit
trees in particular are thought to need a lot of rain when in blossom;
—the rain at this time is known as *sabn ler* (rain fruiting). The
association between water and fruit has already been noted. Furthermore, the main ingredient of a healing *nöpoh* is the dew brought
by the *bi hali* (from the leaves of trees), or from Earth Six. The
patient is bathed in this dew in the morning as the seance ends. The
dew serves to fortify rather than heal, and its coolness, as well as its
moisture, is regarded as beneficial. It is the same desirable combination of moisture and coolness contained in fruit which make the
bi asal of Earth Six immortal.

Perhaps the most graphic example of this association between
moisture and life, is with regard to rivers. Rivers (*tam*) are also talked
of in terms of whether they are alive or dead. A dead river is a dry
river. Similarly, old people are said to dry out as they reach old age.

In the case of human beings, another manifestation of vital principle is also present, apart from *ruwai*, namely *njug* (breath). Again, if
we consider their creation myth, we will remember how Tohan told
his Nabi to make humans out of earth. This the Nabi did, but the
figures were not alive. Tohan gave him breath to be blown into the
mannikins, and upon receiving this they stood up and were alive.
Conversely, someone is declared dead when his or her breath has
ceased. Breath rather than blood is associated with the pulse, both on
the wrist (*njug tyaz*, breath of the hand), and on the neck (*njug
tangkòg*, breath of the neck). The same applies to animals. There is,
however, an identification between *njug* and *ruwai* in certain circumstances. When asked who gave them *ruwai*, the Chewong will
say that Tohan did, and then proceed to tell the creation myth
although employing the word *njug* throughout. They are adamant in
their protestations that Tohan has nothing to do with the perpetuation of *ruwai* or *njug*. He only initiated the process of human
life.

To sum up the discussion so far: to the Chewong, *ruwai* in this most general usage is a prerequisite for life; in a sense it is life, and its manifestations are breath and/or *tam* (sap, water, moisture), and by extension, movement and growth. The reverse is death, whose manifestations are lack of breath, dryness, immobility, and decay.

RUWAI AS CONSCIOUSNESS

Ruwai is often used to indicate something much more specific than vital principle. So whereas on one level all humans, animals, trees, and plants have *ruwai*, on another all humans, but only some animals and plants, have what, if examined in detail, is a different property, also called *ruwai*. In this limited sense, *ruwai* may be translated as consciousness.

For a further discussion of what this means, I wish to take as my starting point a passage from Maurice Leenhardt's book on the Canaque of Melanesia, because, as I hope to demonstrate, there are many parallels between their ideas and those of the Chewong. In a chapter entitled 'The structure of the person in the Melanesian world' Leenhardt says:

> The Melanesian knows the being we glimpse in the word only in its human form. He calls it *kamo*, 'the living one'. We translate it by 'personage' and the term is as applicable to mythic beings as to human beings. The two are always situated in a social or socioreligious ensemble where they play their roles. For example, a lizard sits on the head of the chief of Kone. The chief's wife seeing her husband bent under the burden of the totemic monster, exclaims, *Ne pa kamo*, that is 'ensemble of personages'. She does not distinguish the mythic personage from the human personage. Together they form an ensemble imbued with humanity.
>
> The *kamo* is thus poorly delineated in the eyes of others. He[1] usually takes the human form and is man in his generality, but he may be any other being invested with humanity. The *kamo*'s body appears as the costume of a personage.
>
> (Leenhardt, 1979: 153.)

Leenhardt's term 'personage' may be aptly applied to this second more specific sense of *ruwai*. When the Chewong say that certain animals or plants are (or were) 'people' (*beri*), they mean that they possess *ruwai* in a specific sense which indicates the presence of

---

[1] Strictly speaking the personal pronoun describing *kamo* should be 'it' since in the French edition Leenhardt says that the term is applied without gender.

consciousness and that in certain circumstances their bodies are those of humans. As conscious beings they are personages, regardless of their exterior form, be this human, siamang, porcupine, lemongrass, or whatever. Furthermore, consciousness is 'humancentric'. By attributing *ruwai* to any non-human species, the Chewong expect from it behaviour which is rational in human terms. As will be shown in the next chapter, however, such behaviour is often relative to the species concerned, and may therefore result in deviations from the human norm in the expression of rational behaviour. The word 'human' throughout this book refers to the Chewong themselves, as one category of beings (albeit the most important one) imbued with consciousness. It does not necessarily include other ethnic groups of humanity.

ANIMALS AND PLANTS

Not all species of animals and plants are conscious beings in the sense described above. By using Medway (1978) and Harrison (1974) both of which include numerous pictures of the mammals of the Malay Peninsula, as well as by asking the name of all animals, birds, and fish either caught or seen, I built up a large vocabulary of the animal world. I also enquired regarding each whether it had *ruwai* or not, whether it was 'people' (*beri*) in the past or not, what rules pertained to eating and cooking it, what other rules were associated with it, its habits and habitat, etc. I accumulated a large dossier on Chewong attitudes to the animate world surrounding them. In the case of trees and plants I was much less diligent, mainly due to my own extremely limited botanical knowledge. Only those species which were brought to my attention as being personages or having specific rules associated with them, have been listed.

The Chewong would often refer to their myths and stories, as well as to their songs, in deciding which animal or plant had *ruwai*. Whenever in doubt, the informant would pause for a moment, consider and say, 'no, there is no myth', or alternatively, 'yes, there is such and such a story about this animal' and then proceed to tell it. The criterion for deciding whether it had *ruwai* or not was in all cases whether the animal or plant in question had shown evidence of consciousness by acting in a rational manner. Thus for example, they said: 'yes, bats have *ruwai*, they carried Bongso to the sea' (see Myth 4, Appendix 1). In this, as in most myths, only one member of the bat species actually helped Bongso. Nevertheless the whole species is attributed with *ruwai*. In other words, 'bat-hood' has *ruwai*, or, all bats are personages. The other two animals which also helped Bongso in the myth, the flying lemur and the flying squirrel, are also said to have *ruwai*.

Apart from the animals which demonstrated their *ruwai* in the myths, those animals which are known to affect humans, such as the *tolæg* animals and those which pregnant women and their husbands may not eat, are all said to have *ruwai*. As such, they are personages and are expected by humans to be able to think, judge, and act. Usually, they do not impinge upon the daily life of humans. Only when a person contravenes one of the rules which specify behaviour, is one member of a specific species given the mystical opportunity to act in a damaging way to one or more members of the human species.

With regard to the botanical world, the Chewong say that all trees had *ruwai*, in the sense of conciousness, in the distant past. As evidence for this they said that trees could once speak. Trees would also cry out in pain whenever they were cut down, so no one would do this. One man gave this as the reason why the Chewong did not clear fields in the past, but only foraged. Here one can trace a direct link between speech and consciousness, and by extension, between the practice of foraging as opposed to that of agriculture. At some distant point in the future, Tohan will turn Earth Seven upside down and he will start afresh making new people, animals, plants, mountains, rivers, etc. As already said, he does this when Earth Seven has become very 'dirty' and hot due to blood, faeces, and urine. What has not yet been mentioned is that shortly before Tohan turns the Earth over, all animals and trees regain their ability to speak. Thus when a Chewong digs for a tuber, the tuber cries out, 'Ouch, what are you doing? You are hurting me.' Similarly, monkeys when hit by a poisoned dart, say to the hunter, 'Hey, what is this that hurts my flank? Did you throw it at me?' According to the Chewong, life would become virtually unbearable at this point. 'How can we go on killing trees and animals and tubers when they talk to us?' they said. This belief shows the affinity that exists between man and the rest of nature, and exemplifies how any being or object may become imbued with consciousness. While this is sporadic and limited as is the case today, the Chewong can cope with it by adherence to specific rules and sanctions. When, however, everything suddenly emerges as conscious beings, the end has to come. There is no way they can continue to live in such a world.

There are still some trees which have *ruwai* and are conscious beings. These are the *gol* tree and the *tangòi* tree. They are among the tallest trees in the forest, and they frequently feature in the myths. The tree from which the Chewong used to make cloth, and from which they still concoct their dart poison, the *dòg* tree, also has *ruwai*, and the poison itself has very strong *ruwai* which has to be protected lest it be lost or killed. The bamboo which is used for making blowpipes, and another species which is used for making quivers, also have *ruwai*. In these cases they are attributed with gender: that of the blowpipe is masculine, and that of the quiver is feminine. The dart itself has *ruwai* (sex unspecified) as does the species of bamboo used for drums during a *nöpoh*.

All those leaves, roots, plants, and trees which are used for medicinal purposes also have *ruwai* in this more specialized sense, as do those with which certain rules are associated. Furthermore, all the different wild tubers that constituted the Chewong staple before they began to plant tapioca, have *ruwai*. It thus appears that all plants which are somehow useful for humans are attributed with consciousness. 'They want to help us' (*tologn*), it is said. This is brought out most clearly in the case of the durian and *payòng* trees, which are still eaten as the main staple when in season. Groups of people migrate to large trees at such times. The durian season is in June and July and the *payòng* become ripe in September through November. According to the Chewong it is no accident that they ripen at different times. If there is a bad durian harvest one year, then the *ruwai payòng* see this and make sure that there is a large *payòng* season, and vice versa. These two species of fruit do not want people to be hungry, and so act accordingly.

Other trees, or possibly parts of them, become imbued with *ruwai* only at certain times of the year. This applies to those trees which bear edible fruits and nuts, during their blossoming and fruit ripening season. At such times the *ruwai* of the fruit and blossoms on Earth Six descend to Earth Seven so that humans may eat some fruit. The fruit *ruwai* do not like it on Earth Seven; they regard it as much too hot and therefore do not want to stay for very long at any one time. Indeed they have to be persuaded to come by singing and drumming in a *nöpoh*. The more pleased they are with the singing, and the more frequently this is done, the more likely they are to descend in large numbers. So, when the flowering season is about to begin, the Chewong conduct nightly *nöpoh* for the express purpose of pleasing the fruit *ruwai* of Earth Six. The singing also pleases the *bi asal* of Earth Six, who are said to throw blossoms down to Earth

Seven. The dew *putao* will go up there during the seances to talk to them. (See Myth 3, Appendix 1.)

But the fruit trees do not have their own inherent *ruwai*; they are not conscious at other times of the year, rather they become imbued with *ruwai* from their counterparts on Earth Six for a limited period only. The reason the fruit seasons have been bad lately is blamed on the laziness of the Chewong in carrying out their *nöpoh*.

Thus *ruwai* can also mean something more specific than vital principle. Anything that is alive is imbued with vital principle (*ruwai*), but some of these are further imbued with consciousness (*ruwai*), and therefore act according to rational principles.

HUMANS

The breath given by Tohan to the first human couple, sometimes identified with *ruwai* is to be understood in the general sense of vital principle. Having considered animals and plants, the human *ruwai* as consciousness, in other words the human personage, will now be discussed. Since the Chewong are 'humancentric' in their elaborations, by understanding their representations of the human *ruwai*, more can be learnt about the *ruwai* of animals and plants, and indeed about the superhuman beings.

Each individual person has his or her *ruwai* which is intimately linked with his or her body. In order to understand the concept of *ruwai*, one cannot discuss it in isolation from that of the body.

An obvious point to note is that in the first instance an individual is identified in terms of his or her body, *bi* (the various meanings of *bi* will be examined later). The new-born baby is manifesting itself as a physical object with certain expected attributes. Immediately following a birth the Chewong check that the body conforms to expectations of normality. Any deviations are attributed to superhuman intervention, and/or failure by the parents to observe a ritual regulation during the pregnancy. If the baby moves its limbs and cries, then it is alive, its vital principle is present; it has *ruwai*. *Ruwai* in the sense of personage, while embryonically present in the womb, as shown in the examination of couvade practices earlier, is not fully developed nor fixed in the body and is easily lost until the body has finished growing. In other words, when an individual is fully grown, and is able to carry out all adult functions, the underlying assumption in Chewong thought is that the personage is also fully developed in the sense that the social responsibilities of the individual may be counted upon. From now on the body and the *ruwai* are intrinsically part of each other, and *ruwai* loss occurs less often and mostly when the individual has broken one of the numerous rules that govern their behaviour, the infringement of which allow superhuman beings to attack. These rules and their implications will be examined in a later chapter. Here it is stressed that the person as a social being does not come into his or her own until the body and the *ruwai* are fully developed and merged. This corresponds to the time when they marry.

Throughout infancy and childhood the unformed personage is marked by frequent loss of *ruwai*. The instability of the personal *ruwai* of the small child is seen by the Chewong as a reason for the many illnesses that children are prone to suffer. There are therefore special ritual precautions already mentioned that the parents must observe with regard to the child.

But the *ruwai* of small children may be lost even when no rules are broken. It may just flow away with the water when an older child is bathing, or the wind may blow it away. Moreover, a child's *ruwai* may fail to find its way back to the body during a dream.

As long as the child is fully dependent upon its parents for survival, the *ruwai* is in its most unstable form. As the child grows up and becomes more and more able to fend for itself, and learns all the rules necessary for interacting with the environment, so the *ruwai* becomes fixed in the body, and the individual slowly develops into a fully conscious, and socially responsible human being.

The examples of necessary precautions regarding children pertain mostly to the development of the *ruwai*. I encountered only two examples of prescribed behaviour that must be observed to ensure the growth of the body. The reason offered for why childrens' hair is shaved regularly is that otherwise it will not grow, but remain the thin fluff of babies. Also, the frequent bathing of babies and infants in warm water, in which certain leaves have been infused, is said to strengthen the body, as well as to make the children early and strong walkers.

Having established that the fixed *ruwai* is essential for a person to function as a full human being, our understanding of the *ruwai* is still far from satisfactory. The Chewong say that it is the real person (*bi lòi*)[1] and that the body is the *ruwai*'s cloak (*bajo ruwai*). This, as

---

[1] *Lòi* is usually translated by the Malay *betul* (correct, true). This is the most common meaning, and exclamations of *lòi* can be heard when someone expresses disbelief at some information. It is also a value-loaded term when discussing similar objects, one of which is said to be the true one. Examples are numerous, e.g.,

explained earlier, is a metaphorical usage to indicate the notion of integument. (See Myths 2, 5, 6, 7, Appendix 1.) When the *ruwai* is absent from the body during dream and trance states, the body is 'as if it were dead' the Chewong say. It is not really dead, however, as can be deduced from the fact that it still breathes; but the personage has gone and is alive elsewhere. When the *ruwai* leaves to travel, it does so in the form of a physical presence also referred to as *bi*. This *bi* is a miniature version of the actual body left behind. If *ruwai* did not have *bi* when out travelling, other *ruwai* would not be able to see it. So when a person is asleep and dreaming that he is meeting other people, it is the dreamer's *ruwai* that meets *ruwai* of other dreamers, and they recognize one another because the *ruwai* have *bi*, and look just like the individuals concerned.

In this context the individualized *ruwai* of animals and plants become significant. All those beings who are attributed with *ruwai*, including animals and plants, may be met with in dreams, when the body of their *ruwai* is that of a human being rather than that of the animal or plant whose *ruwai* they are. This gives meaning to the Chewong's assertion that they do not eat the flesh of those animals which are their spirit-guides because they are people (*beri*). They have met their *ruwai* in the shape of a human being. There is, however, always something about these *ruwai* bodies that tells the human dreamer that he is not meeting merely another human being. For example, they may be wearing something that denotes their true status. The following story will elucidate the point. One man, now dead, once came across a large snake while out hunting. He shot several darts at it and the snake vanished. The following night he dreamt that he met a woman whom he did not know. She said to him that she wanted to be his wife. When he looked more closely at her he saw that there were several darts protruding from her body, and he realized that she was the *ruwai* of the snake he had met the previous day. So when the Chewong say that the body is 'only the *ruwai*'s cloak' (*bajo ruwai nai*) the actual situation is not as simple as this statement would imply. The relationship between the two is one of affective interlinking. The *ruwai* takes on attributes of the body, both permanent and temporary ones, and when the *ruwai* is lost or caught by superhuman beings, the body suffers.

---

step-children are called *wòng gòi* (child who is carried), whereas a biological child is a *wòng lòi*. *Lòi* is also used to emphasize something, as when one wants something very much (*imeh lòi*) or the weather is very hot (*abud lòi*).

1 Woman in traditional costume

2 Burning off the fur of a monkey in the main house fire

3 Monkey being cooked in the main house fire and
porcupine on a temporary fire outside the fireplace

4 Burning off the fur of a wild pig in the jungle

5 Cutting trees for a new swidden

6 A new swidden ready for planting

7 A temporary settlement with lean-tos

8 Women gathering materials for a new house

9 Building a more permanent house

10 A nöpoh

11 Bride and groom feed each other from the same bowl

12 Grating the tapioca for bread

13 Playing in the river

Similarly, the hair trimmings and nail-parings of a child, but not those of an adult, are linked with the non-physical aspect of the individual. They must never be casually thrown away, but always wrapped carefully in some leaf and left in the roof of the house. Some aspect of the personage is supposed to be attached to these biological parts, and were these scattered around, the *ruwai* of the child would be affected: and when the *ruwai* is effected, so is the body.

The word for body is *bi*. *Bi* is also used to mean person or people, but not humanity as a whole, which is *beri*. *Beri* is the emphatic form used to separate human beings from other creatures. Thus they say that Tohan made *beri*, or that certain animals were *beri* in the past, or that some still are *beri* as evinced from a dream encounter. *Bi* on the other hand are sub-groups of humanity. The Chewong refer to themselves as forest people (*bi brete*) as opposed to, say, English people (*bi ingris*) or Chinese (*bi cina*). Furthermore, *bi brete* are sub-divided into our people (*bi he*), the Jah Hut (*bi jah*), Batek Nong (*bi nong*), etc. *Bi* can also be translated as 'substance' as, for instance, when they say that the recently planted tapioca does not yet have *bi*, they mean that the tuber has not yet been formed.

Bi does not refer exclusively to the physical aspect of things, however. It can also mean power, or energy. For instance, I was told that there is no point in trying to cure someone with spells and incantations during lightning because the spells then have no 'body', and it has returned to the forest (*hö bi. Ka oweg kö brete*). The dart poison may lose its *bi*, in which case the animals struck do not die. The Chewong have various armbands and amulets made by their *putao* and by those of the Jah Hut, which are to protect against bullets from the Malays and the communists (*bi komunis*) as well as from dangerous animals. If these are allowed to fall on the ground or are worn on prohibited occasions, then they lose their *bi*. It can be restored by infusing them over *oż taba*. A final example, from Western technology, is the batteries used for torch lights which are finding their way into Chewong life. Whenever these batteries have run out, the Chewong say that their *bi* is finished. Thus, in one context the word denotes substance; in another, essence.

The relationship between the body and the *ruwai* of an individual is such that they are mutually dependent and one *ruwai* will not 'fit' another's body. During a *nöpoh*, therefore, when several *ruwai* of various *putao* are moving about outside their bodies, there is a danger of them entering the wrong one upon their return. The Chewong regard this as enough of a possibility to warn against it in their songs when they sing 'do not enter a different body' (*hö masuk bajo masign, la rugn[1] lain*). If the *ruwai* of one individual were to enter the body of another, both would most likely die. Neither aspect of an individual can live beyond a certain length of time without its true counterpart. The presence of an incorrect *ruwai* in a *bajo* would mean that the individual would be unable to act. The *ruwai* needs its own body to be able to depart and return freely. The 'cloak' of the Chewong is not therefore directly equivalent to the 'costume' of the Melanesians since it is not irrelevant which cloak the *ruwai* finds itself in at any given time. The two take on attributes of each other and affect each other throughout the life of an individual.

When a person loses his or her *ruwai*, he or she becomes sick (*dödn*). Loss of *ruwai* of adults may come about in several ways, each with a corresponding means of retrieval. Straightforward *ruwai* loss in a dream is often resolved by the *putao* blowing the smoke of *öz taba* in the four cardinal directions. The scent of the incense attracts the *ruwai* which then follows the path of the smoke back to its body. The *ruwai* may also return of its own accord, being blown back by the wind. In such cases only minor illness is suffered by the individual. If the *ruwai* has gone to a very pleasant place such as an island in the ocean where it can sit and play with beautiful and sweet-smelling flowers, it may not want to return, and has to be persuaded to do so by the *putao* who finds it during a *nöpoh*. Another, and more serious, type of *ruwai* loss may occur when it is taken by a superhuman being who brings it to 'its own house' (*hya' punyeh*). When this happens, the *putao* goes to the house and exchanges his headband or his bandolier for the *ruwai*. Once the *ruwai* has returned to the body, the person recovers. If days go by without the *putao* locating the *ruwai*, or if it has been eaten by a superhuman being, the sick person dies.

RUWAI AS SPIRIT-GUIDE

Yet another, and even more specialized meaning is also conveyed by the term *ruwai*, namely that of spirit-guide, or familiar. One animal or plant of a species which is known to have *ruwai* can establish a special relationship as a spirit-guide with an individual Chewong. An animal or plant of other species, as well as any object, may also

---

[1] *Rugn* is another word for body encountered only in songs. It is possible that this was used in common speech in the old days before *bajo* became common usage. According to Blagden, derivations of the word *brokn* meaning 'body' are found among the Senoi of the Ulu Pahang area and in Perak (Skeat and Blagden, 1906, vol. 2: 541).

reveal itself to an individual as being imbued with *ruwai*. In such cases the knowledge is personal, and although the rest of the Chewong know about the relationship through the appearance of a new song, this knowledge is not usually extended and absorbed into the general collective representations regarding the species as a whole. In other words, outside the context of the relationship, the species in question is not attributed with *ruwai*.

I was puzzled for a long time by being asked if I had *ruwai*, and the amusement that my affirmative answer always provoked. I thought that it meant 'soul' or some vague equivalent, so when I returned the question and asked individuals if they had *ruwai*, I was even more surprised to hear their denials. It became apparent that the Chewong interpreted my question not as to whether they possessed[1] a consciousness—this was taken for granted—but whether they possessed a spirit-guide. More specifically, whether they had met the *ruwai* of a non-human animate or inanimate being in a dream or trance with whom they had established a relationship cemented by the gift of a song which, when sung in the ritual situation of a *nöpoh*, would bring the *ruwai* to the scene and enlist its support in the healing process.

In return for help, a person who has a spirit-guide gives the smoke from *òz taba* which the *ruwai* eats. The *ruwai* also need humans to sing their songs. When the song is no longer sung because the person to whom it was given has died, the *ruwai* also, in a sense, dies. Its manifestation as personage ceases unless it establishes a new relationship with someone else.

Ruwai in the sense of spirit-guide can be anything non-human, but usually it is animal or plant. When a person has met such a *ruwai* his attitude to that particular species as a whole alters. He will refuse to eat any member of it, knowing that they are 'people' (*beri*). This is accepted by everyone, but unless others have had a similar encounter they do not act upon the knowledge, beyond whatever restrictions already operate in relation to the particular species in question. It is an idiosyncratic restriction. The wide range of objects which may thus reveal themselves as being personages can be appreciated from the example cited earlier of the man who met the *ruwai* of the Japanese aeroplane.

---

[1] To possess, or to have something, is always expressed in Chewong by the word *wò*. Thus 'I have a knife' is *ing wò wang*. The word is also used to indicate a presence of something, as in 'are there bananas in the house?' (*wò tiòg lam hyak?*) to which an affirmative answer would simply be '*wò*'.

The *bi hali* discussed in the previous chapter are in fact the *ruwai* of the leaves and flowers of certain trees and plants who have revealed themselves to individual humans as personages. When their songs are sung during a *nöpoh* they arrive in large numbers to place themselves in the *riding*, filling the house with their sweet-smelling scents. Although *bi hali* is the generic term for them, they are usually referred to simply as *ruwai*. In a myth (not listed) the 'wives' of Bongso, who sing during a *nöpoh*, are mentioned. Their song is so lovely that everyone listens with pleasure, but only Bongso can see them. These wives are in fact *bi hali* whom he requests to come during a *nöpoh*. During a *nöpoh* the Chewong say that they are waiting for the *ruwai* (meaning *bi hali*) to arrive, and that when dawn breaks the *ruwai* return to their own lands in the leaves.

By saying that the spirit-guides, as well as those non-human animate and inanimate objects attributed with *ruwai*, are 'people', the Chewong are saying no more than that they are personages, in the sense outlined by Leenhardt. The point is stressed so as to link it with the other Chewong statement that the *bi asal* and *bi inhar* are 'people like us' discussed in the previous chapter.

There are, however, two types of spirit-guides, the *wòng hieng* already mentioned in the previous chapter, and the *ruwai*. In general conversation the two terms are used loosely and interchangeably, but there is in fact a qualitative difference between them. Whereas most older men, and some women, will admit to having one or more *ruwai*, only two men confirmed that they had a *wòng hieng*. The rest rejected any possibility of having a *wòng hieng* by pointing to their chests and saying that nobody was living inside. 'We have met *ruwai* in our dreams only,' they would say, 'we do not have any inside our body.' A *wòng hieng*, also called just *hieng*, merges with the individual and lives permanently in his body. When a *putao* sends out his *ruwai* during a *nöpoh*, he is in fact sending out his own *ruwai* and the *hieng* together. The two are one. If the *hieng* is caught by a *bas* or a *yinlugen*, then the individual dies.

Moreover, the difference between the two kinds of spirit-guide is further stressed by the type of relationship envisaged as existing between the individual and the spirit-guide. The *putao* and his *wòng hieng* are perceived as standing in a parent–child relationship. The *ruwai* on the other hand is a spouse, and the relationship is of a much less stable nature. The *ruwai* does not merge with the personage of the individual as does the *hieng*. An individual refers to his or her *ruwai* as his husband or wife, and the relationship is one of continuing reciprocity and exchange. The two may also quarrel and sever the relationship. The designations are therefore significant. Whereas husband and wife may, and often do, divorce, a parent–child relationship cannot be terminated institutionally in any way.

6

Other Aspects of Consciousness

IN the previous chapter, the discussion of *ruwai* as consciousness was applied to human and other species, and the intimate link between the body and the *ruwai* was noted. This chapter will begin by exploring this relationship in more detail, and then turn to other aspects of the personage: the smell, the ghost, the liver, and the name.

BODY AND THE CONCEPT OF SPECIES

It was said earlier that the *ruwai* of one human individual may not enter the body of another. The *ruwai* of a human being may, however, enter the body of an animal or a plant. In the past this was often done, and there are many myths to this effect. (For examples, see Myths 5 and 6, Appendix 1.)

Today only the big *putao*, are able to do this. Similarly, the *ruwai* of some animal or plant might don the *bajo* of humans. (See Myths 7, 17 and 18, Appendix 1.) These myths demonstrate that there is something fundamentally human, on the one hand, and fundamentally *bayæz* fruit or dog, on the other. In the first type of myths there are men who had obtained various animal *bajo* which they wore in order to pretend to other humans that they were the animals in question. When they were found out, and their animal *bajo* destroyed, they reverted to being human only. In the other type of myths the situation is reversed: various animals and trees donning human *bajo* and pretending to be human. In the final instance all these beings whether human or non-human, return to their own true state.

It is interesting to note that in all the myths which were collected dealing with these topics, we find that where humans wear animal *bajo*, the individual in question is almost always a male, and that he fools everybody including his wife. It is the wife, however, who discovers what can only be described as a fraud, and who destroys the *bajo*, thereby forcing her husband to live exclusively within the domain of humanity. By contrast, the animals or plants who don human *bajo* are in most cases female. Her husband is told from the beginning what she really is, whereas the rest are deceived. It is her mother-in-law who, by innocently comparing her to the species that she actually is, forces the woman to return to her true state, and as a result, the husband follows his wife and turns into the same species.

In another myth (not listed) a girl is lent a squirrel *bajo* by a squirrel. She wears this, and a man, taking her for a real squirrel, shoots her with a poisoned dart whereupon she dies. In death, however, she reverts to her true form, and the hunter finds a human corpse rather than that of a squirrel.

The Chewong language has no word for animal as an all-inclusive group of non-human creatures. Rather, each species has its own name, largely arrived at in an enumerative instead of a classificatory manner. The Malay word *binatang* (animal) is understood by the Chewong, and they will use this when talking to outsiders, but it is never employed when talking among themselves. Sometimes the word for meat (*ai*) is used to convey the general meaning of animal, as when they say for instance that *ai* have eaten all the *durian* fruit. Generally speaking, however, they refer to the specific species of animal concerned. There are generic terms for birds (*kawaw*); fish (*kiel*) and snakes (*talòden*) but the remainder of animals and insects are named individually. This lack of a conceptual all-embracing class of non-human animate beings seems to support the theory that to the Chewong human beings are only one species among many different kinds of animate creatures. The fact that it is possible to slide in and out of the various classes of beings, donning the *bajo* of the non-human being in question, further strengthens the point. When we consider that this is a two-way process, one that goes from human to animal (plant) as well as from animal (plant) to human, the suggestion that the Chewong do not divide the world into human versus the rest of nature and supernature is further supported. Rather they distinguish between those beings or objects who are personages (have *ruwai*), and those who are not. Among the former may be non-animate beings. Despite the possibility which exists of exchanging *bajo*, there is nevertheless some aspect of the personage which is immutable, something which remains itself no matter what kind of *bajo* it is wearing.

On examining the myths about people as animals, and animals as people, it can be seen that in all cases the emphasis, as well as the point of reference, is upon humanity. Thus the animals as people behave, while in their human *bajo*, just like humans—that is they work, and enter into the kinship system and systems of reciprocity and exchange of humans. They also observe all the various rules governing human social behaviour. Whenever their credibility as humans is being challenged, albeit inadvertently, they decide to abandon their human status and return to that of their true nature. They may also revert to their true nature while pretending to be human, as in the case of the dog man of Myth 17 who could not prevent himself from eating the blood and the stomach contents of the game that he and real humans hunted. When he was found out, he was destroyed by his human affines.

The people as animals (humans wearing animal *bajo*) on the other hand, are expected to continue to behave according to human standards and values rather than those in whose *bajo* they are clothed. But sometimes the characteristics of the animal whose *bajo* they are wearing begin to replace the human characteristics, as can be seen in another myth (not listed) in which people as cockroaches are mentioned. They are humans who put on cockroach *bajo* when visitors arrive. One day they are prompted by a child, also wearing the cockroach *bajo*, to attack the human visitor and eat him. This alarming breach of decorum results in the people losing their humanity altogether and metamorphosing into cockroaches. They cease entirely to be humans. In Myth 8 there is a man who changes into a real tiger after having eaten an abnormal fruit. There are several other examples in the myths to this effect, but they have not been included in the Appendix. (See Howell, 1982 for a complete collection of Chewong myths.)

However, even though the *bajo* and the *ruwai* do affect each other mutually, it is nevertheless possible to agree with the Chewong assertion that the *ruwai* is the true person. In those myths where humans put on animal *bajo* they are still acting according to their human collective representations, even though they often pretend otherwise. The mere fact that they are able to pretend, shows that the human personage is directing the animal *bajo*. Similarly, animal or plant *ruwai* clothed in human *bajo* pretend to be human. Whenever the wearing of the *bajo* affects the personage inside it to the extent that he is unable to control it, the individual ceases to be the personage he orginally was, and metamorphoses into the personage of the being in question. But this rarely happens. Normally the *bajo* does not effect the personage, but the personage the *bajo* instead. The *bajo* is activated by whatever personage is inhabiting it. It is only when the correct *ruwai* is in the correct *bajo* that it becomes uncertain which of the two is the 'true person'.

The Chewong concept of personage, of whatever species, may be likened to that of an actor. While performing in a play the actor dons the costume relevant to the part, and acts accordingly. Once off the stage, in his own clothes and environment, he is 'himself'. The roles may vary but, within the parameters of the present argument, the actor always reverts to the same 'self'. So the personages of the Chewong world change *bajo*, but in most cases, they revert to their own true being whenever the correct *ruwai* is in the correct *bajo*. And as the myth about the girl who wore a squirrel *bajo* demonstrates, if death occurs while someone is wearing an inappropriate *bajo*, then in death there is a return to the correct one.

SMELL

There is another aspect of the person which has not yet been mentioned. Smell (*moni*) is as intimately part of the individual as is the *ruwai*, but in a slightly different way. One may lose one's smell as one does one's *ruwai*, but when this happens, and someone becomes ill as a result, most people seem to think that this is less serious than losing the *ruwai*. The smell may be lost while bathing, when it flows away with the river until it reaches the ocean. In such cases a *putao* is required to retrieve it. If the smell is lost while someone is out in the forest, either it returns of its own accord or one may go in search of it. Sometimes one's smell is left behind when visiting other settlements. The symptoms of this are restlessness and a yearning to return home. Once back in one's own house, and reunited with one's smell, all is well.

As with *ruwai*, it is small children who are most prone to lose their smell. When their nails are clipped, the parings are placed in the hair on top of the head. Although the parings soon fall down, this is said not to matter since the smell of the clippings stays with the child. Moreover, when a man has to leave his small child for a few days, he will cut a piece off his loincloth and tie this like a necklace around the child's neck. The smell of the father is thus present with the child who, consequently, will not miss him.

Smell differs from *ruwai* in that the latter has substance, *bi*, and the former does not. Secondly, *ruwai* is more important because loss of it may lead to death. Thirdly, *ruwai* is more of an independent entity in so far as it has substance and can act consciously by going off on its own accord in dreams and trances, whereas the smell is lost only inadvertently. In certain respects the *ruwai* is an active agent whereas the smell is always a passive component.

Smell is also associated with the ghost, *yinlugen*, of people, and it is my contention that smell represents the physiological aspect of an individual, whereas the *ruwai* represents its essence.

Chewong vocabulary in connection with smell is fairly rich, and they distinguish between the noun, *moni*, and the verb, *oin*. The chief distinction with regard to smells is that between *haod* and *soòben*. *Haod* means bad or rotten and is used about meat that is 'off', about faeces, and about a corpse which is not buried shortly after death has occurred. *Soòben* by contrast means sweet, delicious, or good, and is used in connection with flowers, the smell of favourite foods being cooked, and about the *bi hali*. As mentioned earlier, humans covet the scent of the *bi hali*. Despite this importance that smell plays in Chewong ideas, I could find no evidence that it is dangerous to mix different smells, as was found among the Negritos (Endicott, 1979).

YINLUGEN

The Chewong acknowledge that death is normal for all beings who live on Earth Seven, and attribute it to these beings having hot blood. The only natural death, however, is that which occurs in old age. The *ruwai* becomes unstable and loses its strength. The body similarly shows signs of deterioration: teeth rot, hair falls out, and the body shrivels, weakens, and becomes unable to carry out heavy work. Finally, the *ruwai* ceases to exist (*hadeitn ruwai*). There is nothing a *putao* can do when an old person becomes very sick. In such cases there is no *ruwai* which is lost and can be retrieved. Rather, the *ruwai* and the body have run out, as it were, and the person in both his aspects stops functioning. Upon death the body starts to rot and disintegrate. This is why the Chewong bury their corpses. Tohan made the first humans from earth, and they are returned to it.

When a person dies, some aspect of him, the *yinlugen*, is activated. The Chewong are very clear that the *yinlugen* is not a part of the *ruwai*, nor is it the *ruwai* in a new form. 'The *ruwai* is different, the *yinlugen* is different', they would say, whenever I tried to find out exactly what the *yinlugen* is.

The Chewong at Dong said that a person's shadow (*bayang*) becomes its *sotn* (they used this word rather than *yinlugen*). I was told the same by some Temuan near the Krau Game Reserve, but the Chewong inside the Reserve denied any such notion. The shadow is not imbued with any special significance among them. However, the *yinlugen* is associated with the body, and it is some aspect of the corpse that becomes the *yinlugen*. One might call it the spirit of the corpse. Some said that it was in fact the corpse itself that became the *yinlugen*. They based this assertion upon the supposed findings of a man who, being extremely brave, had dug open the grave of a recently buried corpse. He claimed to have found nothing—hence the belief that the corpse had gone to Pulao Klam. It was a belief not adhered to by the majority of the Chewong, however, who stated that the body rots in the grave and becomes earth. Despite the lack of general acceptance of this idea, the incidence nevertheless demonstrates the close association envisaged to exist between the body and the *yinlugen*.

The answer as to the identity of the *yinlugen* may be found if we return to ideas and practices already referred to connected with birth practices. It will be remembered that when the father of a new-born child wraps the placenta and the umbilical cord in an old mat and places this in the branches of a tree, it turns into the older sibling (*tòh*) of the child. It is also known as the ghost of the afterbirth (*yinlugen tomoni*) and it goes to Pulao Klam where it lives without any contact with the human world until such time when it is reunited with its younger sibling upon his death. At some stage after the death (some people said it was before burial, others that it was after) the *yinlugen tomoni* arrives from Pulao Klam and goes to its younger sibling, and says to him, 'Where is your *tòh*?' Upon hearing this the corpse sits up, and must reply, 'You. You are my *tòh*.' Then the *tòh* who is now also known as Ta' Sranre, spits on the corpse. This spittle is said to be blood—an implicit reference to his origin as the placenta. From now until they are expelled together on the sixth night after the death, the merged identity of older and younger sibling, or the *yinlugen* of the afterbirth and the spirit of the corpse, roam the jungle and the settlements. Their presence terrifies the living, because it is assumed that the newly-dead does not yet know about its new state, and that it misses its children, spouse or parents and will try to take their *ruwai*. It will also eat the *ruwai* of the game and tubers in the vicinity of any settlement which has not yet been informed about the death. Every night bowls of *òz taba* are placed in all Chewong houses in order to create alternative paths for the *yinlugen* to follow—away from human habitat.

When a baby dies, the conically-shaped flower of the banana plant is placed in the grave with the corpse, the pointed end being put in the baby's mouth. This constitutes a substitute breast in order to prevent the *yinlugen* from returning to its mother and causing her illness by suckling at her breasts.

Food is placed on the grave for the first five days after death. Whoever brings the food says, 'We two have finished meeting one another. You are going away to a different place,' while putting the food down.

By these various beliefs and acts the Chewong acknowledge the liminal stage between the death and the expulsion of the *yinlugen*. There is a fear that the person may not be dead at all, that the *tòh* has not yet joined the spirit of the corpse; hence their practice of sitting by the corpse until it is buried. But even after burial the *yinlugen* of the afterbirth and the spirit of the corpse are neither one thing or another: not a human being, nor a proper *yinlugen* either. It still lives on Earth Seven, but it sleeps during the day and goes about at night. It misses its life as a human being in so far as it wants the company of its close relatives and it wants to eat food (*ai* and *ratn*). It is in the process of transformation, however, in so far as it moves at night and sleeps in the daytime, and by it seeing the *ruwai* as the real object. By this is meant that it sees the *ruwai* of its relatives as the actual person and that the *ruwai* of the food is seen as actual food. The *ruwai* stands for the object. Until the proper and final fusion of the spirit of the corpse and the *yinlugen* of the afterbirth (or *tòh*, or Ta' Sranre) is effected, when together they are expelled by the community of the living, this entity is slowly being made accustomed to its new state by being bidden farewell by the living who feed him.

The world of the *yinlugen* is thus perceived as the reverse of that of the living. All its joints are loose, it moves at night, and it mistakes the *ruwai* for the actual object. Furthermore, an armband made out of the same leaves as are used for *riding* is twined around the left wrist of the corpse and a smudge of soot is made on its left cheek. During the expulsion ceremony the living make a similar bracelet, but put it on their right wrist, and they make a sooty smudge on their right cheek. The deceased and the living are by these acts both united and separated; united in the sense that their common humanity is stressed by identical adornments, separated by reversing the application. I was told that what the living call left (*yal*), the dead call right (*t'òben*).

They have thus been relegated to a world whose members have different denotations from those of ordinary humans. In my discussion about smell it was said that this was an aspect of the person which is associated with the *yinlugen*. A further examination of what this means will now be made. From hearing how people would discuss death, the corpse, the grave, and the *yinlugen*, it was apparent that smell (*moni*) has a strong association with these concepts. The smell of the corpse is talked about, as is the smell of the *yinlugen* of the afterbirth/Ta'Sranre. From a purely materialistic standpoint, odour is of course the one aspect of a person that not only does not cease to exist upon death, but which actually increases.

The Chewong also stress the smell of the afterbirth (*tomoni*), and I was told that the slow loris, into which some part of the afterbirth also metamorphoses, smells badly. One reason for not eating this animal is that 'when we smell it, we are reminded of what it is' i.e., themselves. One may ask whether it is a linguistic accident that smell is called *moni* and the afterbirth is called *tomoni*. I am, however, unable to demonstrate any link, not knowing the role of the prefix *to*.

The life-span of an individual is marked by a physiological beginning (when the baby and the placenta are separated), and a physiological end (when the *yinlugen* of the placenta and the spirit of the corpse are reunited). Both these events are marked by odour. One might push this argument a bit further and suggest that the placenta and the corpse act as intermediaries of smell—smell here being an active aspect. On the model of separation, it could be argued that for a person to remain alive, the smell of its afterbirth must not be mixed with the smell of its own body. When this occurs, death also occurs.

FUNERALS

On the sixth night the whole community conducts an expulsion ceremony. Members from all the Chewong settlements come to participate, and food is gathered and prepared as for a feast. Those who do not come, perform the expulsion ceremony in their own settlements. They drum and sing as in a *nöpoh*, but the funeral ceremony is known as *bremon*. (See Appendix 2 for a funeral song.) During a *bremon* the Chewong also dance. This is the only occasion when they do so. They also shake their bodies while sitting down. These movements are meant to frighten the *yinlugen*/Ta' Sranre/*tòh* into thinking that the people he is observing cannot be his family because they are behaving in such an unusual manner. The bamboo which is burnt on the path between the grave and the settlement and which 'sounds like a gun' also frightens him, and the combination of these two events induces him to abandon the grave and the forest and go to Pulao Klam. The *putao*'s *ruwai* will guide him on his way to Pulao Klam where he lives henceforth. Once expelled, the *yinlugen* does not return to Earth Seven to bother the living. The Chewong do not abandon their settlement once a death has occurred, but they do destroy the house where a death took place and build a new one. The reason I was given for this act was purely sentimental, 'we do not want to live where our mother (or whoever) has died', they say, 'our livers (see below) are not good'. However, if several deaths occur in the same settlement, this will be abandoned because it is assumed to be a place where *bas* abound.

There is, however, a sanction upon conducting a proper burial as well as a proper expulsion ceremony. If the grave is not made according to all the rules, the *yinlugen* will try to harm its close relatives who have thus failed in their duties toward him. Similarly, at the 'big eat' all the *yinlugen* from Pulao Klam (all dead Chewong) arrive in order to participate. This meal keeps them satisfied until the next death occurs. Again, if this is not done they go hungry, and as a result will take the *ruwai* of the living, or the *ruwai* of their food—both *ai* and *ratn*. Social responsibilities therefore exist beyond death. The rule of *maro*, to give food to one's guests, applies not only to humans in their relationships with each other, but also in their relations with their dead. By feeding the *yinlugen*, they, by extension, ensure their own health (no loss of *ruwai*) as well as their own sustenance (no loss of the *ruwai* of their *ai* and *ratn*). At this level, society is extended to include the afterworld.

PUTAO

The above procedures apply to all except the great *putao* who do not die, but only shed their *bajo* when this becomes old or deficient, exchange it for a new one, and go to live on the mountain with all the other great *putao* of earlier times. In these cases the body dies, but the *ruwai* does not, which is consistent with the Chewong assertion that the *ruwai* is the true person. Unlike the *yinlugen* who is something different from the personage when he was alive, and who forgets about his relatives once on Pulao Klam, the dead *putao* are not really dead. They remove themselves from this life, but they continue to be the same personages that they were while alive on Earth Seven. They do not forget the living but keep a watchful eye on all that befalls them, and contrive to help them in times of danger and distress. As already mentioned earlier, the *putao bi inhar*, as these are called, are in daily contact with the living through the medium of incense and prayer.

Another name for these *putao* is *putao salitn*. *Salitn* means to take off a covering and put on another, and is mainly used in the dressing of sores and wounds. When they apply the term to *putao* the Chewong are explicit that it refers to peeling off, as it were, the old body and putting on a new one, both in life, during trance, and upon death. But the term also refers to these *putao* having had their blood exchanged with cool blood from Earth Six. No living *putao* is referred to as a *putao salitn*. Whenever one dies, the people still carry out a *bremon* on the sixth night (and even did so in the days when they left his body in a *sanrugn*), but a living *putao*, rather than accompanying the *yinlugen* to Pulao Klam, goes instead to the mountain of the 'dead' *putao* of the past and searches there for the recently dead one. If he finds him, he returns and informs the rest of the community that the individual has become a *bi inhar*. He will also be referred to from now on as a *putao salitn*.

If a comparison of the treatment of the placenta and the corpse is made, certain similarities may be discerned. Both are wrapped in a mat but whereas the placenta is placed above the ground, in a tree, the corpse is placed in the ground. The *yinlugen tomoni* (*yinlugen* of the placenta) however, then proceeds to Pulao Klam which is situated below Earth Seven, and this is also where the *yinlugen* of the dead live.

The *putao* on the other hand is not buried. He, like his placenta, is placed in a tree. Both conceptually and spatially he joins his *tòh* where this was placed originally. The *yinlugen* of the placenta is therefore unable to join him—there is no corpse in the ground. As a result of this failure to merge below the ground, the *putao* does not become *yinlugen*, and no aspect of him goes to Pulao Klam. Rather, his *ruwai* does not die, but in a new body goes to join his spirit-guide wife in a mountain, or other 'dead' *putao* of the past in their land on a mountain. The *putao* thus remain associated with the above after death—a direct contrast with the fate of ordinary human beings. So, although during his lifetime, the *putao* went everywhere, after his death he is associated with the world above only.

Human beings' *ruwai* die, but an aspect of their body becomes *yinlugen* and continues to exist. The *ruwai* of the *putao* does not die, his body is shed, in favour of a new one, and he does not become a *yinlugen*, but continues to live as he was, but in a different world from the living.

A third category of death is that effected by Bujægn and Ponjur, whereby a person is killed in an accident in which blood is shed. The *ruwai* is in these instances brought up to Plantor where it marries either of the two superhuman beings. In doing so, however, the *ruwai* can be said to be transformed because it forgets everything about its previous existence as a human being. The body remains and is buried, and a *yinlugen* comes into existence.

A fourth category of death exists, which mediates the two just described. It will be remembered that those who are swallowed by the Original Snake, given to Tanko's dogs, eaten by a tiger, or swallowed by the two *bas* Kwakö and Ta' Glohul are extinguished totally. Thus not only is the *ruwai* destroyed, but so also is the body. Their deaths constitute complete extinction, the *ruwai* and the body not being properly separated.

By creating the separate category of *putao*, the Chewong are defining the concept of personage as applied to the ordinary human. As was found to be the case in their attitudes towards the super-human beings of Earths Six and Seven, that their different attributes are compared and contrasted to those of the ordinary mortals, so the Chewong clarify their notions regarding themselves by comparing their own attributes with those of the *putao*. By focusing upon those aspects which they regard as ideal—coolness, absence of disease, and immortality—the conclusions they tend to draw regarding them-selves are that they do not measure up to the superhuman beings nor to the *putao*. It is in this sense that they regard themselves as inferior *vis-à-vis* these beings. As has been stressed throughout this work, the Chewong emphasize similarity rather than differences among the various beings in relation to themselves. This does not mean, however, that there is an absence of values from their belief system, rather that in daily life these are not stressed.

LIVER

So far I have been discussing the individual in terms of his body, his *ruwai*, his *yinlugen*, and his smell. I have not as yet touched upon the person as a psychological being, nor do I wish to do so, except in terms of the collective representations concerning the self. Else-where (Howell, 1981a) I have discussed the limited psychological vocabulary of the Chewong, and I tried to explain this in terms of the way the numerous rules governing behaviour demand a suppression of emotionality. Here I shall merely elaborate upon their notion of the liver (*rus*) as being the seat of thoughts and feelings. This may seem strange in view of what has been claimed for the *ruwai* as personage. However, the Chewong rarely refer to their *ruwai* in general daily conversation, and when they do, it is only mentioned in terms of whether or not it is present or under attack. Psychological and mental states are never discussed by reference to it. It is the liver that is the seat for these, and any changes in them are expressed via the liver, much as we express emotional changes by reference to the heart when we say for instance, 'my heart is broken' and mental ones to the head as in 'my head is not functioning properly today'. But whereas we distinguish between thoughts and emotions, the Chewong make no such conceptual separation. There is no word for either thought or feeling. Both are verbally expressed through the medium of the liver.

Thus they will say, 'my liver did not remember' (*han mud rus ing*); or 'my liver was tiny' (very ashamed) (*rus ing kanin*); or 'my liver is good' (I am feeling fine) (*rus ing sedap*).[1] They told me that the only way to learn the Chewong songs would be to 'follow them in the liver' (*odiaz lam rus*) while they were being sung. The English language equivalent is of course, to repeat the words in one's head, or to learn the songs off by heart. This particular example notwithstanding, there is generally a clear dichotomy in Western thought between the intellect and the emotions, commonly symbolized by the head and the heart respectively, whereas the Chewong do not endow either the head or the heart with any symbolic significance: the liver is the only organ thus endowed.

Other beings attributed with *ruwai* are also assumed to possess liver in this figurative sense. Thus when someone breaks a certain rule the retribution of which is an attack by a tiger, the tiger sees the offence in its liver (*endagn lam rus*), and hence knows who and where to attack.

The liver is not prone to loss as are the *ruwai* and the smell of an individual. Unlike these, the liver is an actual physiological organ. As such it nevertheless has super-physiological attributes, being the seat of individual consciousness, and the medium via which emotional and mental states are expressed.

[1] *Sedap* is Malay for 'pleasant, nice, agreeable'. It has been assimilated into common Chewong usage to mean the same.

NAME

Unlike another Mon—Khmer speaking aboriginal group in the Malay Peninsula, the Temiar (see Benjamin, 1968), the individual Chewong does not mark by a change of name his passing through the various life-crises. Nevertheless human beings are individualized by name, each person being given one shortly after birth. The name chosen may be that of a tree, flower, animal, river, or mountain, any of which is equally suitable for a girl or a boy. It is, however, forbidden to name a child after anybody, alive or dead. Each individual must be given his own original name. To use another person's name is to show disrespect (*tolah*) to that person and he or she would die as a result. Similarly, it is *tolah* to resemble one's parents very closely. 'Each person is different from everybody else' they say, and for this reason they are given different names. These two kinds of *tolah* are further examples of the importance attached by the Chewong to the principle of separation, or differentiation. Moreover, as each individual is different from every other, so is each species of conscious beings unique in some way.

As soon as a child has been named, it is then referred to and called by that name by everyone. This is the real name (*chò lòi*) of an individual. At some later stage a nickname (*chò punlao*)[1] is also given to most people. There is no prescription upon this, however. There are a few people who did not have a nickname, but I could find no reason for this.

Nicknames may also be derived from natural objects and animals, and they often refer to a particular instance in the person's life, frequently one that was thought amusing. One man whose real name is Gadogn (a species of fruit) is known by all as Chalag (monitor lizard). This refers to an occasion when as a young man he was chasing a monitar lizard, trying unsuccessfully to kill it by hitting it with a stick. In some cases one person may have several nicknames, either because different settlements associate him with different events, or because a new and important event may precipitate a new name. An example of the latter is found in one of Patong's nicknames, Pinto. *Pintu* is the Malay word for door or entrance and is used as such by the Chewong as well. In this instance, it refers to the fact that Patong entered *pinto gahogn*, the headwaters

---

[1] *Chò* also means 'what', as in 'what is that?' or more specifically 'name it' (*chò noh?*). I do not know what *punlao* means, it did not appear in any other context.

of a river, where certain *bi inhar* live. This, of course, closely resembles the Temiar practice of changing a personal name upon an important event. The difference is that whereas the Temiar cease to employ the previous name, the Chewong just add the new one to the existing list. Patong's other names are Maning (a flower) and Ta' Gajah (grandfather elephant), the name he is usually known by.

Members of certain affinal categories may not refer to each other by the real name, but always employ the nickname, or a teknonym. The persons thus constrained are parents- and children-in-law of either sex, and spouse's siblings of either sex. In all cases they represent actual genealogical links, not classificatory categories. In practice, however, people tend to address each other by the nick-name. The real name is always given to outsiders, and is the one that features on their identity cards when they have them. They regard their nicknames with some embarrassment, which would seem to indicate that these are ritually more important, but there was no further evidence for this.

They rarely refer to each other by relative kin term; the only exception being when ritual restrictions forbid one to use the real name. For instance, a man may refer to his son-in-law as his daughter's husband. This may take place in an actual encounter as for example when Beng calls out to his son-in-law Kwe, 'Nyom's husband do you have some poison to give me?', or when referring to such persons in general conversation. However, he would never call him 'son-in-law' (*besewa*) when talking to him.

7

Relativity in Perception

IN the preceding two chapters the various aspects of the conscious individual, or personage as I have also termed him, have been discussed whether he be in human, animal, plant, or some other form. Because most of my data relate to the human personage, and because the Chewong are 'humancentric' in their attributions of other species, I have mainly concentrated on their concepts regarding humans, but pointed out parallels and differences whenever possible. In my conclusion I suggested that each personage is species-bound, that is to say that there is something unique to each species of personage, manifested not only in their different bodies, but also in the collective representations of the species. This discussion will now extend into the field of perception, as the beliefs of the Chewong in this area are illuminating and provide further evidence for my general thesis. In effect I shall be arguing that all the various species of personage have different ways of perceiving reality, and that these differences are explained in terms of the eyes. Different conscious beings have, as a species, different eyes (*med masign*). The importance attached by the Chewong to the eyes is exemplified by their belief that it is the eyes which are made first of all when a foetus is being developed inside its mother's womb.

The presentation begins with the Chewong concept of hot and cool eyes, by which they make one boundary between human and superhuman beings. A discussion of beings with different, rather than cool eyes, is then presented and the conclusion reached is that eyes and perception are intrinsically species-bound. The chapter concludes with a consideration of hot and cool as symbolic agents for thinking about humans as opposed to superhumans.

HOT AND COOL EYES

It has already been mentioned on several occasions that one way of distinguishing the superhuman beings from ordinary humans is to attribute cool eyes (*med sedeig*) to the superhumans, and hot eyes (*med abod*) to humans. In what follows I wish to elaborate upon this distinction, particularly with reference to the *putao*, who, despite their humanity, are attributed with cool eyes. In fact they are often referred to simply as 'people who have cool eyes' (*bi wò med sedeig*). This is also a common way to refer to the *bi inhar*. Strictly speaking, only those *putao* who have dew as their spirit-guide, and whose hot blood has been exchanged for cool blood by the *bi asal* of Earth Six, are so described. In practice, however, any of the more knowledgeable *putao* may be included. In the human context a number of abilities are associated with cool eyes. Not only can the possessor see the superhuman beings, but he can also discern the 'true' (*lòi*) nature of things, beings, and states, thus allowing deceptions to be unveiled and illnesses to be diagnosed and cured.

Ordinary people do not see the superhuman beings. 'Our eyes do not meet them' (*med he han yao*), they say. During a *nöpoh* only those who have cool eyes are able to find the lost *ruwai* of the patient. The rest cannot see it; nor would they be able to see the *bas*, *yinlugen*, or whoever had taken the *ruwai*. In a *nöpoh* all those who have a spirit-guide (and here I refer to *ruwai* rather than *wòng hieng*) are able to watch the progress of the *putao*'s journey. The rest of the people present are unable to see any of this. They cannot see the *bi hali* who arrive at the house, but they can smell their sweet scent. Nor can they see any other superhuman beings who might arrive, but they are told about them by the *putao* in their singing.

The great *putao* are able not only to see a superhuman being, but also to summon them during a *nöpoh* or a dream. To do so outside the context of a *nöpoh*, with its singing and drumming and various other paraphernalia, however, is regarded as a superior way of making contact.

I witnessed one such encounter when Al was asked by Beng to come to Gambir. There had been a lot of minor illnesses at the Latah Tujuh settlements, and Beng felt that a contact with some friendly superhuman beings might alleviate the situation. All members from the two settlements were summoned, and some people accompanied Al from Sentao and Gandah. Great excitement preceded the event, with the women preparing for a feast and the men providing the game to be eaten, since the encounter would be followed by a 'big eat' (*cha manung*). Like a *nöpoh*, this ceremony could take place only after dark, as no superhuman beings may be contacted during daylight. Towards afternoon, Al, Lamait, Laneg, Beng, Kwe, and several of the adolescent boys went up to the waterfall at Latah Tujuh to bathe. They wanted to make their bodies cool (*bi sedeig*) for the ceremony. When they returned, Al began to prepare several bowls of *òz taba* with the special wood chips and lit these in all corners of the house some time before everyone gathered inside. Al took fistsful of the incense smoke and blew it many times in the four cardinal directions. No special order seemed to be observed. This was done to attract the attention of the *bi inhar* whose presence he wanted. When night fell, everyone went inside. Al, Beng, Kwe, Lamait, and Laneg sat apart on a lower extension to the main part of the house. Al and Beng in turn blew the incense and uttered an abbreviated version of the nightly 'prayer'. Then all lights were extinguished and everybody was told to be quiet. Total silence reigned for about fifteen minutes, after which Al sighed and said, 'I want to sleep.' Beng then gave instructions for the lights to be lit. 'They have all gone home now', he said. The only activity carried out during the period of silence was the constant tending of the *òz taba* bowls, which under no circumstances should be allowed to go out.

During this time eight female *bi inhar* had arrived at the platform where the men were sitting. Al, who was responsible for summoning them, expressed the great effort this involved by saying how exhausted he was. Apart from him, only Lamait, who had not previously encountered any superhuman beings, saw the *bi inhar*. This was important since as far as the rest of the Chewong were concerned, it established Lamait as a 'person with cool eyes'. One of the *bi inhar* women, who were from the source of a nearby river (*pinto gahogn*) and 'very beautiful', became his wife on this occasion. The other three men just said, with disappointment, that their eyes were hot and that they had not seen the *bi inhar*.

Cool eyes also enable the possessor to see other objects and deeds invisible to those with hot eyes, and, for example, to see through outward deceptions such as when a human being is wearing an animal cloak.

There are many myths that deal either explicitly or just in passing with the ability of the *putao* to see the actual state of affairs, the 'real' or 'true' (*lòi*) personage of the being, be it human, animal, plant, or superhuman. Often the *putao* pretends stupidity or incompetence, whereas in fact because of cool eyes as well as his powerful spirit-guides he can see what is happening anywhere and who it is who is acting. In Myth 2, for instance, Bongso knew that the pandanus woman's vagina was full of thorns, which was why he made himself tiny in order to enter her safely. In Myth 8 Bongso knew that the *howaw* fruit without thorns was really a tiger so he refrained from eating it when the fruit was offered to him. In another myth, in which the ghost of a young girl appears to Bongso's brothers as horrible and frightening, Bongso could see through her disguise and perceived her as she really was, namely lovely.

The ability of those with cool eyes to see the true nature of things is not limited to the unveiling of deceptions (of which there are numerous other examples in the mythology). For instance, Aeh's father was by all accounts a great *putao*. To illustrate this man's mystical powers, the following story is told. One day he was up on Gunong Benom with a group of other men when they saw a siamang. Nobody had brought their blowpipes with them, but some *bi inhar* gave a blowpipe to Aeh's father. The others could not see this. He shot at the siamang and it fell. When the others saw the ape fall they became very frightened. They thought that it had been killed by *bas*, but Aeh's father told them to go and fetch it. Despite their reluctance he insisted, and when they came to the fallen siamang, they saw a dart protruding from its side. Aeh's father could thus not only see the blowpipe and use it, but he could also make the previously invisible dart visible.

Cool eyes are also essential in healing. Ideally a *putao* should be able to see the cause of any ailment. He should see who has attacked the patient, what the attack consists of, and how to effect a cure. In the same way that to contact the superhuman beings without the aid of a *nöpoh* is superior, so it also displays a *putao*'s great healing powers if he can do this without conducting a *nöpoh*. The great *putao* of the past disdained to conduct *nöpoh* and to employ all their paraphernalia. There was no problem for them. 'No need to sing and drum, no need to wear headbands and bandolier', people used to say. What these *putao* did instead was to *bla med*. *Bla* (cf., Malay *belah*, cut open) normally means to cut something in half, but in this instance they *bla med* ('cut the eyes') by cooling their eyes in the incense smoke of an *öz taba* bowl and saying powerful spells. Then they were able to see the cause of a disease as well as curing it.

How various superhuman beings may attack and cause disease in humans, and how these attacks may manifest themselves as *ruwai* loss or in bodily pain were discussed earlier. A *bas* for instance sets up traps all over the forest to catch pig *ruwai*. A human being may be inadvertently caught in one, and injured, although he is unable to see this for himself. The cause being invisible to the ordinary hot eye, the result is also invisible, and it may manifest itself in symptoms such as sharp pains in the body, a sore throat, or a fever. A great *putao* may be able to see what the problem is, and furthermore, he may be able to make it manifest by extracting the weapon used by the *bas*.

On three occasions, I was able to observe this. The *putao* in all cases was Cheī, deftly assisted by his wife, Gòl. Cheī began by cooling his eyes, face, hands, and torso in the smoke from the *òz taba*, all the while muttering spells. Gòl similarly cooled herself, but less visibly. So far as could be seen she did not make invocations. The patient sat in front of Cheī, and the house was full of people watching expectantly. Cheī appeared to be completely absorbed and unaware of his surroundings. He blew smoke through his right fist all over the patient's body, concentrating on the painful spot. He then infused some leaves over the bowl, muttered spells over them, and with these held in his right hand, rubbed the painful spot while blowing smoke on it through his left hand. Finally he removed the leaves and placed them in a bowl prepared for the purpose. This he handed over to another man who concentrated very hard on the bowl with the leaves (having already cooled himself in the smoke). He muttered spells, took the leaves out of the water, placed them on another leaf on the floor and unwrapped them. On each of the three occasions witnessed, there was something inside. Once it was an animal tooth; this indicated that a *bas* had bitten the patient. On the second occasion it was a fish bone; this indicated that a *bas* had thrown his spear at the sick person. The third time it was a piece of wood which was the dart from the blowpipe of a *bas*.

In each of these instances the injury suffered by the human patient was inflicted by a *bas* attacking in a manner similar to that employed by humans in hunting. The difference lay in the perception of the weapon used. To a *bas* a fish bone *is* a spear, a piece of wood *is* a dart, etc. When a *bas* is confronted by a fish bone, he sees a spear. This brings us to another distinction made by the Chewong in their concept of seeing, namely that all species of conscious beings have different eyes, and according to Chewong thought, a different way of perceiving reality.

DIFFERENT EYES

The behaviour of non-human conscious personages is explained by the Chewong in terms of each species having different eyes, not only from each other, but also from humans. When asked 'why do *bas* eat *ruwai?*' people always replied that *bas* have different eyes (*med masign*) and that when they look upon a *ruwai* what they see is meat (*ai*). This of course conforms to my earlier assertion that the Chewong do not accuse the superhuman beings who attack them of malevolent intentions, since they are only carrying out their necessary activities, just as humans do; but that they perceive the objects required as food differently.

Similar examples occur in the case of animals attributed with *ruwai* in the sense of consciousness. It was explained that dogs, for example, which eat human faeces (generally those of babies, under the house or elsewhere in the settlement) only do this because when they look at faeces they see a banana. As far as humans are concerned, to eat faeces is dirty (*kama*). The Chewong were ambivalent in their attitude to dogs and they were always eager to proffer this explanation, thereby, as it were, absolving the dogs from an otherwise unacceptable act.

The story about the man who became a tiger and then pursued his human family in order to eat them is also illuminating (Myth 8, Appendix 1). Towards the end of the story, when the tiger has been killed by Bongso, Bongso revives him briefly, by blowing smoke from *òz taba* over him, in order to ask him why he wanted to attack them. The tiger replies, 'I do not remember. All I wanted was meat. When I looked at you (plural) all I saw was meat.' In other words, the brother had changed into a real tiger and looked at the world around him with the eyes of a tiger. Consequently, to him humans were nothing more than potential meat, just as monkeys are to humans, said the storyteller adding that when the Chewong see monkeys, they only think of eating them.

This story also provides further evidence for my earlier conclusion about personages being species-bound. Bongso had killed his metamorphosed brother, and the view might be held that he had in effect killed his brother. The tiger-brother had, however, ceased altogether to be human. This is not a case of someone changing his cloak temporarily, it is a total metamorphosis. The point is brought out by Bongso posing his question—a question important enough to necessitate revivifying the tiger—since the answer absolves Bongso of any suspicion of fratricide. Bongso was entitled to kill him since his brother had entered wholly into the world of tigers, and by so doing had adopted the collective representations of the tigers' social world.

The same point is illustrated by Myth 9 in which a father changes into a keòi (the sort of bas who eat human bodies rather than their ruwai). Again the transformation is complete, and it was caused by the man licking his knife in order to alleviate his hunger. That these examples represent metamorphoses rather than the possession of an alien personage must be emphasized. The Chewong are quite clear on this point. There is a complete transformation of the human personage into a tiger personage in one case and into a keòi personage in the other. In both myths it is stated that the eyes of the main characters changed, and that following this change the personage viewed the external world in a different manner, and according to different values, from that of human personages. They became, or turned into, a tiger (ka yedi kle),[1] or a keòi (ka yedi keòi). In neither of these myths is it possible to reverse the metamorphosis. Only death can put a stop to the activities of these beings. In the myth about the man who turns into a tiger, his body changes as well as his eyes (and personage), and it is obvious for all to see what has happened. In the case of the man who becomes a keòi, it is only his eyes (and his personage) that change, whereas his body remains the same. It is not possible for people to know that he is a keòi, although I was told that if a person with cool eyes had been present, he would have seen the true state of affairs. Furthermore, the corpse of the tiger-brother is that of a tiger. Unlike the myth about the girl who wore a squirrel bajo and who in death reverted to the human form, in this case the man remained a tiger thereby demonstrating the transformation.

As Myth 9 demonstrates (as does Myth 16 about nlab, said to be very similar to keòi) as well as other myths not included, it is in the 'nature' of keòi to pretend to be human. The keòi know that if they seek human flesh, or that which they covet even more, human blood and stomach contents, they must pretend to be ordinary humans. But the point that must be emphasized yet again is that the Chewong explain the behaviour of keòi in terms of their having different eyes.

---

[1] The word yedi is probably taken from the Malay jadi, coming into existence, becoming, accomplishing its purpose. The Chewong use yedi in all myths when they describe the change from one state to another. They may also say 'have' (ka) as when they say 'he had (got, obtained) different eyes' (ka med masign).

There is never any intimation that they are regarded as malevolent, or evil in any abstract sense. They only behave according to their 'nature', as it were. So whereas humans must be on their guard against them, and are entitled to kill them should they ever be attacked by one, they do not represent an evil force opposing other forces which are inherently good.

There are numerous examples of how the Chewong envisage the animate conscious world around them (i.e., those species with *ruwai* in the sense of personage) as perceiving reality differently from both humans and other species of personages. The story that perhaps sums this up most succinctly is Myth 10 about Bongso in the elephants' land.

Elephants have *ruwai* and are personages. In their own land, which even has a name, Moödn, they appear as human beings (*beri*). Bongso's spear in the elephant's flank ceases to look like a spear once the elephant returns to Moödn and becomes a man. This spear's presence is then manifested by a severe illness. The other elephant people cannot see it, but Bongso can—presumably because it is of his own world—and he removes it, thereby curing the elephant-man. The analogy with conceptions about attack by *bas* on humans is obvious. When *bas* shoot their darts or spears at human beings, these cannot be seen, but they do cause illness. The *putao* can, through the aid of the smoke and spells, both see and extract these weapons. The same applies to the elephants. Although they appear in human form, they are not really human personages, otherwise they would perceive reality in the same way.

Numerous other examples may be quoted in support of this argument, but I will restrict myself to mentioning just a few more regarding different sorts of beings. When there is a *talaiden* storm, one way to appease the Original Snake is for the *putao* to take a piece of bamboo and fly down and give this to her. When she looks upon the bamboo she sees a bushknife, and since she cannot obtain these in her own world she accepts this as sufficient recompense, and the storm ceases.

When someone has died, the *yinlugen* roams the settlement seeking to abduct the *ruwai* of the living. At night the *putao* sits at the opening of the house and waves an attap leaf in the air. When the *yinlugen* sees this it is frightened and runs away. This is because it sees the leaf as a spear.

The final example concerns a change in Chewong collective ideas regarding the non-human world. It was said that the canes known as

Malacca cane (*seg manao*) have *ruwai* and 'are people' and this was the reason given for not cutting them down and selling them despite the high prices offered. One day some young boys could not resist the temptation any longer and sold a few lengths. The resulting radios, biscuits, and other consumer goods seduced the rest of the Chewong, and within three weeks it had become general practice despite the earlier protestations to the contrary. Everyone was, however, extremely uneasy about their behaviour, fearing that disease would ensue. Then one night Al had a dream in which he met some *bi inhar*. They told him that they were angry with the Chewong for taking all their 'sweet potatoes'. It turned out that the Chewong had been mistaken in their assumption that the canes were people who should not be killed. Instead they were the sweet potatoes of some *bi inhar*. The offence was still there, certainly, but its severity had been reduced. It was explained that when the *bi inhar* encountered humans cutting down the cane, they saw porcupines digging their sweet potatoes. It was therefore to be expected that they would erect their traps around the cane, just as people would if porcupines were eating their crops. Because of this, whenever someone planned to go in search of the cane he would make a special invocation the night before to the *bi inhar* in question and offer them the smoke instead of the cane. Apologies for the act were made.

CONCLUSION

The discussion of the idea of personages has been extended into the area of perception, and it has been shown that each species of personage has eyes which are different from those of other species. What this means is that they all perceive reality differently. There is therefore a uniquely human way of seeing the world, a siamang way, a tiger way, a *keòi* way, a *bas* way, a *bi asal* way, etc. Whether the totality of objects and beings is perceived differently by the various species is unimportant. As far as the Chewong are concerned the principle is established, and can be drawn upon to accommodate whatever may arise out of specific circumstances. As such the principle of differential perception provides the Chewong with an interpretation of acts and events which are otherwise inexplicable. It forms one aspect of their theory of causation. Another, and a related one, is one principle of rule-governed behaviour to be discussed in the next chapter. The examples that occur of different perceptions chiefly relate to food and disease, concerns with which the Chewong are particularly preoccupied, and also areas where they most frequently encounter non-human and superhuman personages.

In view of the above, one may suggest that the Chewong posit a relativistic view of reality. As far as members of a particular species are concerned, the world that they view is the true one. Indeed, if this were not the case they would be unable to act. What is interesting, however, is that implicit in the Chewong conception is a basic belief in the 'psychic unity' of all personages regardless of their being human, animal, plant, or superhuman. The Chewong do, however, display a distinctly 'humancentric' view of other species in so far as they posit the same wants, needs, and modes of rationalizing for all personages. What differs between these personages is their notions as to what constitutes food, weapons, and other objects, both cultural and natural. So whereas one object looks like a piece of bamboo to the Chewong, and is used accordingly, the Original Snake when looking at the same piece of bamboo will see a knife and uses it as such. What humans see as smoke from a bowl of *òz taba*, the *bi hali* see as their staple, and so on.

As discussed earlier, the eyes are really part of the identity of a personage. When someone dons the body of another species, he continues to see and act according to the mode of his original species. If a man puts on a tiger cloak, for instance, he continues to see the world as would a human being. Similarly, when a *keòi* appears in human shape he continues to see the world as a *keòi*, although he may, when in contact with humans, pretend otherwise; as does the human in tiger body when encountering true tigers. It is only when a complete metamorphosis has taken place, as when the personage changes from a human to that of a *keòi* or a tiger, that the vision also changes.

There is a state of illness called *totn med* which is described as attacks of severe dizziness. I do not know what *totn* means, but it has connotations of going round and round. In this expression (unlike others where *med* is also used, such as in *med kato*, 'eye of the day', i.e., the sun) *med* is in the grammatical position of a qualifier which would indicate that something is happening to the eyes. To be *totn med* is to see the world upside down, and it occurs after an attack by the *bas* Ta' Tyo'. People who suffer from *totn med* are said to be 'mad' (*gila*) (cf., Malay *gila*, mad, insane). Although this usage of *gila* may not correspond to conventional notions of madness, it is nevertheless interesting to note that the only time this word is employed is in connection with the eyes. You are 'mad' if you perceive reality upside down, or, in other words, differently from the other members of your own species. Human beings have hot eyes. Only the *putao* who, in some contexts is classed with the superhuman beings, has cool eyes. The human *putao* is unique in being the only personage able to see, when in the different non-human and superhuman 'worlds', in the same way as members of those worlds see their reality, without losing his ability to see as a human being at the same time. As such the *putao* occupies a very special place in the Chewong cosmology. He is the only being within their extended social universe able to travel to all the different worlds within it, as well as being able to see in the same way as the inhabitants of these different worlds. He thus represents the pivotal point of this universe. It is through the medium of the *putao* that the rest of the Chewong obtain their knowledge about the non-human and superhuman worlds.

HOT AND COOL AS SYMBOLIC CATEGORIES

I have noted on several occasions the importance the Chewong attach to the distinction between the two states associated with temperature: hot and cool. I have suggested that these concepts are used symbolically as a means for distinguishing categories. These concepts will now be examined in more detail since they appear to be of extreme importance in Chewong symbolic classification. The two states are always opposed to each other, and coolness is invariably superior to heat. The significance of the opposition will now be considered.

The first and obvious contrast in th Chewong use of the concepts is that established between human beings and their world on the one hand, and superhuman beings and their worlds, on the other. At the simplest level of analysis everything human is hot and everything superhuman is cool. Earth Seven as it belongs to humans, plants and animals, whether conscious personages or otherwise, is hot. Earths Five, Six, and Eight, Pulao Klam, Plantor, as well as the habitats of the various personified *bi asal* on Earth Seven and elsewhere, and the different worlds of the *bi inhar* on Earth Seven, are all cool. What does this distinction signify?

Cool indicates health, immortality, and fertility. It is because of its cool sun that it is cool on Earth Six and that the fruit trees there bear all the year round. It is because the various superhuman beings have cool blood that they do not fall ill and die. Conversely it is because human blood (and bodies) are hot that we suffer illness and death, and it is because the sun of Earth Seven is hot that the fruit season is so short and occurs at such long intervals. This has all been stated before, when it was suggested that the Chewong are in a dilemma regarding their own state because theoretically they have the means to dispel the heat of their own bodies (although not that of their habitat) yet they will not do so. The *bi asal* and the *bi inhar* are frightened by the heat on Earth Seven and have to be induced to come here, and even then they will stay only for short periods. The *putao* is an anomaly in this instance, he has cool eyes (and in some cases cool blood as well), but he lives under a hot sun.

So far the words 'hot' and 'cool' have been used as if they were self-explanatory. In order to understand what they mean in the Chewong context, I will consider each in some more detail. *Abod* (hot) is used to describe the feeling of heat in the body. If one sits or works outside in the sun, one seeks shelter because one is *abod*. The eyes and blood and bodies of ordinary humans are *abod*. The body of a person with a high temperature is *abod* (it may also be said to be *hale*). The area close to the fire is *abod*, but the fire itself and food, including boiling water and saucepans just removed from it, are *lòig*. Similarly, although the sun on Earth Seven is *abod*, it appears to be its effect on humans which is *abod*, and were the Chewong ever to come very close to the sun it is likely that they would say that it was *lòig*. Hot weather as opposed to overcast, rainy, etc., is known as *pòr*.

Tokad (cold) is the opposite extreme to *abod*. Few states or things in the Chewong environment warrant the application of this word, but there are sufficient examples of usage to give a gloss on it. Whereas unheated water is usually known as cool water (*tam sedeig*) the waterfall at Latah Tujuh is *tokad*, and when people jump into it they shout '*tokad!*' Children having spent a long time bathing come up shivering, saying they are *tokad*. Whenever someone is shivering with cold in a fever they are said to be *tokad*, and the Chewong do not like to go high up on Gunong Benom because it is very cold there at night and, they say that because of this they fall ill after such a visit. The two states of *tokad* and *abod* are therefore seen as equally undesirable. They are both associated with disease, they are both actively avoided, and they are classed together as opposed to the desirable state of coolness (*sedeig*). *Sedeig* is of course the state of the superhuman beings, with whom the Chewong contrast themselves.

A quick bath makes the body *sedeig*, the forest is *sedeig*, ordinary unboiled water is *sedeig*, and smoke from *òz taba* is *sedeig*.

If human beings want to communicate with those superhuman beings regarded as helpful, they must induce a state of coolness in order to facilitate the contact. The best mediator is the dew *putao* who has had his blood exchanged with the cool blood of the super-humans and who has dew as one of his spirit-guides. In these ritual contexts he is classified with the superhuman beings. The dew *putao* can travel to the worlds of the various superhuman beings, and up to Earth Six. When people talk about the dew *putao* they always emphasize their coolness. They are said to be able to work in the hot sun without perspiring, they can hold hot embers in their hands without being burnt, and they are able to see the superhuman beings and non-ordinary realities because their eyes are cool.

The emphasis on coolness in connection with adeptness in esoteric matters is found among other Orang Asli groups also. The Batek for instance, say of a shaman (*hala' te*) that he can 'be recognized by his having the clear, colourless blood of the *hala' asal*. Also he would not sleep near the fire like ordinary Batek' (Endicott, 1979: 129); and the Temiar, though not employing the same metaphors, can never-theless be seen to associate coolness with shamanistic behaviour. The spirit-guides are related to water. According to Benjamin, the spirit-guides 'make their appearance as the watery emanation aspect of the upper-body soul of their everyday form' (1967: 246). And again, 'the spirit-guide appearing to the shaman as a "rain-like object"—he [the shaman] holds out his hand to meet them, and they collapse into his palm, liquifying into the watery state of *kahyak*' (247).

Putao who are not dew *putao* but are nevertheless able to conduct a healing *nöpoh* need to make themselves cool before contact may be made with the superhuman world. As mentioned earlier, Al went to bathe in cold water before he summoned the *bi inhar*. He did this explicitly because he wanted a cool body (*bi sedeig*). Similarly, Cheī cooled his face and body in the smoke from *òz taba*. Again, the reason was made explicit. When I first observed this action I was reminded of someone washing with smoke instead of water. It was therefore tempting to think in terms of pollution and of the smoke as a means to achieve a state of ritual cleanliness. This is not, however, the correct interpretation of the Chewong behaviour; the aim is ritual coolness. This assertion is further substantiated when we consider the Chewong prohibition on sexual intercourse before and during a series of healing seances. This prohibition is encountered in many other cultures, but it is usually interpreted as preventing the pollution of the participant for his encounter with the 'sacred'. This may perhaps be an ethnocentric interpretation by the Western ethnographers. In the Chewong context, at least, the notion of pollution does not enter into the consideration of why a *putao* must not indulge in sexual intercourse at such times. Rather, it is the heat that is seen as ensuing from such an act that must be avoided, since the heat would preclude the *bi inhar* from descending to help the *putao* in conducting a successful healing operation.

It is not just the *putao*'s responsibility, but that of the whole community, to ensure that a successful interaction with the superhuman world takes place. I was told that there had been times in the past when they held *nöpoh* and the *bi inhar* and other spirit-guides refused to come because of the immense heat that had been generated by the enthusiastic love-making of the entire adult population.

The smoke from the *òz taba* is cooling. The *putao* employs it not only to cool himself, but also to cool the patient by blowing the smoke all over him in the manner already described. When one is sick one is said to be either hot (*abod*) or cold (*tokad*) and many of the healing activities consist in making the body cool (*sedeig*). These two states can therefore be seen as classed together for the purposes of defining disease. There is an implicit opposition between hot and cold on the one hand and cool on the other. Placing the body of the patient in a symbolically cool state can be interpreted as an attempt to place him in an ideal state, contrasted to the two extremes. He is also thereby brought closer to the superhuman beings.

The dew *putao* always brings back some dew from Earth Six in which he bathes the patient. This is the most powerful cooling agent. Lesser *putao* who are unable to enter Earth Six, are given dew by various *bi inhar*, especially those who are already associated with cool places, such as those who live in the underwater pools which are the sources of the rivers, or those who live high up on Gunong Benom.

When someone is being cured by spells rather than by a full-scale *nöpoh*, smoke is again utilized. But often the spells do not 'take' (*chab*) in hot places, which is why people will sometimes leave their houses and the settlement in order to 'sleep on ground' (*abn ka te*) having made several unsuccessful attempts to cure with spells and smoke. They go to the forest and spend some days in a lean-to. The forest is cool, and the ground is cool, so they expect the spells to take effect there.

The above discussion may be summarized by the following series of analogues:

Cool : hot :: forest : field :: smoke : fire :: ground : house :: health : sickness :: superhuman + *putao* : ordinary human :: immortal : mortal :: seeing : not seeing :: *ratn* : *ai*.

Chewong ideas regarding hot and cool may be interpreted in terms of a nature/culture dichotomy. On the ideological level, as cool is preferred to hot, so nature is preferred to culture. As mentioned earlier the house and the field, both of which may be said to constitute 'culture', are hot and unhealthy, whereas the forest, the epitome of 'nature', is cool and healthy. However, it must be remembered that the characteristics of nature are those of Earth Seven before the culture heroes introduced the Chewong to culture and to society. There is thus a conflict of values. On the one hand society is more highly valued than individual existence. On the other, the advent of society results in undesirable conditions.

Foods are classed implicitly according to whether they are hot or cool. The Chewong do not explicitly state that certain foods are hot and that others are cool, but the following may constitute sufficient evidence for the connection to be made. The Chewong are unambiguous in their assertion that human beings have hot bodies (and blood) as a direct result of eating meat, and the *bi asal* on Earth Six have cool bodies (and blood) because they eat only fruit. The helpful *bi inhar* also have cool bodies (blood is unspecified) because they eat only the smoke from the *òz taba*. Furthermore, the Chewong make a linguistic distinction between the two types of food. Meat and fish of all kinds are called *ai*, whereas all types of staple vegetable foods and fruits are known as *ratn*. The Chewong say that when *bas* and *yinlugen* eat *ruwai*, the *ruwai* is their *ai*. When they look upon a *ruwai*, they see *ai*; when they go hunting for *ruwai*, they are in their own terms hunting for *ai*. Concomitantly, it is asserted that the fruit of the *bi asal* and the smoke of the *bi inhar* are their *ratn*. When one further considers that those who eat *ai* are hot, contract disease, and die; and those who eat *ratn* are cool, healthy, and immortal, one may posit the thesis that, implicit in Chewong modes of thought is the assumption that *ai* is hot and *ratn* is cool.

In view of the above discussion the inclusion of the last set of pairs in the list of analogues *ratn* : *ai*, is justifiable. Despite what has just been said, there is one occasion when the elements under discussion are inverted. A new-born baby cannot leave the house, its head must be covered at all times, and it must be bathed in warmed water only. Both it and the mother spend all their time lying next to the hearth. The explanation for an inversion of normal attitudes may perhaps be found in the inherent attributes of a new-born human. It is not yet incorporated into the society as a human being. It needs to be culturized. It is deliberately exposed to everything that symbolizes human society: the swidden, the house, clothing, transformed (that is, heated) water, and fire. Conversely, contact with nature, that is the forest, the ground (outside the house), untreated water, nakedness, and coolness must be avoided.

The corpse, on the other hand, cannot be washed in heated water but must be washed in cool, untreated water. 'They have died', it was said as an explanation for this rule. At death they are reversing the practices prescribed on birth. In this case they are separating the dead from society, or culture.

At times of other life-crises one finds a symbolic dissociation from what one may for present purposes call culture, imprecise though this term is. During healing processes, menstruation, and death a state of symbolic coolness has to be induced in order to facilitate the passage from one state to another. Coolness is the antithesis to the human condition.

Menstruation, with its prolonged show of blood, may be said to place the menstruating woman in a state of heat. By denying herself meat, she is protecting her body from increased heat, from the blood in the meat. This may be what underlies the Chewong assertion at such times that 'blood must not be mixed with blood'. The same applies to a woman following childbirth, when meat cannot be eaten until the post-partum bleeding has ceased. The new mother has to be kept warm by staying close to the fire, but this is a means of returning her to society.

A patient must take active steps to maintain the induced cool state achieved by the application of dew and smoke, by refraining from eating any of the foods which would make his body hot again. He must not eat meat (*ai*) of any kind because he would be eating blood, and blood as mentioned earlier is hot and induces heat. He must only eat vegetable matter (*ratn*) which, being cool, maintains his state of coolness. Moreover, the *ratn* cannot be cooked with any condiments, such as salt, chillies, lemon-grass, and oil, which, if eaten, would render his body hot. These condiments are not in themselves said to be hot, and the reason for their prohibition may be that they represent a sophisticated cooking method, cooking being quintessentially human. None of these prohibitions has to be observed if no ritual curing has taken place, even if a person is sick. This leads me to suggest that they are all directed at maintaining the cool state induced by the healing methods. Any breach of the sickness *pantang* (see next chapter) would reverse the healing process.

According to the Chewong, human beings will die if they do not eat meat and salt, so the enforced abstention from these foods is in effect a symbolic classing of themselves at such times with the superhuman world. The healing person is placed outside of society and culture, where it is assumed that the healing may be effected. This is substantiated by the temporary abandonment of house and settlement for the forest which occurs when the spells do not take effect, and the ritual cooling methods are not sufficient.

So, to return to the set of analogies, the same relationship that obtains between hot and cool, also obtains between humans and superhumans, and between culture and nature. It is in this loose sense that the last two terms are employed.

FIRE AND SMOKE AS AGENTS OF TRANSFORMATION

It is an anthropological commonplace to say that fire is quintessentially the means of converting natural substances to human use. Cookery is the most obvious example, but in the Chewong context it is also true about their swiddens. Fire is a destroyer, but it is also a transformer, and I suggest that to the Chewong it may be the heat of the fire rather than the flame that is significant in its role as transformer. When talking about a fire generally, it is the heat aspect of it that is emphasized. Its colour or the movement of the flames is not referred to. The concept of heat is also (possibly because of this) used metaphorically to indicate transitions of less mundane kinds.

In several myths mention is made of persons who change irrevocably from one species of personage to another, signalling this change through sudden and inexplicable heat. All attempts at alleviating this sensation fail. Bathing in cold water does not help. In Myth 8 one sees how the man who ate the *howaw* fruit began the transformation into a tiger when he became unbearably hot. In another myth (see Myth 18, Appendix 1) the star that came to earth and married Bongso became unquenchably hot after eating the maggots; she then ceased being human and returned to the sky.

In the same way that fire (heat) transforms raw food into cooked food, and jungle into field, so heat symbolically transforms physical beings from one species to another. Fire (and heat) are associated with the transformation of actual physical objects, of individuals, or of states.

Coolness, which in the Chewong context is the antithesis to heat, can correspondingly be seen to stand for the transformation of states effected through the medium of smoke. Smoke is used as an agent whereby disease is transformed into health. Similarly, by referring to the myths, one sees again and again how Bongso revives his dead siblings by blowing smoke over their bones. These are instances of a transformation of the state of death into the state of life. Of course not all smoke serves this function. It is only the smoke from *oz taba* used by a *putao* who knows all the right spells, which are sufficiently potent to ensure the transformation. As fire is seen in terms of heat, smoke is seen in terms of coolness. Smoke is used metaphorically to stand for coolness. When an amulet has lost its power due to one of the restrictions connected with its use being broken, its power can only be restored by symbolically cooling it in the smoke from *òz taba*. The change effected in this case is one from inefficacy to efficacy. By the same token, batteries used in radios are given a similar treatment when they begin to run down, or 'become hot' as the Chewong would say.

One might ask why two aspects of a single phenomenon, the heat and smoke of the fire, are used to symbolize both heat and coolness, states usually thought of as antithetical. The answer may be found in the nature of fire itself. Burning can be seen as a self-generating perpetual transforming action of flames into smoke. The flames are hot, the smoke is cool. Furthermore there is a transformation of colour: flames are red (*sowòd*),[1] smoke is white (*puteh*). The dichotomy is contained not only within the same phenomenon, fire, but also, and more importantly, within the same process.

Smoke is used as a symbolic vehicle for several unrelated significations apart from coolness. We have seen that it is blown in the four cardinal directions at times of impending storm in order to provide alternative paths for the descending *bi asal*. Sweet-smelling smoke is blown to the helpful *bi inhar* in exchange for their help. In these cases

---

[1] Chewong colour classification is simple. They do not distinguish between red and yellow, both of which are called *sowod*, or green and blue which are known as *bolowoden*. Brown, black or any very dark colour is called *se'eng*; and white or any pale or shining colour is called *puteh* (cf., Malay *puteh*, white). None of these words or close approximations are listed by Blagden.

the smoke is their food. Bad-smelling smoke is blown out in order to frighten *bas* when atmospheric conditions indicate their presence. (Whether the smoke is good or bad depends on the wood chips which are put in the bowl used for these purposes. The Chewong said that some incense smells good, and others bad.) Smoke is also used to signify the presence of human beings when they want to alert *bas* to the fact that they, rather than animals, are present. It can be used to cool an object or a sick person, thus acting as agent for metamorphosis.

These examples serve to demonstrate again that one object or phenomenon may, within the same society, be made to stand for different and often unrelated ideas. In this case, smoke among the Chewong is a multifaceted vehicle for symbolic thought.

PART III

RULES AND CLASSIFICATION

INTRODUCTION

IN this final part, attention is focused on questions which, though separate, are connected in terms of my exposition; namely the rules which constitute the dominant restraint upon Chewong behaviour, and the question of classification in Chewong modes of thought. Much of the data given in Chapter 8 forms the major basis for my discussion of Chewong classification which follows.

Chapter 8 thus describes in detail the numerous rules which govern Chewong behaviour; both the kind of acts that are forbidden, and the repercussions which will ensue. There are four propositions which underlie my examination: firstly, that these rules constitute an important part of Chewong understanding of their universe, since they, together with the myths and the received knowledge about the superhuman beings, form the body of Chewong knowledge about their environment, their society, and their culture, i.e., the interaction between individual and society; and between human society (including individuals) and nature and super-nature. Through the medium of the rules the superhuman beings are drawn directly into the day-to-day life of the Chewong. The fact that the consequences of all breaches of the rules are administered by superhuman or non-human beings, may account in part for the absence of a legal/political machinery among the Chewong. The rules inform the individual how to conduct himself or herself in order to pass through life in harmony. They are thus a means by which the individual is involved in the mechanism of order. Individual breach is often the trigger to social/universal destruction.

Secondly, the rules constitute a theory of causation regarding disease and mishaps of most kinds. Ideally, such mishaps do not occur unless a specific transgression has been committed, and the Chewong therefore conduct *post facto* investigations of behaviour in order to establish a diagnosis of a particular disease or accident, or an unusual natural phenomenon.

Thirdly, a number of the rules either prohibit the mixing of different things, for example different types of food, or (which is in effect the same) prescribe that certain categories and activities must be separated correctly. The sharing of certain objects is also prescribed. The issue of whether or not this latter type of prescription also constitute a manifestation of the importance of separation is an issue I shall return to in the conclusion of this chapter.

Fourthly, a close examination of the sorts of behaviour prohibited in the rules, reveals a remarkable emphasis upon control of the emotions. With the exception of those rules which are directly concerned with food, the rules prohibit most kinds of extravagant behaviour. But whereas most emotions are required by the rules to be suppressed, those of fear and shyness are positively encouraged.

Chapter 9 attempts to further test the conclusions drawn at the end of Chapter 4, where I found that no underlying patterns could be discerned in the Chewong system of categorizing superhuman beings. Attributes were scattered throughout the different nominal classes, the only binding factor appearing to be the class names attributed to them. This finding was sufficiently unusual to prompt me to examine other areas of Chewong thought where named categories could be seen to exist, the most obvious being the rules discussed in Chapter 8, and I have therefore submitted these to a very close scrutiny.

While I was in the field, I realized that the rules were not immediately accessible to systemization, and in view of this I tried to elicit as much information as possible about the kinds of acts which were forbidden, the objects and properties involved, and the repercussions, with a view to subjecting these data to more rigorous analysis.

As a starting point I presented much of the material obtained in tabular form, but was even then unable to discern implicit principles of organization, and could establish none of significance. Wishing to test these findings further, I submitted my data to a principal components analysis with the use of a computer. The result differed from that usually obtained from similar analysis (in psychology for instance) in that it suggested an absence of any significant pattern in the classification under study. In view of my own findings, supported by the computer analysis, I have suggested a redefinition of what may be said to constitute a class (in the sense of a multiplicity of elements united by a single name), namely that no other factor may be common among members of an assigned class beyond their membership of it, the criteria of membership being contingent.

8

Rules Governing Behaviour

IN this chapter the various rules which govern Chewong behaviour will be examined. Some of these rules have names which correspond to Malay words which mean 'forbidden', 'prohibited', or 'taboo'. What is prohibited in Malay folk tradition, as well as the kinds of repercussions envisaged, however, differ quite considerably from the Chewong rules and repercussions. It is likely that whereas the names have been adopted from Malay usage at some time, the content has done so to a lesser extent. Several of the names are employed for similar rules among other Orang Asli groups, and brief mentions of these are made under each heading. For instance, the Chewong rule of *talaiden* whereby laughing at animals leads to thunderstorms, is found among all the Senoi and Negrito groups in very similar form. Others, such as *maro* and *mali* seem to be unique to the Chewong. But even where similarities exist, the Chewong place different emphasis and interpretation upon their prohibitions so that the body of the rules can be seen to be an expression of the Chewong world view and moral and social values. They certainly regard them as uniquely their own, different in significance, though maybe not superficially, to rules and practices known to exist among neighbouring Orang Asli. To the Chewong, the rules constitute part of their traditional knowledge, and they are the chief means whereby children are socialized. Since the rules encompass most daily activities, children soon learn their names, the various activities associated with them, and the results of specific transgressions.

The rules to be discussed are *talaiden, punen, pantang, maro, tolah, tolæg, tika,* and *tanko,* and each will be dealt with in turn.

TALAIDEN

What is clearly the same word is found among the Negritos, and is used to denote similar ideas to those of the Chewong. Thus Schebesta writes of the Kenta–Bogn of Kedah that, 'A transgression of one of Kaei's laws is called *telaidn*. . . . The result of a *telaidn* is called *dos* (Malay, *dusa*), guilt' (1928: 222). He also found the same word among the Kensiu of Kedah (253, 255), and among the Batek of Pahang (276). Endicott reports the use of the word *talan* among the Batek Nong to mean 'ordinary offences against the thunder-maker and the earth-snake' (1979: 69, 155). Evans came across the term among the Batek Hapen who said that 'Lai-oid lives under the earth. She makes *talain*. . . . if we laugh at, or play with ants, *talain* comes' (1937: 146). According to Dentan, the Semai use the word *tarlaid* to mean 'to act in a way that might bring on a natural calamity' (1968: 23).

Among the Chewong there are two types of *talaiden*, snake (or wind) *talaiden* and tiger *talaiden*, and these are differentiated both by the cause that makes them happen and by the ensuing effect. Thus wind *talaiden* (*talaiden hong*) also known as snake *talaiden* (*talaiden talòden*), is caused by laughing at animals, and is punished by the Original Snake beneath Earth Seven. By breathing heavily through her nostrils she produces a special kind of wind on Earth Seven. It blows along the ground only, and when it occurs during a thunderstorm, the Chewong know that someone has committed *talaiden* and is about to be swallowed by the Snake. There is also an accompanying upwelling of water. The conciliatory measures which may be entered into to persuade the Snake to cease have already been described (Chapter 4). Although the Chewong stress that the Snake will swallow (*ogòd*) one if one commits *talaiden* by laughing at animals, no one could give any examples of this having ever occurred in the myths. The following legend, on the other hand, was always told to me as an example of how the Chewong know about *talaiden* and the repercussions of committing it.

Once there was a man who killed a large snake [they would always say that it was a boa constrictor]. He brought it home and cooked it. There was lots of good fat, and the man, his wife, and the other people ate it. It tasted very good. His son-in-law would not eat it and he told his wife not to do so. Nobody knew about *talaiden* in those days. When they had eaten the snake, a strong wind blew up, it blew along the ground, and water began to well up from the earth. Water flooded everywhere and everybody climbed tall trees. After seven days the wind ceased. The people climbed down, all except the couple who had not eaten the snake. The houses had fallen down into holes in the earth. The snake was waiting for them, and all the people fell down the holes and were gobbled up by the snake. Only the couple who had not eaten snake meat were safe. Since that day the Chewong have been frightened of eating snake, even though the meat has lots of fat.

The above is the version from the Chewong in the Krau Game Reserve. I was told the following version at Kampong Yol (Dong).

A long time ago some people killed a large snake (*naga*). They cooked it and ate the fat. There is a lot of nice fat on snakes. They did not cook the head, however. This they cut off and put on a nearby tree stump. All the people partook of the snake fat. When they had eaten, it began to rain and storm. Water welled up from the ground and the people climbed up a tall tree. The snake head which they had left became a complete snake again and when the people climbed down from the tree the snake swallowed them all. One couple only managed to escape. They ran towards a tall mountain. The snake followed, but they did not realize this. When they had built a small house, the wife, who was pregnant, went to bathe in a nearby river. After she had bathed, she sat down to comb her hair. She chose to sit on what she thought was a tree trunk, but it was the snake's head. She did not know this. The next day she was no longer pregnant. Her husband looked at her stomach and asked, 'where is the child in your stomach?' The wife did not know what had happened. Not only had she lost her unborn child, from then on she was barren. Once the snake had eaten all the people and made the woman barren, it became a *bi inhar* and moved to the sea which is its real homeland.

Though the details vary, these two myths tell virtually the same story, namely that to eat snake meat will be punished by the Original Snake who causes storms, winds, and upwelling of subterranean water, and then gobbles up the offenders. In the Dong version there are no innocent bystanders who escape the waters, but the theme of a fleeing couple is there, although in this case they were not innocent, and the woman was duly punished by miscarriage and later barrenness—a different form of death. What is curious about these myths is that they make no reference to laughing at animals, the common cause given today for *talaiden talòden*, yet whenever I asked for some explanation of why the Snake eats people I was always told the above myths, and many people will refuse to eat snake meat, saying that to do so is *talaiden*.

The prohibition on eating snake meat is not universally accepted. It is significant, however, that those who do eat the meat always seem to feel the need to justify their behaviour by stating that to do so is in fact not *talaiden*. On the other hand, everybody is explicit that it is *talaiden* to laugh at animals, whether alive or dead, and that this will be punished in the way just described. I came across no one who did not adhere to this rule.

Although I was told about numerous incidents in which *talaiden* storms had occurred as a direct result of someone having laughed at an animal, and observed several myself, I was never told a myth which directly display the same causal link. Yet the Chewong are very specific regarding the restriction on laughter. They say that it is *talaiden* to laugh (*oglug*) and would make noises like 'ha, ha' whenever telling me about it. In the next chapter the actual animals involved in the storm *talaiden* rule will be examined. For the moment I wish to stress how strongly the Chewong adhere to this rule, and how diligently children are brought up to observe it. Expressions of levity must not occur in connection with animate non-human beings.

The term *talaiden talòden* and *talaiden hòng* are used interchangeably for either offence (eating snake meat and laughing at animals). When children are found teasing some animal boisterously, or playing noisily near a carcass or meat being cooked or eaten, they are sharply told off: '*Talaiden!* The Snake will gobble you up' (*talaiden! Ogòd talòden*).

The following legend was also told to me as another example of the cause of a *talaiden* storm. It was, however, never recounted spontaneously as *the* explanation for *talaiden* and why the Chewong observe the rule.

A man and his fiancée caught a live squirrel. They took it home with them. They placed the squirrel in a baby sling which was suspended from the ceiling, and rocking it to and fro they chanted '*bowei, bowei*' just as they would a baby. It rained and stormed and water welled up from below. The house and the people were flooded out and gobbled up by the Snake. To do what they had done was very much *talaiden*.

In this case the people concerned did not actually laugh at the animal, but they could be said to be teasing it. The story parallels one told by Evans about dressing up a monkey in human clothing which also resulted in thunderstorm and destruction (Evans, 1923: 203). It is possible that the underlying reason for the prohibition is that one should not submit other species to activities which mimic human behaviour. Thus, the implicit message seems to be that different species of animals must be kept separate according to their characteristics. Each has its own role to play, and proper behaviour on the part of humans *vis-à-vis* them must be observed. To 'marry' a cat with a dog is *talaiden*, further suggesting that boundaries between classes of beings must be upheld.

In a recent article, Blunt (1981) shows how the link between boisterous behaviour towards animals and punitive thunderstorms can be found not only in the Malay Peninsula, but throughout the Austronesian world. It would appear, however, that the precise manifestation of the rule varies between societies. In the case of the Chewong, the rule certainly fits well in relation to the numerous others that proscribe their behaviour.

The second type of *talaiden* is known as tiger *talaiden* (*talaiden kle*) and does not concern the expression of inner states. It is invoked by mixing certain types of meat with certain other types, or with specific vegetables or fruit. The foods in question may not be eaten together at the same meal, cooked over the same fire, or even carried together in the same backbasket. If this is done, a tiger will attack and kill the offender. The Chewong have several legends that expound the dangers of tiger *talaiden*. (See Myths 11 and 12, Appendix 1.) Furthermore, to eat elephant meat is elephant *talaiden* (*talaiden gadja*), and would lead to being attacked and killed by an elephant. Myth 12 is interesting in so far as it shows someone purposefully exploiting her knowledge of the *talaiden* rule in order to attract the tiger.

The rule of *talaiden* thus refers to two very different acts (in addition to the eating of snake or elephant meat), namely that to laugh at animals leads to fatal thunderstorms, and that to mix certain types of foods leads to being attacked and killed by a tiger. The former rule refers exclusively to the matter of laughter, and the latter to acts of eating; thus one concerns the expressions of emotions, the other the diet. Both, however, display a preoccupation with the principle of separation.

Modn once tried to explain the word to me. She took a leaf and said, 'There are two different *talaiden*, one side is *talaiden talòden* (and she indicated one half of the leaf whose central stem was clearly marked) and the other side is *talaiden kle* (and she indicated the other half of the leaf)'. From this one might deduce that it means nothing more than 'prohibition' or 'forbidden', and that it might stand for 'taboo' as this word has come to be used. This would be a false interpretation, however, as is demonstrated by the fact that there are a number of other rules, in addition to *talaiden*, which forbid specific acts and which are applied in various contexts. The Chewong language makes no distinction between what one may call the name of the rule, e.g., *talaiden*, the act that will lead to a punitive reaction, and the punitive act itself. In other words, they do not distinguish linguistically between cause and effect in these particular instances. One may ask what an adult actually means when she calls out '*talaiden!*' to a child who is laughing at or near an animal. Does she just mean 'forbidden', by which the child is expected to cease whatever it is doing? This is clearly not sufficient. The act of the child leads the adult to choose which particular word to admonish him with. Thus had he not been sharing his food, she would have called out '*punén!*' (see below), etc. So the act and the consequences of committing them are united in the Chewong mind, and it is not possible to say which the word in specific cases actually is referring to. There is an added difficulty, namely that several of the rules encompass different causes and effects, for example, snake *talaiden* and tiger *talaiden* discussed above. In all cases, however, the offending act identifies the repercussions to be expected. It is therefore not necessary to state what kind of *talaiden* is being committed when admonishing someone, the offender knows by his act whether it is wind *talaiden* or tiger *talaiden* and it is necessary only to call out '*talaiden!*'.

An interesting aspect of the laughter *talaiden* is that it does not apply only to human beings, it is equally *talaiden* for non-human beings to laugh at members of other species. Thus they said that to go to Gunong Benom is always fraught with danger because *talaiden* may be caused by the superhuman beings who live up there, and whose bodies are green. Whenever these beings see humans, they cannot refrain from laughing. 'They find us ugly because our bodies are brown.' But by laughing at us they provoke a *talaiden* storm, in which the humans might be hurt by falling trees, although they would not be swallowed by the Snake.

This example is yet another piece of evidence for my submission that the Chewong universe extends beyond the human world to include the superhuman beings, and that they attribute to other species of personages similar values and constraints. In this particular instance, the identical rule is operational in both worlds, and the repercussions are also the same.

PUNÉN

The Malay *kempunan* means 'a calamity, misfortune, owing to not having satisfied an urgent desire to eat some particular thing' (Coote, 1976). Similar words are used by various groups of Orang Asli. The

Semai, for instance, employ the word *punan* to mean 'a sort of "taboo" that keeps people from breaking the rules of food distribution' (Dentan, 1968: 55). Elsewhere he defines it as '1) A frustrated desire that makes one sick or accident prone. 2) An action which produces such a mental condition, for example hurting someone's feelings. 3) The rule against committing such actions. 4) More generally, taboo at all times. 5) The sicknesses or accident-proneness resulting from *punan* acts' (107). The Semelai use the term *penon* to describe injunction on the consumption of certain types of food as well as 'to describe a certain state of psychological vulnerability which someone is put into if he or she fails to consume certain categories of food at certain times' (Hood, 1978: 110).

Among the Chewong there are several kinds of *punén*, most of which are concerned directly with the suppression of emotions. Transgressions are in all cases punished in an attack by a tiger, snake, or poisonous millipede. The actual animal may bite, or its *ruwai* may do so, and in either case the result will be an actual wound on one's body or some form of disease.

The first type of *punén* has social ramifications since it prescribes the sharing of food and other objects, and prohibits the nursing of ungratified desires. In the Chewong world, desires are most likely to occur in connection with food. If someone is not immediately invited to partake of a meal which he observes, or if someone is not given her share of any foodstuff seen to be brought back from the jungle, that person is placed in a state[1] of *punén* because it is assumed one would always wish to be given a share and hence experience an unfulfilled desire. As already stated, to 'eat alone' is the ultimate bad behaviour in Chewong eyes, and there are several myths that testify to this. (See e.g., Myth 13, Appendix 1.) The sanction on sharing out food originates in the myth about Yinlugen Bud (quoted in Chapter 4) who was the chief instrument in bringing the Chewong out of their pre-social state by telling them that to eat alone was not proper human behaviour. *Punén* thus has two aspects in common with some of the other rules: first, it is concerned with the emotions (desires); secondly, it prescribes the sharing of food. The ramifications are of particular significance since the identity of the 'offender' depends on what one regards as the pertinent aspect of the rule. Thus, is the

---

[1] *Punén* may be used as a verb. Thus it is said that someone has '*punéned*' his parents-in-law, *no ka punén klòg*, or that one '*punéns*' oneself, *ka punén punyeh*. It is in this sense that I feel justified in using the expression 'puts one in a state of *punén*'.

'offender' the person who experiences an ungratified desire, or the one who fails to gratify someone else's desire by not sharing? The Chewong take all possible precautions against provoking *punén*. All food caught in the forest is brought back and publicly revealed immediately. It is then shared out equally among all the households. The women cook it and then share the food in equal portions among all the members of their own household. As soon as a carcass is brought back, and before it has been divided up, someone of the hunter's family touches it with his finger and makes a round touching everyone present in the settlement, each time saying '*punén*'. They usually touch with their right index finger on the hand, lower arm, or ankle. This is another way of announcing to everyone present that the food will soon be theirs, and to refrain from desiring it yet awhile. Similarly, when it is being cooked, the woman responsible will call out to those present, 'It is very slow in cooking, but it will soon be ready', thereby again ensuring that no one need fear that he or she is not going to receive their full share. If guests arrive while the hosts are in the middle of a meal, they are immediately asked to partake. If they refuse, saying they have just eaten, they are touched with a finger dipped in the food, while the person touching says '*punén*'.

Once a desire has been voiced, the person who can satisfy it must immediately do so. If he refrains, the person refused will suffer the consequences of *punén*. But unvoiced desires are just as liable to provoke the same repercussions. In fact people hardly ever make overt requests for anything, and the fear of *punén* may easily have prevented people from requesting gifts from me. I can recall only one instance when I was solicited to give. An old woman, Mag, asked me to give her a whetstone, which I duly did. The rest of the Chewong, when they heard what Mag had done, commented unfavourably upon her behaviour. Of course, if I had refused, it would have been because of my failing to satisfy her desire that Mag would have been bitten by a tiger, snake, or whatever. To desire for oneself can be seen to be bad on two counts. First, it is an overt emotion. Secondly, it emphasizes the individual at the expense of the social.

Whereas all food must be shared out under penalty of *punén*, only certain non-foodstuffs are subject to the same injunctions. These are objects brought from afar (*tyòtn*). Thus bamboo for baking the tapioca bread must be shared equally among all households if the gatherer had to go very far to obtain it. If the bamboo grows close to the settlement, one may collect enough for oneself only. The difference is expressed as bamboo far away (*lao tyòtn*) or bamboo near by (*lao duah*). If the nearby river dries out and water has to be carried some distance, it again has to be shared, but daily water collection from the usual source need not be shared. I suggest that a possible explanation for this is that daily requirements which are easily fulfilled are not thought to provoke any desires in others whenever these are observed to be satisfied, but if special efforts are necessary to meet ordinary needs, then desire for such objects might easily arise in those who had not bothered to provide for themselves, and hence *punén* is invoked on such occasions.

Even if one does not want something that has been brought back, one has to be made publicly and specifically aware of the existence of the thing, by touch if not by the receipt of an actual share. The following exemplifies this: I had once gone with a group of people for a visit to Pyapoz where everyone chewed nuts from a betel-nut tree which grows near by. No one offered me any, knowing full well that I would decline. Shortly afterwards I was walking into the forest on my own and was much frightened by a sudden encounter with a large snake. When I told about it, everyone immediately stretched out their betel-nuts for me to touch, while exclaiming '*punén! punén!*'. When I suggested that it could not be *punén* since I did not want any betel-nut, they insisted that maybe I wanted some, just a little bit.

I have said that the consequences of placing someone in a state of *punén* is that that person will be bitten by a tiger, a snake, or a poisonous millipede. In these cases the Chewong do not distinguish between the actual animal and its *ruwai*. I have several times heard people say, 'If it is not a tiger that bites, then it is a snake; if not a snake then a millipede; if not an actual tiger, etc., then its *ruwai*.' The attack may manifest itself as an injury or as some disease. Kwe once came home saying that he had been bitten by a snake on his big toe. He had not seen the snake, but he had a sharp pain in the toe. He had dug around in it to see if it could have been a splinter but had found nothing, so he assumed it was caused by a snake. It started to swell, and became more and more painful as the days went by, and people began to think back to locate the cause. They soon realized that when, a few days earlier, some of the men had brought back from Gunong Benom an ingredient for making dart poison, they had not given Kwe any. It was assumed that he did not need it and Kwe claimed not to have wanted any at the time. But now it was realized that *punén* had in fact been committed, and Kwe was certain that he had been bitten by the *ruwai* of a snake rather than by the snake itself. In this case the bite of the *ruwai* of the snake was manifested as a wound, not as an illness which would have been caused by a bite on the person's *ruwai*.

Punén can also be self-imposed by not fulfilling a desire which it is within one's power to satisfy. For instance, if one wants to smoke, one must stop whatever one is doing in order to gratify this wish. In these two aspects of *punén* the emphasis is upon not only the suppression of the expression of the emotion, but, more importantly, upon the suppression of the emotion itself. In one case the rule is directed towards social behaviour and responsibilities, in the other the responsibility is only towards oneself. In both cases the repercussion is attack by a tiger, snake, or millipede, whether the actual animal or its *ruwai*.

The next two varieties of *punén* have the same consequences of being attacked by the animals mentioned, but the causes are quite different. Furthermore, in both cases it is the actual animals, never their *ruwai*, that attack. These *punén* are both invoked by 'speaking badly' (*klugn yabud*). One form of speaking badly is to cry out in the event of personal misfortune. The words *krid*, *mas*, and *gibed* are associated with this sort of act, but I am unable to give any gloss. Whether they are the actual swear-words that may not be uttered, or whether they mean the equivalent of 'to swear' I cannot state with certainty. My impression is that they are probably both. The sort of misfortunes envisaged whereby one might speak badly are times when one falls and hurts oneself, or when one discovers that one has lost something. In cases of *krid*, etc., rather than being attacked by an animal, the result may be a failure to shoot any game (*osial ai*).

If one discovers that one has lost an article, or left it behind in the forest, not only is it *punén* to cry out at the discovery, it is also *punén* to state what it is one has lost or forgotten. A substitution word has to be used. Similarly, many other objects, when gathered or collected from afar (those that have to be shared out), cannot be referred to by their real name, but euphemisms must be employed, or what I here call '*punén* names'. For instance, if a person is going to gather some tobacco leaves from plants some distance away, she must use the *punén* name. If she is cutting leaves from a tobacco plant in the field, then the word for tobacco may be used. To use the real name in the former instance is *punén*, and if one sets off after having spoken badly in this sense, a tiger will wait on the path and attack (see Myth 15, Appendix 1). Table 8.1 is a list of these *punén* names. It con-

Table 8.1
Punén Names

Object	Punén Name	Meaning
*Be (uncooked rice)	ai le beseng med	little eyes
*Bladen (spear trap)	ai talòden[1]	snake
*Dòg (dart poison)	ai le eg	ruwai of blood
Galeh (tapioca)	ai manung bi	large body (root)
Goll, tangòi (sp. trees)	ai le njug	breath
*Hekrid (grater)	ai lemon	teeth
Kiaei (sp. tuber)	ai le Ta' Toi	man by this name who did not share kiaei
*Lao (bamboo)	ai le darægen mò ai le hate	nostril tail
*Macaw (tobacco)	ai le chinhöi	clearing (in jungle)
*Plò tanyog (sp. fruit)	ai mahum	blood
*Plò genti (rambutan fruit)	ai le sòg	hair
Sarign (fish trap)	ai le yinhagen ai le tabod	biting difficult to eat
*Saròng (sheath)	ai le hò	skin
*Seg (cane)	ai le wòrr	intestines
Silah (sweet potato)	ai le selor	sneak up
Tagad (sp. tuber)	ai chinbugn[2]	spider
*Tam (water)	ai haradj	sweat

Table 8.1 (*continued*)

Object	Punén Name	Meaning
*Tenlaig (dart)	ai tatinyogen[3]	porcupine quills
Tiòg (plantain, banana)	ai le Ya' Rud	female culture hero
*Toka (sp. fruit)	ai le kain	sarong, cloth
Totogn (root)	ai le keeb[1]	poisonous millipede
*Tuwang (durian)	ai le gile	thorns
*Wang (knife)	ai loka	claws
Yagògen (maize)	ai le wegn	tooth

[1]Snake *punén*.   [2]Spider *punén*.   [3]Bear *punén*.
*Indicates 'sympathetic signatures'. This will be discussed in the text.

stitutes the most common ones which various informants gave me. In most cases each informant listed all of them. The paraphrasing was identical in all cases.

Three main points emerge from the list of *punén* names. Firstly, *punén* names are only applied to non-meat foodstuffs and to inedible objects. The Chewong have no restriction on calling animals by their real names. The food and objects which have *punén* names are the very common ones, things which are eaten or used virtually every day and, in the case of food, not normally subject to the sharing restriction imposed by the *punén* rule. It is thus only when something becomes significant which under normal circumstances has little importance, that special precautions are imposed.

Secondly, it will be noticed that all the *punén* names start with the word *ai*. *Ai* means meat. In certain circumstances it is used figuratively to denote 'animal'. In the case of *punén* names the word *ai* actually refers to the tiger. The Chewong are explicit on this point. It must be remembered that to speak the real names of the things provided with *punén* names is tiger *punén* and that if one transgresses, a tiger will lie in wait to kill one. Furthermore, most of the *punén* names are direct references to different parts of a tiger's body. Thirdly, and arising out of the second point, all the *punén* names marked with an asterisk denote the presence of 'sympathetic signatures'. By this I mean that there is a correspondence between the properties of the actual object and the part of the tiger's body (or other objects to which it is likened) which serves as its *punén* name. In other words there is a conceptual resemblance between the object symbolized and the symbol itself. So when the *punén* name for knife is 'tiger's claws' we can readily understand the perceived resemblance between knife and claws. Or, the red juice of the *tanyog* fruit as well as the red dart poison, are both associated with blood because of their red colour and are therefore known as 'tiger's blood', or '*ruwai* of tiger's blood'. The question of sympathetic signatures and the place this mechanism has in Chewong symbolic thought will be returned to later.

It is not just the oral expression of a thing's real name which is prohibited; one may not even think of it, or in Chewong terms: 'say it in the liver' (*bad lam rus*). When a young man, Beng was once asked to collect some special herbs for his mother's delivery. It is *punén* to mention the name of these herbs when searching for them. Beng came across a tiger because he kept thinking of its real name. Luckily it was asleep, and Beng managed to escape. The important point to note is that thinking and the expression of a thought are not distinguished. They both have to be suppressed in specific circumstances, just as the *punén* on unfulfilled desire is both on the expression of a wish, and on the actual feeling itself.

A different *punén* is yet another form of 'speaking badly'. In this case it concerns the anticipation of a pleasurable event. Again it is not just the expression of the anticipation which is to be suppressed, but the actual emotion itself. Myth 14 is about this sort of *punén*. Here a boy (who incidentally is old enough to be expected to know the rules and behave accordingly) is anticipating a meal consisting of *payòng* nuts and monkey meat, a combination much liked by all the Chewong. He knew that the people at home were preparing *payòng*, and when he saw the monkey his father shot fall dead to the ground, he said that they would be eating monkey and *payòng* that night. There was no doubt that both the monkey and the *payòng* were there, nevertheless such a pleasurable fact must not be referred to, nor must it be anticipated. In other words, to express the emotion of anticipation is to speak badly.

Finally, the last type of 'speaking badly' is for a husband or a wife to command their spouse to do something. This is tiger *punén*. An example would be for a husband to tell his wife, 'Go and fetch some *hodj* fruit!' or for a wife to tell her husband, 'Go and shoot some monkeys!' In other words, the role-associated behaviour of a husband and a wife should not be demanded. To command something which is really a duty, is to step outside the proper role of a spouse. Conversely, by not fulfilling one's duties one is provoking an unfulfilled desire in one's spouse.

There is yet another type of *punén*, which bears no resemblance to the others, and to the outsider it would appear more suitably as a type of *pantang* (see below) than one of *punén*. Nevertheless, all the Chewong insist on calling it *punén*, and its specific name is corpse *punén* (*punén bankai*). It refers to pregnant women, who must under no circumstances look upon a dead body. Were they to do so, the foetus would be damaged, either physically, mentally, or both. Examples of this having occurred have already been given (see Chapter 3), when I suggested that the underlying reason for this rule is that while life (body plus *ruwai*) is in the process of being created, it must not be put in contact with death (body only).

There are thus several different kinds of *punén*, some of which may be said to forbid the expression of emotions, others which are less directly concerned with this. Among the first is the prohibition on wanting something which cannot immediately be gratified, and the constraint upon people not to provoke such desires in others. Then, there is the rule which forbids one to express one's dismay in face of pain and misfortune, and the one that forbids one to express anticipation of certain pleasurable events. The *punén* names which have to be employed when goods are collected from afar might be said to be linked to the prohibition associated with anticipation. Wanted goods should not be named until they are actually within one's grasp. Not naming lost goods is another way of repressing any emotion that this event might produce.

PANTANG

In Malay, the word *pantang* means 'forbidden' or 'prohibited' (Coote, 1976). In Chewong, the usage is similar, but most of the *pantang* prohibitions are invoked during and following major life crises such as pregnancy, birth, marriage, disease, and death. They also apply during menstruation, and there are several people who have individual *pantang*, restricting their diet in specific ways. Most of the Chewong rules are preventive; that is they specify that behaviour which if indulged in, will incur specific consequences. The *pantang* rules on the other hand are mainly protective. They specify restrictions on behaviour once certain events outside the control of humans come about. They ensure a safe passage from one stage in a person's life to another, whether it be from non-life to life, disease to health, or whatever. For convenience of exposition, the *pantang* will be discussed in connection with these various stages. They are largely concerned with restrictions on the individual's diet and movement.

BIRTH

The *pantang* associated with birth were discussed to some extent in Chapter 3 where it was suggested that the *pantang* restricting both parents of a child could be interpreted as a couvade, whereby the parents' behaviour affects the body or the *ruwai* of the foetus. Here the main points of the birth *pantang* will be reiterated in order to show their relationship with the other *pantang*.

Expecting parents may not eat fruit bats, horse shoe bats, flying foxes, bamboo rats, one species of river tortoise, or scaly ant-eaters. In addition, many informants told me that the slow loris and the otter may not be eaten either, but these two animals are part of the *tolæg* animals, none of which expecting parents may eat since the *yinlugen* of the species concerned will take the *ruwai* of the unborn baby. The rule of *tolæg* will be discussed later in this chapter. The reason that the other animals may not be eaten is that this would lead to a slow and difficult birth (*otugò wòng*) because all animals in question are said to have an unusually strong clasp. This is therefore another example of use of sympathetic signatures in Chewong symbolic thought. A further manifestation is the rule that pregnant women, but not their husbands, are forbidden to drink the water of coconuts and bamboo.

During the birth itself the mother does not give much vent to her labour pains. She may, at most, cry out '*adi!*' (a Malay interjection). But louder and more uncontrolled behaviour is not restricted by a *pantang* or any other rule. Since, however, women often talked about the pains of childbirth, and expressed fear at the prospect, the reason they behave in such a restrained manner at such times cannot be attributed to the benefits of so-called 'natural childbirth' methods, but must be seen in the wider social context of subdued behaviour in the face of emotional crises.

The umbilical cord must be cut by a sharpened bamboo. To use a metal knife is *pantang*. It is *pantang* for the mother and the new-born child to leave the house for the first few days following the birth. They have to spend the whole time lying next to the fire with their heads covered. Whenever the woman has to go outside for reasons of personal hygiene, she must keep her head covered. Were she not to do so her head would burst open and she would die. Both mother and child must wash in heated water only inside the house. Whereas this particular *pantang* holds for the baby until it can walk, the mother may bathe in the river once she starts her ordinary occupations again. Throughout the main *pantang* period when mother and child are confined to the house, nobody from another settlement may enter.

Finally, certain foodstuffs are *pantang* for the mother for the period while she is still bleeding after the birth. She may not eat any meat, fish, salt, chillies, oil, or any bought goods. She can only eat tapioca, wild tubers, and rice. In fact she must abstain from *ai* and confine herself to *ratn*, but this *ratn* must be eaten hot, and fruit for this reason is forbidden. In the last chapter I suggested that the mother's exposure to 'culture' together with her new-born baby is a manifestation of the conceptual link envisaged between mother and child during the first few days after the birth. The *pantang* operational on birth are strongly concerned with diet, and with confinement. The mother and child are restricted to transformed food (cooked and heated) and transformed washing water (heated water). They themselves have to be transformed by being heated by the fire. They are confined to the house and to the settlement, that is to say that they must be kept separate from the forest, the ground, and members of other settlements. Furthermore, their bodies are confined by clothing, in the case of the baby its whole body is wrapped completely, in the case of the mother the head only is wrapped. The separation of the baby from its mother's womb has been effected physiologically, but for the first few days after the birth the two are not yet separated conceptually—hence their subjection to the *pantang* rules. The actual restrictions strongly mark an immersion in 'cultural' concerns.

MENSTRUATION

Menstruating women, like newly delivered women, may not eat meat, fish, chillies, oil, etc., but only *ratn* without additives. In this case, as opposed to that of lying-in women, she may eat cool *ratn*; in fact this is specifically stated to be better. The dietary restrictions operate in both cases until the bleeding ceases, but I suggest that reasons are different in the two cases. Post-partum bleeding is a continuation of the birth—hence the conceptual identification of mother and child. When the bleeding ceases, the separation between the two is also completed. The menstrual flow, on the other hand, is expressed by the euphemism 'I don't want meat', explained by the statement that 'blood may not be mixed with blood'. As suggested in the discussion on hot and cool as symbolic categories, a menstruating woman must take steps to cool her body; one means of achieving this is to abstain from eating meat. This is therefore a rather particular example of the ban on mixing, since the two substances are both the same—blood; but they derive from two different sources: animal and human.

It is the consumption of meat that is *pantang*, not all contact with it. Thus menstruating women handle, cook, and share out all meat given to them either by their husbands or by women of other households. In Chewong society, unlike many others, menstruating women are not regarded as polluting. They accompany men on hunting expeditions, handle blowpipes, quivers, darts, as well as dart poison. They mix freely with members of both sexes, and they bathe in the rivers with the rest and may do so upstream as well. It is only in respect to their own health that *pantang* prohibitions have to be observed. It is significant, in view of this, to note that the most common colloquial expression for menstruation is 'I don't want meat' (*inyeden ai*). Other terms for the condition is 'moon children' (*wong keché*); 'moon blood' (*mahum keché*); or 'Tanko's children' (*wòng Tanko*) (see Chapter 4).

SICKNESS

As has already been stated on many occasions, disease to the Chewong is all caused by superhuman beings in one way or another. Sometimes the cause is transgression of one of the rules, sometimes it is an accidental encounter with a non-human being who regards *ruwai* as their *ai*. Disease means a loss of the equilibrium of the personage, and steps are taken to redress the balance. This is done by the *putao*, and in the Chewong case cure is rarely effected through the taking of medicines. It is most frequently done by spells, incantations, and the full shamanistic seance. Whenever any of these has been carried out on a sick person, he or she is bound by various *pantang* rules. After a full *nöpoh*, meat may not be eaten for three days, nor may anything which the Chewong say is 'spicy' or 'hot' (*pesed*), this includes salt, chillies, and sugar. Following a less elaborate curing ritual, only the spicy foods are to be avoided. In other words, there is a distinct emphasis on neutralizing the things which are consumed by a person in a liminal state between disease and health.

It is also *pantang* to leave the house before a lapse of one to three days after a curing ceremony of any kind, and, as was the case for post-partum women (but not menstruating ones), bathing in the river is *pantang*. Heated water inside the house must be used for washing.

It must be pointed out that if no curing has been attempted, no *pantang* rules need be observed. Only when disease is publicly acknowledged, and made socially manifest through curing techniques is the individual placed in the liminal state between disease and health, and thus requiring special observance of precautions.

DEATH

I never witnessed either a death or the funeral rites. What follows is therefore based on what I was told, which, to judge by other events which were described to me before I actually witnessed them, may entail some omissions. Some of the practices have already been described and only those designated as *pantang* will be discussed.

Once someone has died, it is *pantang* for those who were in the same house with the dead to leave the house until the 'expulsion of the ghost' (*halao yinlugen*) takes place on the sixth night. If they do leave, the *yinlugen* of the recently deceased will take their *ruwai*. They may only go out quickly to perform the necessary bodily functions, and while doing so they must cover their head and not speak or make any rash gestures or movements lest the *yinlugen* catches sight of them. Conversely, it is *pantang* for anyone else to enter the house. Those directly in touch with the deceased are separated from the rest of the community.

The singing session known as *bremon* which takes place on the sixth night is the ritual act which ensures a correct separation of the dead from the living. It is not actually *pantang* for people to show their grief too openly; 'we cry a little, but not much', they said. This would appear to parallel the situation in childbirth when the woman is not forbidden to cry out, but nevertheless refrains from doing so. In this instance the Chewong reason is that the dead person misses his family, and if his family shows that they are unhappy by his death, he may not want to go to Pulao Klam. Since the acts on the sixth night are designed specifically to frighten the *yinlugen* away, loud lamentations at the same time might be regarded as detracting from this main purpose.

The Chewong frighten the *yinlugen* in two ways: they burn bamboo on the path between the grave and the settlement, and they dance. The fire makes a loud crackling noise which 'sounds like gunfire', and this terrifies the *yinlugen*, who then wants to run away. The dancing, from descriptions and demonstrations,[1] is fairly extravagant. The people sit either on the floor or on the ground, and sway their bodies to and fro, or they dance around in a jerky, but rhythmic, fashion. They do not swing their arms about. The songs which are sung on these occasions (see Appendix 2 for an example) are much less varied in their content and imagery than are the songs given by spirit-guides. The theme of moving and shaking the body is repeated over and over. When the *yinlugen* sees the people behaving in this way it becomes very frightened indeed. The two acts carried out during the funeral ritual are done in order to make the dead person leave the human beings and retreat to the afterworld.

One may consider that what is in effect a reversal of normal Chewong behaviour is indulged in during the funeral ritual just described. Usually restrained in their behaviour and dealings with each other, on this occasion alone do they engage in energetic dancing. Whether they are emotionally abandoned at such times is impossible for me to say, but even if they are not, they are still behaving as if they were. By contrasting this with everyday mores, the Chewong must be said to display non-human (i.e., non-Chewong) characteristics on these occasions. It could be argued that by adopting this 'uncivilized' stance, they are alienating the *yinlugen*, who therefore does not recognize them as his family and friends, does not understand what is going on, and in true Chewong fashion, runs away from the unfamiliar and the threatening.

MARRIAGE

Marriage among the Chewong is not focused upon as a great ritual event. In effect, the lack of prohibitions is implicit evidence that it is

---

[1] Demonstrations of the dances were very half-hearted, and very short, done just to give me an idea of what they were like. The Chewong may not perform these or the special songs outside the context of a real expulsion of the *yinlugen* ceremony. Were they to do so, they would die. Knowing how much I wished to record the funeral song, Kwe on my very last night at Gambir, sang two of them admist much nervous laughter from himself and the rest. I spent the afternoon and evening on the overnight stop in the forest on my last journey down transcribing the songs from my tape and having them explained to me by Laneg and Modn.

not a particularly dangerous occasion during which the participants have to protect themselves against superhuman influence. As already noted in the discussion about the procedure and ceremony, there are a few regulations which have to be observed. The young couple must consummate their union in the forest and in secret before the ceremony can take place. The only named rule invoked in connection with the wedding, is that it is *pantang* for the couple to leave the house and go into the forest on the day following the nuptial. Were they to do so, they would be attacked by a tiger.

Marriage is pre-eminently a social event. The couple's incorporation into the social system in a new status is thus marked by their confinement in the house, and by a separation from the forest. As such it parallels the exposure of the new-born child to cultural objects and values. Moreover, it must be remembered that the Chewong practice matrilocal residence. For the groom the marriage night also means the first night in which he sleeps in his parents-in-law's house. By keeping him there for the first day he is incorporated into that household which will be his for the years to come.

MISCELLANEOUS

Finally there are several other prohibitions, all of which are also designated as *pantang*. They differ from the ones discussed so far in two main respects. Firstly, they are, unlike the rest of the *pantang* rules, preventive rather than protective; and secondly, they are not part of any life crises or rite of passage.

Idiosyncratic *pantang* are often encountered among the Chewong and are linked to individual revelation. I came across examples of these only in connection with dietary restrictions, but I believe they might occur as behavioural restrictions as well. Such *pantang* may be connected with the relationship with one's *wòng hieng* or *ruwai* spirit-guide. Thus Cheï would not eat siamang meat because his *wòng hieng* was a siamang. But it may also happen that a person encounters in a dream the *ruwai* of a particular species of animal or plant who does not become his spirit-guide, but who asserts that henceforth it is *pantang* for the person to eat members of that species, and that if he does so disease will ensue. This encounter may take place before any disease has struck, or after, or as part of the healing. Thus Yareng would not eat the leaves of the tapioca plant because he had once met tapioca *ruwai* in a dream and it had told him not to. Beng had a similar experience. Once when he was ill, his *ruwai* met in a dream the *ruwai* of a monitor lizard who told him that he was ill because of the monitor lizard he had eaten just before taking sick. This meat is poison (*böl*) to Beng, and he refuses to eat it, saying that he has a *pantang*.

Certain diseases are directly linked with particular *pantang*. People who are known to suffer from convulsions may not eat eggs, including fish roe, as this will bring on an attack. They express their refusal of eggs by saying 'there is *pantang*' (*wò pantang*).

There are also several situational *pantang*. The preparation of dart poison is not subject to any rules, but on the day that poison has been prepared, it is *pantang* to throw the washing-up water on to the ground underneath the floor if one has been eating any meat shot by a poisoned dart. The bones of two animals: squirrel and rhinoceros hornbill (both of which are killed by poisoned darts) cannot be thrown on the ground under the house, but must be placed in the thatch of the roof. This again is expressed in terms of *pantang*. Failure to observe them would lead to loss of potency in the poison. These two examples of *pantang* appear to prohibit a mixing of elements from two different spheres, namely air and ground, or off-the-ground and on-the-ground. Both the Temiar (Benjamin, 1967) and the Semai (Dentan, 1967) have strict rules to maintain the boundaries between the ground and the off-ground, and in these two cases the Chewong harbour similar notions. However, these two instances are the only such examples among the Chewong and they are not part of a wider symbolic classification scheme based on such concepts of division. Whether they are remnants of a larger system now forgotten is difficult to say, but in view of my conclusions regarding Chewong principles of classification discussed in the next chapter, I regard this as unlikely.

Once a settlement has been left in favour of a new one, it is *pantang* to return to the same spot and cultivate the land until secondary growth has completely covered the fields and new trees have grown tall. If one does so, then either (according to some informants) one will die, or (according to others) everything that is planted there will die. While inhabiting a settlement which still has viable fields and is therefore not to be abandoned for some time, one may, however, clear and replant a patch of a field where all the tapioca has been dug up.

At specific times of the moon's cycle, it is *pantang* to undertake certain kinds of work. At full moon and eclipse (when the moon is about to give birth and when she dies) one may not cut trees, clear a new swidden, plant, or give birth. The *pantang* lasts for three days on both occasions, and were one to break it the moon would become sick and nothing planted in the new field would grow.

I think that these two periods of *pantang* correspond to those observed when humans give birth and die. It is also *pantang* to engage in any of the above activities (with the possible exception of childbirth) after a night of heavy rain and thunder. Again, the plants will not grow. The reason given in this instance is that *bas* abound on such nights.

As regards a woman giving birth at these times, it is said that were she to do so, she would suffer heavy bleeding. The menstrual cycle, it will be remembered, is associated with the moon's cycle, one of the names for menstruation being 'moon children'.

Finally, the amulets already described, which are made and sold by the *putao* for protection against *gob*, communists, wild animals, etc., have the power to protect because of the spells incanted over them while infused by the smoke from *òz taba*. The various types protect against different dangers, and are also linked with different *pantang*. The most powerful, and incidentally the most expensive, is that which has fewest *pantang* restrictions. Examples of these *pantang* are: one must not wear such an amulet outside the house, or in the forest and one may not urinate or defecate while wearing it. In no circumstances must the amulet be allowed to fall on the ground. If the *pantang* associated with a particular amulet is contravened, it loses its power to protect. The *pantang* operating in connection with the amulets are thus not only numerous, but also, apparently, disparate. The only common thread that appears to run through them all is the importance attached to keeping the amulet apart—whether from certain places, objects, activities, or even times of the day.

SUMMARY OF PANTANG RULES

It is interesting to try to elicit any common features among the various *pantang* rules. Three main concerns seem to stand out: the importance of confinement to a specific place, the emphasis on keeping specific 'things' and activities apart, and, finally, the numerous dietary restrictions. Confinement to the house or the settlement, comes into operation at times of major life crises; namely at birth, marriage, and death, as well as during the passage from illness to health. Social and cultural cohesion is at such times paramount, and the person(s) is confined to the domain of culture: the house and/or the settlement. (It will be remembered that a cure is often effected by a sojourn in the jungle, because of the coolness, but even there the same *pantang* apply, although the house is replaced by the lean-to.) At death the living are confined to the settlement whereas the corpse is placed outside it. Furthermore, at certain times, the head must be covered (confined) by a cloth.

Secondly, there is a concern with separation—manifested most clearly in the *pantang* rules regarding certain foods being kept off the ground, and in those relating to the amulets. But the emphasis on separation relates also to the concept of confinement, since the prescription on confinement to the realm of culture, on the occasions listed, may also be interpreted as a proscription on the mixing of domains.

Thirdly, the protective *pantang* include dietary restrictions. Again, this may be viewed in terms of separation, or of not mixing certain foods at certain times. In fact, it is the separation of the two categories of food—*ai* and *ratn*—which is required at such times. Only half of the ideal meal is allowed while a person is in a liminal stage between giving birth and being reincorporated into society, between illness and health, and while waiting for the menstrual flow to cease to make one fertile again.

MARO

I have been unable to find any correspondence to the Chewong concepts of *maro* among the Malays or other Orang Asli groups. There are two kinds of *maro*: one brings disaster upon oneself, the other upon others. Firstly, whenever a visitor arrives from another settlement, he must immediately be given some food. Not to do so is to *maro* oneself;[1] one becomes ill, and if one persists in this stinginess (*kenjed*) the ultimate consequence is death.

Maro it will be remembered, was originally given to the Chewong by the culture hero Yinlugen Bud. However, its manifestation today is somewhat different from that of the original myth. The injunction on sharing all food caught or found in the jungle is today covered by the *punén* rule, whereas this was called *maro* in the myth. As practised today, *maro* still emphasizes the need to share one's food, but it applies only to visitors to one's house.

The second type of *maro* is invoked by failure to inform the whole tribe that one of its members has died. If this is not done on the day

---

[1] As with *punén*, *maro*, may similarly be used as a verb as when it was said that the people from Sentao had '*maroed*' their friends at Gambir by not informing them that Mag had died (*ka gödn maro bom*).

following the death, or as soon after as is possible, those left in ignorance have been *maro* (*ka maro bom*) by the relatives of the deceased. The *yinlugen* of the newly dead roams around all the places where it has been while alive, and it goes to see all its friends and relatives. If some of these are not informed of its existence, the *yinlugen* will eat the *ruwai* of all the game, fish, fruit, and tubers in the vicinity of that settlement. As a result its inhabitants will be unsuccessful in their search for food, and if they remain uninformed they will finally die of starvation. Even were they to shoot some animal, this would taste so horrible as to be inedible. It will taste rotten, an indication that it is dying, its *ruwai* having been eaten. Another sign of *maro* is that the *yinlugen* may enter the body of an animal recently shot. In such cases the animal moves some limb after it has been proclaimed dead and is about to be thrown on the fire to have its fur burnt off. The meat cannot be eaten in such cases, but must be abandoned immediately. Also, all tubers, wild and cultivated, rot and cannot be eaten. As soon as the people are informed of the death, the *yinlugen* no longer eats the *ruwai* of their food.

Both types of *maro* stress the social unity of the tribe. It is when the bonds that keep them together as one group of people, as opposed to all other groups, are in danger of being broken, that *maro* is invoked. Firstly, the laws of hospitality extend to members of the group only. It is *maro* not to feed all visitors who are acknowledged as *bi he*, 'our people'. Visiting members of neighbouring groups may or may not be fed, depending on the closeness of their relationship and the degree of fear and shyness of their hosts, but it is not *maro* or any other rule that compels hospitality.

Modn told me a very illuminating story about the time when she and Beng accompanied Ogilvie to Kuala Tahan where they lived for about one year as his guide and bearer. This was Modn's first encounter with Malays and Malay way of life. Needless to say, she was terrified. 'I knew nothing then', she told me, 'I did not understand when they spoke to me (she is the only Chewong woman who today can speak Malay), I did not know I had to give them food, or tell them to enter my house.' She was referring to her encounter with not only Malay women, but also other Orang Asli, chiefly Batek Nong. Today she knows the ways of the world, and does offer all visitors food, but she is unique in this respect.

Secondly, the disruption that a death entails to such a small group of people is severe. The concept of *maro* ensures that the cohesion of the group is maintained. Whereas gossip travels around all settlements and people hear about births, sickness, activities, etc., in the course of time, death must be notified immediately; at the latest before the sixth night, so that everybody can be present at the expulsion of the *yinlugen* and its subsequent rebirth in the afterworld. At this event the tribe reaffirms its solidarity and group identity. With no leaders and few institutionalized rituals, the thread that binds the Chewong together and gives them a sense of group identity is very tenuous. *Maro*, in both its manifestations, more than any of the other rules stresses the group identity, and as such helps to ensure a continuous cohesion despite the far-flung settlements.

TOLAH

The concept of *tolah* among the Malays means 'a calamity consequent upon sacrilege or extreme presumption' (Coote, 1976). The Batek use the word *tolah* to refer to 'a large number of socially disruptive and disrespectful acts, especially those that are directed towards older people' (Endicott, 1979: 81). In the case of the Chewong, the meaning of *tolah* closely corresponds to the two just quoted. It means to show disrespect either towards certain categories of persons, or towards certain types of non-meat foodstuffs. (See also Myth 9, Appendix 1.) The former specifies that in-laws of either sex must always refer to each other by nickname and the polite 'you', *gitn*, as opposed to the more familiar 'thou', *mö*. Otherwise, people in such relationships should behave, in all their dealings with each other, with circumspection. Not to do so is *tolah*, and the offender will suffer severe swellings of the hips and lower abdomen. It is also *tolah* to laugh or play near *ratn*. The repercussions are the same as for *tolah* in regard to affines.

In *tolah* one may also discern a preoccupation with separation, in this case that between kin and affine. As categories these two have to be kept apart, and this separation is ensured through linguistic means. This is particularly interesting because the Chewong language does not include terms for either 'kin' or 'affine'; each specific relationship has its own term, but there is no overall term to act as a class signifier. However, by insisting upon a change in the terminology relating to individuals who change their status *vis-à-vis* a particular person following a marriage and by employing the terms rather than the personal names, they are in effect forming a class of affines constituting those categories of persons who have to be approached according to the rule of *tolah*.

Both forms of *tolah* prescribe restrained behaviour, one towards an identified set of individuals, the other towards a category of food. In the second case there is of course a direct parallel between *tolah* and *talaiden*, both of which refer to a suppression of laughter in the vicinity of food. In the case of *talaiden* the prohibition concerns meat (*ai*), and in the case of *tolah* it concerns staple vegetable foods (*ratn*). The conceptual complementarity already discerned between these two categories of food is here further enhanced.

It is also *tolah* to quarrel with one's spouse, yet another expression of emotionality. This leads to a failure to obtain any game, thus upsetting the balance of an ideal meal. It can lead to other general misfortunes as well.

MALI

The Malay *pemali* means 'forbidden' (Coote, 1976). The Batek Teh say that the prohibitions on cooking certain foods together are known as *pemali* (Endicott, 1979: 80), and similarly, the Semai rule that 'mixing together types of food that should be kept separate; and the calamity such mix produces' is called *panali* (Dentan, 1968: 107).

There are several, seemingly unrelated, kinds of *mali* among the Chewong. Firstly, two which are directly and explicitly concerned with the suppression of unrestrained behaviour: to whistle, and to swing one's feet in an abandoned manner are both *mali*, but the consequences differ. Whistling alerts the attention of Bajægen and Ponjur (see Chapter 4). These two who are always on the lookout for new spouses take the whistling as a sign that the person wishes to marry them. In the case of a woman whistler, Bajægen will cause her to have an accident that involves the spilling of blood so that he can take her *ruwai* and bring it up to Plantor and marry her. When the whistler is a man, Ponjur does the same to him. The presence in the early morning of a certain kind of red cloud is said to mean that '*bas* are near-by'. In fact it is Bajægen and Ponjur who are near. Their earth, Plantor, is red, the association almost certainly being made between its red colour and blood. A person whose mother has died may take some ashes from the house fire, put it on the tip of the bush-knife and throw it up in the air. If someone whose mother is still alive does this, it is *mali*, and her *ruwai* will be taken by Bajægen.

Swinging one's legs alerts the attention of the Original Earth Ghost and she will take, according to some informants, the *ruwai* of the transgressor; according to others, the *ruwai* of his or her mother.

The Chewong say that as long as one's mother is still alive one may not swing one's feet.

It is also *mali* to shout out in anger when one falls on the ladder leading up to a house. 'It is *mali* to be angry with the rungs of the ladder', is how it was put to me. This resembles the *punén* rule of 'speaking badly'.

Again, it is *mali* for someone who still has a mother to throw out after dark the washing-up water, from a plate on which an animal shot by a blowpipe is eaten, on to the area underneath the house. It must be kept until the following day and then be thrown away from the house. The reason always proffered for this behaviour is that underneath the house is children's urine, and the water from the meat must not be mixed with this urine as it would lead to the hunter of the house failing to find any more of the same game. So in this instance one may distinguish a need for keeping dissimilar things apart; but this does not explain why many animals, and all fish, are excluded, nor why the prohibition operates at night only. The restriction concerning throwing the washing-up water onto the ground is very similar, and in parts identical, to the *pantang* which has to be observed in connection with the dart poison. In the case of *mali*, all daytime animals shot with the blowpipe are thus included, whereas the *pantang* singles out just two, and for a different reason. I am at a loss to explain the significance of the role of the mother in these instances of *mali*.

TOLÆG

The next two rules to be discussed both concern eating habits, and not the expression of emotions. The first of these, *tolæg*, has already been discussed in the chapter on the superhuman beings, so only the pertinent points are restated here. No child may eat any of the following animals: gibbon, water monitor lizard, otter, mountain tortoise, slow loris, and, in some cases only, the macaque. Were they to do so, the *yinlugen* of the species concerned would take their *ruwai* and bring it to the land of the particular *yinlugen*. Unless a *putao* manages to find and retrieve the *ruwai*, the child dies. Pregnant and suckling women may not eat these animals either, because they would pass the effect on to the foetus or child. They themselves would not suffer.

As already described in Chapter 3, those who are prone to epileptic fits may not eat macaque, as this means that the macaque *yinlugen* have a special relationship with the sufferer. In such cases the prohibition applies throughout the individual's life, although the condition is still referred to as *tolæg*.

The Chewong display much circumspection in their handling of the *tolæg* animals. Usually the fur or skin is burned off in the forest with the explicit rationalization that this minimizes the danger to the children. The meal is prepared outside the house, on the ground near the outskirts of the settlement. Children are told not to go near it, nor touch the carcass as they tend to do with other animals brought home. Even the adults who eat any of the *tolæg* animals display extra care while eating. They also take their plates and saucepans to the river to wash afterwards, rather than washing them in the house and letting the water fall on the ground underneath where children play. So although the prohibition is only on young children, adults clearly feel a responsibility to ensure that the children do not come into contact with any part of *tolæg* animals. Children less than nine or ten years old cannot eat this meat; in other words while they are still largely dependent upon their parents rather than the peer group. Once they start roving, and leading fairly independent lives, they may eat the meat.

All the *tolæg* animals are said to have 'big' *ruwai* (*ruwai manung*) and to be personages. To put them in contact with children whose *ruwai* are small—or at any rate not fully developed and fixed in the body—is fraught with danger. (The characteristics of the various *tolæg* animals will be discussed in the next chapter.)

TIKA

In Malay the word *cika* means 'colic' (Coote, 1976). Otherwise I have found a reference to it only among the Batek where it is prohibited to make humorous word-plays on names of foods, 'because this will cause anyone who eats that particular food that day to contract "*cika*", severe stomach or intestinal pain' (Endicott, 1979: 80). The Chewong rule of *tika* also has as repercussion severe stomach pain, but this is produced by some beings (*bas*) who enter the stomach of the sufferer and claw away at it until the person dies. The condition is caused by the mixing of certain kinds of food in the stomach, or in the cooking process. Unlike the foods which are tiger *talaiden* and are prohibited only in specific combinations, the *tika* foods may not be mixed with anything else, except *ratn*. Of those animals which may not be cooked together, those which are not *talaiden* are almost certain to be *tika*. But the worst kind of *tika* is to mix meat with something sweet, usually fruit, and several examples of recent deaths were attributed to this kind of *tika*. One woman died because she was eating some monkey meat off a plate where papaya had been kept a short while before, and the plate had not been properly washed.

It is also *tika* to smoke immediately after eating pig or monitor lizard. This is known as '*tika* of the mouth' (*tika hain*) and is not deadly, but very unpleasant stomach-ache will ensue. Finally, it is *tika* to eat a carcass found in the forest. Only meat killed by man may be eaten. Further implications of the rules regarding food will be discussed in the next chapter. Here it is sufficient to note that the rule of *tika* is a particularly clear example of the Chewong injunction upon separation.

TANKO

The question of incest (*jawab* or *tanko*) was dealt with earlier when discussing the superhuman being called Tanko who punishes one form of forbidden sexual intercourse. Tanko punishes *tanko* by sending a thunderbolt into the hip or knee joints of the offenders—rendering these stiff and painful. If the case is very serious, i.e., persistently indulged in, the persons concerned will die by being given as meat to Tanko's dogs. *Jawab* only applies to sexual intercourse taking place between siblings, and it is punished by the attack of a tiger.

The Chewong do not appear to regard *tanko* and *jawab* as more serious offences than *talaiden*, *punén*, or the other rules. As with several of the rules, the actual things—or categories—forbidden may vary depending upon circumstances. (This will be taken up in the following chapter.) In the case of *tanko*, sexual intercourse (or marriage) is only forbidden between parents and children, and between a man and his brother's daughter, or his father's brother's daughter. It is also *tanko* for parents and adult children of the opposite sex to sleep close together, for older siblings of the opposite sex to sleep close together, and for 'those who have drunk at the same breast' to marry one another.

It has already been suggested that the role of *tanko* is one that demands separation of whatever is defined as 'alike'. So, according to the view of conception, it is to 'mix the same blood' for members of the forbidden categories to marry each other. It is, however, more precisely, the mixing of the life-giving fluids which must be avoided. Those made from the same semen, or those who have drunk the same milk must be kept apart. In order to create new life (and this is what the union between men and women is chiefly about in the Chewong view) the products of the same fluids must be divided and not be allowed to reunite.

CONCLUSION

In this chapter the various rules observed by the Chewong have been examined. The different points which were mentioned in the Introduction to Part III and which were raised in the discussion of each rule whenever relevant, will now be drawn together in order to establish what may be concluded from them in regard to Chewong modes of thought.

First, an examination of the rules, from the point of view that they constitute a major means by which the Chewong can conceive of order will be made. Whereas I was unable to discover any one word which could be seen to denote 'order', I will nevertheless argue that such a concept is indeed implicit. Disease and mishaps of various kinds are the two chief disruptions of smooth growth and development. The need to provide some explanation for these phenomena is present among the Chewong as in other societies. Where the Chewong differ from many is that disease and mishaps are attributed exclusively to supernatural causes. They have no concept of sorcery or witchcraft. On the whole, the superhuman beings who cause misfortune do not move in mysterious ways. In general, they are only activated when human beings transgress one of the rules, allowing the being in question to attack. The superhuman, or non-human, beings cannot act upon humans unless a human being breaks a rule. The rules are thus a structured means by which the Chewong order their universe. Adherence to them provides people with a means to prevent chaotic and idiosyncratic events taking place, and they therefore constitute the chief method for making a diagnosis of an unfortunate event. The rules are an idiom for explaining disease or 'bad luck', and the consequences of transgressions are justified through, and administered by, supernatural agencies. The rules cannot be thought about without also thinking about the superhuman beings associated with them.

Athough the rules may be seen as replacing a political and legal machinery, they must not be interpreted as forming a strait-jacket on Chewong behaviour. This is far from the case. Whereas the Chewong appear to the outsider to be timid, self-effacing, and undemonstrative, they are also extremely confident in their relationship with their environment. The rules define the boundaries of their mobility. By knowing what will cause disease and mishap, they also know how to avoid incurring them. Knowledge about them provides the individual with a certain amount of freedom. Every adult knows all the rules and the results of transgression, and by acting upon this knowledge they can be said to control their own destinies to a large extent. They also control the destiny of their universe, since the consequences of many breaches upset the cosmic balance.

Other rules also exist, which were discussed in Chapter 4, in connection with specific superhuman beings. These also guide the Chewong in their daily lives and help them to avoid illness and accidents. Each is directly linked to the superhuman being in question, and may for instance involve nothing more than avoiding certain areas known to be inhabited by *bas* or taking shelter at times of unusual atmospheric conditions. These rules are more difficult to observe, however, since hitherto unknown places may become inhabited by superhuman beings, or one may not always be able to take shelter. It is also possible to fall inadvertently into a trap set by a *bas* for pig *ruwai*. All these are contingencies for diagnosing disease where none of the known rules and prohibitions appear to have been transgressed. They are thus an alternative means of establishing causation.

It is clear from the plethora of rules, and the complexity of many of the acts proscribed, that this is a particularly rich aspect of Chewong culture. From the description of the numerous different rules, and the apparently wide diversity of some of the acts proscribed, it appears that no simple unifying theme can be found to underlie them all. Nevertheless, there are certain threads running through which can be profitably examined and, perhaps, connected.

Firstly, all those rules which restrict and even prohibit the expression of inner states should be considered. I have suggested elsewhere that one manifestation of the suppression of emotions is the limited psychological vocabulary of the Chewong language (Howell, 1981a). I will not elaborate upon this aspect here, but will repeat my argument, which is that the rules suppress the emotions, that they are an externalized idiom which both acknowledges that psychological states are experienced, and controls and suppresses these. We have seen how uproarious laughter in the vicinity of, or at, animals of all kinds (*talaiden*) or at staple foods (*tolah*), is forbidden; how wishes of all kinds must be gratified immediately or suppressed (*punén*); how whistling and swinging one's feet in an extravagant way must be avoided (*mali*); and how pleasurable events must not be expressed (*punén*), or even be thought about; and anger or pain must not be displayed when accidents occur (*punén*). Altogether, most emotions commonly acknowledged in the West are suppressed by the Chewong. That they experience them, or at any rate are aware of their existence, must be assumed because of their being specifically forbidden. By contrast, there are two emotions which are openly acknowledged by them; namely fear (*höntugen*) and shyness (*lidya*). Whereas children are daily admonished for extravagant behaviour by shouts of '*talaiden!*', '*punén!*', '*mali!*', or '*tolah!*' and soon learn to control the expression of their emotional states, they are encouraged to develop fear and shyness. Parents constantly taunt their children by telling them that a *gob* or a tiger is waiting to catch them, and they laugh rather proudly when terror-stricken children scream, saying that they are very fearful. Similarly, a parent would appear pleased at the timidity of a child confronted by me in the early days of my field-work, saying that he was extremely shy. Adults are reserved when meeting each other, and guests openly admit that 'we are very shy in other people's houses'. In view of all this, it may be said that emotions are subject to socialization procedures whereby fear and shyness are encouraged, while pleasure, anger, frustration, anticipation, exuberance, are suppressed.

A second, more elusive thread, is the importance of separation and division (or conversely, the prohibition on mixing[1]). This appears to be of great significance in Chewong modes of thought, underlying many of their ideas and practices. It is difficult to establish how far this may be associated with other less evident threads which have been remarked upon in earlier chapters. The emphasis on confinement (*pantang* rules) may be regarded as a manifestation on the prescription of separation; the dietary restrictions as interdicting the mixing of foods; and relating back to an earlier point, the ban on laughing at animals and staples, might be interpreted as a ban on the

---

[1] The Chewong use the word '*jampor*' (cf., Malay *champor*, to mix) whenever they talk about mixing something together. It is not usually employed to explain the rules forbidding mixing different foods together, however. Then they just say 'cannot eat gibbon with pig' (*timoh bi gau han kom cha*), or 'to carry siamang and binturong in the same basket is tiger *talaiden*' (*siamang bi kintoa lam nai lugn, o talaiden kle*).

expression of emotions, or of mixing categories, or of both. Furthermore, is it correct to regard the prescription on sharing as another manifestation of the principle of separation? Although separation necessarily precludes sharing, the connection may be regarded as rather tenuous. However, it is surely of significance that the myth which first introduced the Chewong to the notion of society at the expense of the individual (the one about Yinlugen Bud), contains the two themes within it. The same culture hero informs humans within the same myth that the sharing of food, and the correct separation of the baby from its mother, as well as the placenta from the baby, are prerequisites for social and family life to operate.

9

Classification

INTRODUCTION

SINCE the days of the *Année Sociologique*, anthropologists have been aware of the immense importance of classificatory principles in human societies. Although Durkheim's and Mauss' essay *De quelques Formes Primitives de Classification* was published in 1903, it was not translated into English until sixty years later. The general ideas put forth in the treatise were, however, included in Durkheim's *Les Formes Elementaires de la Vie Religieuse*, published in France in 1912, and in an English translation in 1915, whereby they reached a much wider audience. Through these two works, classification became isolated as 'an aspect of culture to which sociological enquiries should be directed' (Needham, 1963: xl).

In *Primitive Classification*, the title of the English translation of Durkheim's and Mauss' essay, the authors distinguish between scientific and symbolic classifications, but they nevertheless assert that:

However different they [symbolic classifications] may be in certain respects from the latter [scientific classifications] they nevertheless have all their essential characteristics. . . . They are systems of hierarchical notions. Things are not simply arranged by them in the form of isolated groups, but these groups stand in fixed relationships to each other and together form a single whole. . . . Their object is not to facilitate action but to advance understanding, to make intelligible the relations which exist between things. . . . Such classifications are thus intended above all to connect ideas, to unify knowledge.

(Durkheim and Mauss, 1963: 81)

To Durkheim and Mauss the origin of all classifications is social; hence they postulate their famous dictum that 'the first logical categories were social categories, the first classes of things were classes of men, into which these things were integrated' (82). The actual development of their argument is not accepted today, but the general notion that there is a link between the social and the conceptual, often manifested in classification, is still part of anthropological thinking and methodology. Lévi-Strauss rejects the separation made by Durkheim and Mauss between scientific and symbolic classifications when he suggests that the various classificatory schemes of 'primitive' societies form a conceptual whole. He says,

What is significant is not so much the presence—or absence—of this or that level of classification as the existence of a classification with, as it were, an adjustable thread which gives the group adopting it the means of 'focusing' on all planes, from the most abstract to the most concrete, the most cultural to the most natural, without changing its intellectual instrument. . . . Commonly [in primitive societies] zoological and botanical classifications do not constitute separate domains but form an integral part of an all-embracing dynamic taxonomy the unity of which is assured by the perfect homogeneity of its structure.

(Lévi-Strauss, 1966: 136, 139)

These beliefs have been widely accepted by anthropologists, and from my reading of numerous ethnographies in which it was shown that the people under study did indeed display analogous principles of classification in their attitudes to the natural environment as well as to their metaphysical universe, I went to the field fully expecting to discover similar principles in the modes of thought of the Chewong.

I was dismayed to discover that not only was I unable to discern the Chewong 'masterplan' of interlinking taxonomic systems, but, more importantly, I could not discern any taxonomies at all, or indeed establish what were their classificatory principles. Their ordering of the environment appeared largely to be based simply on naming and enumeration rather than on traditionally accepted principles of classification. On the symbolic level also, I was unable to reveal any meaningful patterns in their construction of categories. The absence of a 'masterplan' need not worry one too much. It is not a totally new phenomenon. Indeed, as early as 1963 Needham says in his introduction to *Primitive Classification*:

Recent investigations make it appear that in cognatic societies the relation of symbolic to social order may be insignificant or minimal, that in simple lineal descent systems the relationship may be discerned in a range of particulars or in isolated institutions but not usually in any comprehensive manner, and that in systems of prescriptive alliance there is such a concordance between the symbolic forms and social organisation that these two orders of facts may be regarded as aspects of one conceptual order, one mode of classification.

(Needham, 1963: xxxvii)

Before embarking upon a consideration of the second point, that much of Chewong ordering and classification is not based upon identifiable principles, it is important to clarify my terminology. In much anthropological literature the terms classification, taxonomy, categorization, and nomenclature are not clearly distinguished. It is not my intention to enter into a debate of definitions, but merely to state how the terms will be used throughout this chapter. Abstract symbols might equally well have been used, or they could have been called Type A, Type B, and Type C, corresponding to the three types of classification that I am isolating.

Classification may be said to be the all-embracing general term used to denote a consistent method of ordering. Classification locates a thing in a conceptual frame or map, and in doing so it relates it to every other thing on the map.

Within any one society there may be numerous conceptual maps and, contrary to the assertions of Lévi-Strauss and others, these need not interlink via the principles employed in constructing each one. My concern here is not to disprove the necessary existence of such a masterplan (see the above quote from Needham, and also Morris, 1976). Neither am I concerned with the current discussion regarding convergences and divergences between the so-called 'scientific classification' of the West and the 'folk classification' of primitive peoples. (For a useful summary of current problems in the anthropological study of classification see Ellen, 1979.) I am not concerned either with formally distinguishing symbolic classification from technological ones according to the model of Durkheim and Mauss (and in a slightly different vein, Bloch, 1977). As should be clear by now, it is extremely difficult to demarcate any boundaries between ritual (or symbolic) thought and mundane thought among the Chewong. Their society and their cosmology coincide, both in terms of ideas and in actual practice. Thus, for instance, their attitude to a particular species of animal does not undergo a structural change whether they are hunting it or encountering its *ruwai* in a *nöpoh*. The person who has the particular species as spirit-guide has a different relationship with it from that of other members of the tribe, but this is carried over into the mundane. He will not hunt or eat it because it is his spirit-guide. In this they differ from the Ma' Bétisek (see Wazir, 1981) who vary their conceptual classification of animals and plants depending on context.

My concern is with what can be said to constitute a class in Chewong classification, and what are its constituent parts. Whereas arbitrariness, variability, structural complexity, and expressions of inclusiveness have been accepted by some as compatible with classification, thus blurring the neatness of any scheme (see e.g., Ellen, 1979), it is nevertheless assumed that members of a class are selected according to *some* common features on grounds of significance and manageability and to correlate either explicitly or implicitly. It is this assumption that I wish to question.

I propose to separate three different types of classification, which it is important to distinguish, by using the terms categorization, taxonomy, and nomenclature. My use of these terms does not necessarily conform to common usage.

In a system of *categorization*, the members of a class are identified as such by virtue of possessing one or more of certain properties. To take a simple example: animals may be categorized according to their habitat, their means of locomotion, their size, their colour, their habits, etc., or a combination of some or all of these. A system of categorization could be quite complex, and may be polythetic rather than monothetic, but it must involve explicit or implicit resemblances, so that some underlying correlations can be discerned.

A *taxonomy* I take to be a special case of categorization in which the concept of hierarchy is also present. Thus a genus does not stand alone; it implies a position in a hierarchical structure. Above are the phyla, orders, and families; below are species and varieties; alongside are other genera. These may, of course, be arranged according to criteria different from Western ones.

Nomenclature, according to my use of the term, consists simply in assigning a common name to all the members of a class. It is based neither on hierarchical principles nor on shared attributes, but may nevertheless be regarded as a type of classification because, by virtue of the consistency of its application, it does locate a thing in a conceptual frame. However, the search for common attributes underlying such a system would reveal that members of a class have nothing more in common than their being named as such. On the basis of my study of the Chewong I shall try to show that it is largely a system of nomenclature that is to be found in their society.

Thus, either one regards it as inadmissible to claim nomenclature as a type of classification, or one must conclude that the concepts of Durkheim and Mauss, as well as Lévi-Strauss, as to what constitutes a classification, are too limiting since neither hierarchy nor underlying principles are necessary attributes.

In order to substantiate my claim that the Chewong do not classify according to identifiable principles (i.e., that they have merely a nomenclature), it is not sufficient to demonstrate that the concept of hierarchy is lacking. One must go further and rule out categorization also, by proving a lack of any discernible pattern, either explicit or implicit, in their classification.

The issue of hierarchy will be dealt with first. In the discussion of the superhuman beings, it was found that there were several different classes of these, such as the *bi asal, bi inhar*, etc., all identified and separated by different linguistic labels and with each class containing several members. But no overall word exists to denote the total class of superhuman beings as opposed to human beings, and no intermediate groupings of members are found. The different classes of superhuman beings cannot, therefore, be mapped onto a taxonomic scheme arranged according to hierarchical principles. This is analogous with much of Chewong classification of the animal kingdom. As there is no overall word for superhuman being, so there is no word for animal.[1] This does not mean that the Chewong do not order their knowledge about the animal world. In fact they take an active interest in their environment, and every man, woman, and child displays a thorough knowledge of the world around them. I never came across a single tree, plant, or animal in the jungle which did not have a name. Indeed, it was my own ignorance and tendency to ignore differences and special characteristics of a particular species that led me, for instance, to call every ant an ant. The Chewong had names for each one, but no encompassing category name, although they clearly understood my wanting to call each one 'ant'.

There are many other examples of the Chewong omitting linguistically to bring together animals which the Westerner is used to thinking of as a class. Thus, there is no word that joins the different species of monkeys and apes into one class, each species is named individually, as are most of the other animals. However, in certain

---

[1] Although *binatang*, the Malay word for animal, is understood by the Chewong, it is not used among themselves. They employ it, however, in their discussions with outsiders.

cases the Chewong cluster together under one linguistic label several animals perceived to be of the same kind. All tortoises, for instance, are called *kòh* with qualifiers for each variety as in the case of *kòh gading*. There is also a class 'bird' (*kawaw*), a class 'fish' (*kiehl*), a class 'snake' (*talòden*), and a class 'butterfly' (*ligwog*). All squirrels are known by the Malay word *tupai* which is used as a prefix to indigenous names for each variety. It is not unreasonable to suggest that the introduction of *tupai* is of relatively recent origin, and that traditionally either there was an indigenous name for the class of squirrel, or that each was named separately by the word which today is used as a qualifier.

Having said this, let me insist that I am not suggesting an 'ineptitude of primitive people for abstract thought' as Lévi-Strauss has accused earlier ethnographers who reported apparently similar findings (Lévi-Strauss, 1966: 1). I am merely making a statement about one manifestation of their modes of thought; a particular tendency found in much of Chewong classification, namely that they tend to enumerate objects and beings around them (including the superhuman beings who are no less part of the environment than are stones or animals) rather than placing them in taxonomic pyramids. When things are classed together, they form a very low pyramid consisting of two levels only, for example, the class *bi asal* and all the various beings named as such. So whether a class is formed linguistically, like that of *bi asal*, or not, as in the case of monkeys, the main emphasis is upon juxtaposition rather than the formation of a pyramid.

Although it is not my intention to introduce yet another element into this discussion, it should be noted that this ordering of the external world is analogous to Chewong social organization whereby no individual, or class of individuals, is placed above any other, either conceptually or in practice, but juxtaposed.

The next issue is to establish, by reference to the Chewong material, whether categorization is a necessary part of a classification. Again, by returning to the analysis already undertaken with the superhuman beings, it was found that although classes of these exist, as verified by named labels for different classes, the elements of each member of a class do not form any meaningful patterns, and in many cases they overlap. I will examine the implications of this statement further by looking at other categories of Chewong thought to see if the same is the case. The rules governing behaviour discussed in the previous chapter are categories of thought, and correlations among the elements of each class will be sought. If none can be established, then it must be concluded that although the Chewong classify, as evidenced by the superhuman beings and the rules, they do not necessarily do so either according to the principles of hierarchical taxonomy, nor on the basis of categorization whereby identifiable principles—explicit or implicit—can be ascertained.

PREVIOUS RESPONSES TO THE PROBLEMS OF CLASSIFICATION AMONG THE ORANG ASLI

I am not the first to have faced this seeming perplexity that what is usually thought of as classificatory principles are absent from the collective representational systems of the Orang Asli. Both Endicott, in his work among the Batek, and Benjamin with the Temiar, have had to cope with similar difficulties. To varying degrees they are reluctant to accept the possibility that such principles are absent, and they attempt to establish that despite the difficulty in discerning meaningful patterns these can nevertheless be found. In effect, they attempt to demonstrate the existence of what I have called categorization. Both of them focus their discussion on symbolic classification and do not say whether taxonomies of natural species occur.

Benjamin's position is somewhat ambivalent. Towards the end of a lengthy section on the role of animals as symbolic vehicles for thought, he concludes, 'It has not been part of the present discussion to wonder why certain species and not others are drawn into the thoroughgoing system of ritual categorisation' (1967: 117). Earlier on, however, he tries to do this, though with little success. He moves between premises of common sense and structural analysis, but neither premise helps him to establish the existence of what he would call a classificatory system. Starting with an examination of those animals involved in taboos, he asks, 'What meaning lies behind the ideas and observances?' and claims that 'The question can best be answered by examining the structural implications of the full "ideal type" constellation of features' (92). Whereas he admits that 'It is hard to detect any regular patterning' (95), he nevertheless persists in trying to do so, and finally comes up with the suggestion that there is 'an incipient patterning involving the variables of culture, *genha*? [type of taboo animals], myth, and tameability' (95). But empirically this argument holds true for only a few of the species, and many are not important in the mythology. Later he explains how certain acts may not be performed because 'these are more or less out-of-the-ordinary. The normal place for their performance would be within an inhabited house' (111). But this is surely an inadequate explanation, especially since there is no explicit native statement to this effect, and it is therefore fair to ask why it is 'normal' to have sexual intercourse inside the house only, or to keep new bamboo there.

Benjamin further suggests that the institution of *misik* (the rule that forbids laughing at certain animals lest thunderstorms occur) serves not so much to avoid the intervention of Karey (the 'thunder deity') as to 'keep the very thought of him alive in the mind of every Temiar' (112). Benjamin's reason why Karey needs to be thus kept alive in the minds of every Temiar is that, according to him, Karey represents evil, a concept which he claims to be fundamental to Temiar thought, and one which must be kept at bay. One should be careful not to impose notions of good and evil as clearly conceptualized categories in alien societies. Hocart warned about this when he said, 'In fact, among most peoples, the idea of evil, pure evil, is completely lacking' (1954: 93). Certainly, in view of what we have seen to be the case among the Chewong, no concept of evil can be attributed to them. As an explanation for a difficult phenomenon such as *misik*, we must consider the concept of evil as unsatisfactory. It was, I think, because Karey—and the assumed accompanying concept of evil—was the only common element in the *misik* beliefs and observances, that Benjamin regards it as the focal point.

This very brief survey of Benjamin's argument is necessarily schematic and leaves out much thoughtful discussion. The reason for including it at all is to highlight the fact that it is extremely difficult for anthropologists to abandon the notion that common principles must link members of a class, and that failure to establish such principles implies that the field-worker just did not manage to obtain the pertinent data. It is this assumption that I hope to query.

Endicott faces similar problems to Benjamin in his attempts at interpreting the Batek acts known as *lawac*, all of which are punished by thunderstorms and the upwelling of subterranean waters. As such they can be seen to be equivalent to Chewong *talaiden* and Temiar *misik*. The prohibited acts include laughing at animals, cooking certain combinations of food over the same fire, pouring certain kinds of blood into the river, improper sexual behaviour, and several others (1979: 70). Failing to identify any common regular features in the various *lawac*, Endicott concludes that the term *lawac* 'is like our term "illegal" which covers numerous acts, from murder to parking violations' and that the unity underlying all of them is that 'they all serve, in their very different ways, to affirm the order of the world as the Batek conceive it' (1979: 70). Later he concludes:

Thus the Batek seem to believe that there is a natural order to the world which is manifested, among other ways, in the divisions of the plant and animal kingdoms. To a large extent, the Batek way of life is considered part of the natural order as well. Because this order was established by the *hala'* [the Batek equivalent to the Chewong *bi asal* of Earth Six] it should be respected by human beings. The *lawac* prohibitions seem intended to prevent man from violating or ridiculing this order.

(Endicott, 1979: 79)

In summary, therefore, Endicott claims that there is an external order imposed upon the Batek way of life, despite the difficulty of establishing its underlying structural principles, and suggests that in the last analysis it is part of the natural order established by supernatural beings. But within each symbolic class he nevertheless searches for underlying principles. The question of attributes of what is forbidden by the *misik*, *lawac*, and *talaiden* rules will be dealt with again.

Endicott encountered the added difficulty in his work among the Batek, that information regarding the *lawac* prohibitions, as well as the superhuman beings, was inconsistent as reported by different informants.

OTHER PROBLEMS OF INDIGENOUS CLASSIFICATION

Before beginning the detailed examination of Chewong formation of certain categories, I wish to distinguish very clearly the kind of problem that I am faced with from others, possibly more commonly encountered by anthropologists, about which more has certainly; been written. These other problems are all couched in terms of the difficulty of discerning a consistent classification. Yet if these are examined closely, bearing in mind the three types I distinguished at the beginning of this chapter, we find that very often the issues are not separated, and that as a result of this, it is sometimes difficult to ascertain exactly the nature of the perceived problem. To illustrate this point, a few relevant papers will be discussed.

Morris in an article on the Hill Pandaram of South India says that these people are unconcerned not only with classification, but also with naming.

> They seem to have an unsystematic and incomplete knowledge of the natural environment in which they live. . . . But though this knowledge [of the forest environment] is detailed it is gained mainly by personal experience and this means that not only are their taxonomic systems limited in scope but they have a relative unconcern with systemisation.
>
> (Morris, 1976: 544)

His subsequent data, however, do not really bear out the above statement. With regard to ascertaining the names of common plants and animals, he found this to be a 'frustrating business' for either no name was forthcoming, or just a descriptive or generic term was given. Despite the fact that the botanical world was classified into three primary taxa, each of which contained several intermediate taxa and numerous terminal taxa, Morris still claims that there is 'no systematic taxonomic hierarchy' among the Hill Pandaram (547).

If we turn to their classification of animals we find—despite Morris' unhappiness about overlaps and absence of high pyramids of clearly ordered hierarchies—that the Hill Pandaram approach the world of animate creatures with clear ideas of ordering them. Thus, 'living creatures' are divided into humans and animals. The class of animals is further divided into birds, snakes, animals, fish, insects, and reptiles. The category 'animal' contains nine intermediate taxa, each of which have numerous terminal taxa.

In view of this, it would be wrong to claim that the Hill Pandaram do not classify the plant and animal world according to principles of hierarchy or common attributes. That the Western ethnographer with a detailed botanical and zoological expertise finds their taxonomies, relatively speaking, to be unsystematic and full of inconsistencies, does not to my mind detract from the fact that the Pandaram both categorize and build taxonomies in their classification of natural species. By comparison with the Chewong classification of natural species, the Hill Pandaram appear fairly sophisticated.

Finally, despite his earlier assertions to the contrary, Morris later states: 'I am highly sceptical of the notion that some societies lack names for different species of animals and plants' (553). Thus his earlier claims, first, that systematic classification of plants and animals is not done among the Hill Pandaram and, second, that they do not assign names to individual species, are, on his own evidence, not correct. He concludes by saying that it is not so much that they do not actually classify natural species, but, having failed to find any correlation between the animal taxonomy and what is regarded as inedible animals, he concludes that the various classificatory systems are not linked together into a conceptual scheme, and that the Hill Pandaram do not have any 'systematic elaboration of culture' (556). So we end up with a different problem altogether, and one that he himself acknowledges takes us back to Lévi-Strauss.

The reason that such a detailed discussion of Morris' article has been included is that it exemplifies certain problems often encountered in anthropological writings on indigenous classification. Different levels of classification are not separated, and consequently the argument may become confused. The *type* of classification somehow seen as deficient, is not conceptualized. Are the people under study not constructing taxonomies, or is there an absence of categorization? Is it quite a different problem, namely that what actually constitutes a class is uncertain? Do different informants give different and conflicting information regarding classes? Is there an absence of detailed naming and enumeration? Is one talking about symbolic or scientific classification; or is it rather an issue arising out of the proposition of Levi-Strauss that all primitive classifications form a totality? In order to advance the complex topic of primitive classification, it is important to distinguish exactly the nature of the problem in question. My proposed typology intended to contribute towards a clarification.

One problem not touched upon by Morris, but which commonly arises, is that of variability in what constitutes a class, either according to different informants or according to different contexts. Two recent examples will be briefly referred to. Endicott's encounter with inconsistent data regarding the *lawac* prohibitions, as well as attributes describing Batek deities, because of variability between informants have already been mentioned. Ellen, in his study of animal classification among the Nualu of Eastern Indonesia, isolates different causes of variability, namely, differences in individual informants' experience of animals due to varying degrees of knowledge and social differentiation; according to context; and, to some extent, due to characteristics of the animals themselves. He concludes by questioning whether homogeneity of knowledge is necessary, or indeed possible, and suggests that, 'Variability is what we must expect, diversity is part of the system' (1979: 357).

Both Endicott and Ellen suggest that one useful way of dealing with such situations is to treat the classes polythetically.

THE PROBLEM IN THE CHEWONG CONTEXT

The problem of variability did not occur among the Chewong. My informants always gave the same answers when asked for names of animals and plants. Once their confidence had been gained, I found that the same applied to all areas of knowledge which I chose to investigate. There was little hesitation, and few variations in the answers. This was surprising as I had gone to the field fully expecting the opposite to be the case, in view of the fact that I knew the Orang Asli to have little formal organization in areas of politics and religion, and that theirs were societies in which much knowledge was acquired through personal revelation. Individual idiosyncratic knowledge was to be expected.

The problem which I did encounter, however, was a lack of pattern underlying the members of various constructed categories of knowledge. Despite the consistency of Chewong replies to questions regarding, for example, which species were included in the various rules, it was not possible to establish any common pattern which united these species in some way. As already pointed out, much knowledge is revealed by superhuman beings to the individual, this is often incorporated into the collective body of knowledge, and is therefore shared by everybody. Although this is unlikely to happen in the case of naming natural species, the choice of which species are associated with which rule is more likely to be so selected. Indeed I shall make this claim, although it is unfortunately one which is difficult to establish with conviction since it requires me to prove a lack of any underlying pattern. In order to substantiate it I have chosen to follow the path of Benjamin and Endicott, and to search for common attributes. This will be done as thoroughly as possible, first by presenting the data in tables and attempting to identify patterns by observation, and then using a computer to conduct a principal-components analysis on animals and the attributes and characteristics of those singled out by the Chewong in the different rules already discussed.

While in the field I compiled long tables of all animals, as well as useful plants and trees, fruit, and staples which I came across or was told about. Alongside each name, I listed locally attributed features, as well as my own imposed ones. In the following tables I have extracted those animals, fruits, and staples which are significant in the present discussion, i.e., those which have a link with the various rules examined in the previous chapter. A longer list of animals, their attributes, and Chewong attitude towards them, was subjected to the computer analysis, and this can be found in Appendix 3. The tables are arranged according to each named rule which specifies restricted behaviour towards specifically named animals and plants. Attributes considered vary between the tables, because of both limitations of space and ease of comprehension, but I have singled out the elements which are either pertinent, or might conceivably be so.

The elements can be seen to overlap in many cases with those tested in Tables 4.4 and 4.5 in which *bas* and other harmful super-human beings were analysed in terms of their characteristics and Chewong attitudes towards them. Again, I try to establish whether the animals and plants have *ruwai* or not, i.e., whether through the mere fact of their being able to affect humans they are regarded as personages. In some cases, the possibility of their being people in the past is included. When this is not affirmed in a single instance, the heading is excluded. Where animals are included, the hunting method is listed in case this should prove to be of importance. The question of where and how a certain food may be cooked is then addressed, and finally, the question of the species' place in space. The remainder of the headings are relevant only to the rule in question. In the computer analysis each animal and plant is tested against all the twenty-five attributes and characteristics included.

INTERPRETATION OF THE TABLES

If we look at Tables 9.1 and 9.2 we can see which animals are regarded as particularly dangerous to eat for people who, in different ways, are not 'normal'. In the one case, children, who as yet are not fully developed social beings with fixed *ruwai*; in the other, pregnant women and their husbands both of whom are involved in the creation process. Both these categories of humanity have to protect themselves in various ways, one of which is to abstain from eating certain meats. From an examination of the attributes of the *tolæg* animals no common factor can be established beyond the trivial one that all *tolæg* animals have *yinlugen* counterparts. Since it is the *yinlugen* of a forbidden animal species which takes the *ruwai* of any

Table 9.1

Tolæg Animals

(Forbidden for small children to eat)

Name	Ruwai	People in the Past	Yinlugen	Blow-piped	Mixed[3] Habitat	Cook in the House
Geriang (water monitor lizard)	×		×		×	
Kòh gading (sp. land tortoise)	×		×			
Manai (otter)	?[1]		×		×	
Timoh (gibbon)	×	×	×	×		×
Tuwò (slow loris)	?	?	?	×		
Yed (sp. lizard)		×	×	$\times^2$	×	
Bawæg (macaque)	×		×	×	×	×

[1]The question mark indicates uncertainty on the part of the Chewong.

[2]The most common way to hunt lizards is with dogs and spears. However, whenever they climb a tree they are shot.

[3]These animals are found, and hunted, in at least two different spheres, e.g., both on land and in water, or both on land and in trees.

child who eats its flesh, it is a tautology to say that all *tolæg* animals have *yinlugen*.

Although most of the *tolæg* animals have *ruwai*, people were uncertain about the otter and the slow loris, and one species of lizard (*yed*) definitely does not have it. This is interesting because it demonstrates that no necessary link is envisaged between what must be regarded as a conscious act of taking a child's *ruwai* because it has transgressed the prohibition, and the possession of *ruwai* by the abductor.

There is an overlap of three animals between the two classes of *tolæg* and *pantang*: one species of land tortoise, otter, and slow loris. These animals were not spontaneously mentioned by everyone as being *pantang* for pregnant women and their husbands to eat, although everyone agreed that no *tolæg* animal may be eaten by them as the *yinlugen* would take the *ruwai* of the foetus. This could be the reason that some people listed the otter, the tortoise, and the slow loris as *pantang* animals. The slow loris, as already said, is not eaten

Table 9.2

Pantang Animals

(Forbidden for pregnant women and their husbands to eat)

Name	Ruwai	People in the Past	Blow-piped	Cook in the House	Mixed Habitat	Sympathetic Signature
Bantoai (ant-eater)	×	×			×	×
Dekan (bamboo rat)	×	×				
Kawad (fruit bat)	×			×		×
Kòh gading* (sp. land tortoise)	×					
Manai* (otter)	?				×	
Pelig (horseshoe bat)				×		
Rangsal (flying fox)				×		×
Tuwò* (slow loris)	?			×		×

*Overlap with tolæg animals.

by anyone because of the association it has with the individual as the metamorphosed afterbirth, so it is difficult to understand why it is included at all. Similarly, I came across no one who had eaten otter.

There is thus no feature that all the tolæg animals have in common, and there is no apparent reason why they should be singled out. In the case of the pregnancy-pantang animals no pattern appears either, except that four out of eight exhibit 'sympathetic signatures'. That is, the Chewong themselves explicitly point to the biological features of the animals, specifying the link between them and the envisaged effect. In all instances, birth would be slow because the animal itself is unusually slow, or because its grasp is exceptionally strong (the assumption being that the baby would be held back in the womb). But again, many other animals display similar characteristics yet these are not forbidden.

Other foods which are governed by specific regulations because of

attributes seen to constitute 'sympathetic signatures' are listed in
Table 9.6. There may be many more examples of these which were
not brought to my attention.

There are twelve animals altogether in Tables 9.1 and 9.2. Five of
these (the scaly ant-eater, the fruit- and horseshoe bats, the flying
fox, and the slow loris) are animals which have presented the
Western taxonomers with problems. The category 'mammal' is not
distinguished by the Chewong, nor is the feature underlying the
term regarded by them as significant. With no overall notion of what
constitutes an animal, and with a general absence of intermediate
taxa (apart from those already mentioned) the notion of anomaly
(see Douglas, 1966) can therefore not be applied as an explanation for
why these particular animals are singled out. Since, on the whole,
there are no conceptual groupings based on common attributes,
there is nothing with which each animal may be compared in order
to determine where they might belong on a conceptual map. There
are no criteria by which to measure any one species of animal. As the
tables have demonstrated, social attitudes to the animals singled out
in the rules are not based on anything structurally inherent in its
make-up, habits or habitat.

On examining Table 9.3, two features immediately stand out:
except for fish, all those animals that can be cooked in the same fire
and eaten together at the same meal are hunted with the blowpipe;
and all, again with the exception of fish, have *ruwai*. Most of them
were also people in the past, except fish, and squirrel which the
Chewong say have only been 'pets' (*botn*). Here another category,
namely *botn*, is encountered. Unfortunately I failed to enquire if
there are any animals which may not become *botn*. In the myths,
squirrels, monkeys, dogs, and tigers are *botn*. In the case of tigers
they are always the *botn* of a Bongso (i.e., a *putao*), and are euphemis-
tically known as their dogs.

To return to the category of animals which may be eaten together,
a sociological explanation may partly account for it, although a
structural explanation eludes one. The blowpipe is the prime
hunting weapon and therefore symbolizes the adult male. It also
symbolizes the Chewong as forest people. Meats most frequently
brought back from the forest are animals killed by using the blowpipe. These meats are also the favoured ones. When a Chewong
complains that he has not eaten meat (*ai*) for a long time, he is
thinking of monkey or ape.

But the blowpipe is not an overriding consideration determining

Table 9.3
Animals that may be Cooked and Eaten Together

Name	Ruwai	People in the Past	Blow-piped	Special Prohibitions	Tika[3]	Talaiden[3]
Bawæg (pig-tailed macaque)	×		×	×	×	
Boweig (banded leaf-monkey)	×	×	×		×	
Siameng (siamang)	×	×	×	×		×
Tayog (long-tailed macaque)	×	×	×			×
Tobowad (dusty leaf-monkey)	×	×	×			×
Timoh (gibbon)	×	×	×	×	×	
Tupai (squirrel)	×		×		×	
Birds (with some exceptions[1])	×[1]		×	×	×	×
Fish (with some exceptions)		×		×[2]		

[1] Some birds with red spots have to be cooked and eaten separately. Some birds have *ruwai*, others do not. There is no correspondence with the presence or absence of red spots.

[2] Fish with red spots have to be cooked and eaten separately.

[3] If the meat is cooked with any other meat not in Table 9.3, the result is either *tika* or tiger *talaiden*.

in all cases where meat may be cooked. Many other animals also killed by using the blowpipe have to be cooked and eaten separately. The bats, the flying lemur, the flying squirrel, the flying fox, and the binturong all of which are shot with the blowpipe, and most of which, moreover, have *ruwai* cannot be mixed either with each other or with any other animals. These animals go about during the night and sleep during the day. They therefore exhibit behavioural traits opposite to those of other animals killed by the same method. The day/night opposition is not absolute, however, since many commonly eaten animals are not nocturnal, yet have to be eaten and cooked separately. Also two species of monitor lizard are often shot with the blowpipe. They are not nocturnal, yet must be cooked separately and cannot be eaten with any other meat. Several species of birds with no obvious, or stated, special feature, cannot be cooked in the house fire. There is even one instance of one daytime animal which is killed with the blowpipe, the banded leaf-monkey, which may be cooked and eaten together with pig, a nocturnal animal caught in traps. Although the Chewong distinguish those animals which 'sleep during the day and walk at night', I could not find sufficient evidence to suggest that this distinction has any ritual consequences.

Fish, but no other water creature, may be cooked in the house fire, and may be eaten at any meal. Certain fish and birds, however, have to be treated separately. If they have noticeable spots of red or yellow, colours which are associated with blood, they must not be mixed with any other meat.

The issue is further complicated when we consider that some, but by no means all, vegetables, fruit, and nuts may be cooked and/or eaten together with meat. Table 9.4 shows these. The only point of convergence is that except for plantains and *toka*, those which are staple (*ratn*) have *ruwai*. But, as has already been stated, *ratn* is usually attributed with *ruwai* because of the central role it plays in Chewong diet. In the days before the Chewong became cultivators, all their staple foodstuffs had to be found in the forest. The wild tubers are available all the year round, whereas nuts and fruit are seasonal. The wild tubers have today been largely replaced by tapioca, but they are still eaten. Of what we would call fruit, only the durian would qualify from the list, the remaining fruit is either *tika* or tiger *talaiden* to eat together with meat. The Chewong invoke *ratn* as an explanation for this—the rest of the fruits are not *ratn*. They do, however, include all nuts, wild vegetables, as well as fruit into the one class of 'fruit', *plo*. The tubers are not *plo*, the only generic term for them was *ratn*, but some *plo* as we have seen can also be *ratn*. The only factor common to all members of the *plo* class would appear to be their seasonal appearance. The category *tarog* includes various species of green leafy vegetables such as the leaves of the tapioca plant. Some are wild, others are cultivated. Unlike *plo*, but like the tubers, they can be found all the year round. There is no prohibition on the cooking and eating of *tarog*, and as such they are treated the same as *ratn*.

Table 9.4
Vegetables and Fruit which may be
Cooked and Eaten with Meat

Name	Ruwai	Ratn	In the Ground	On the Ground	Tree	Special Prohibitions
			Habitat			
Galeh (tapioca)	×	×	×			
Hodj (sp. nut)	×				×	Must be cooked with ash of *malor* bark
Howaw (sp. tuber)	×	×	×			
Kiæi (sp. tuber)	×	×	×			
Payòng (sp. nut)	×	×			×	If kept raw next to sleeping place: *tolæg*
Pre (sp. nut)					×	
Ranté (sp. tuber)	×	×	×			
Silah (sweet potato)	×	×	×			
Siwai (lemon grass)	×			×		If cooked with all monkeys, apes, tortoise: *talaiden*
Takad (sp. tuber)	×	×	×			
Tarog (leafy vegetables)				×	×	
Tiòg (plantains)		×			×	
Toka (sp. fruit/nut)		×			×	
Towæng (durian)	×	×			×	

The Chewong cannot conceive of eating meat or fish on its own, these have to be complemented by *ratn*. There is no injunction to this effect, but no meat or fish is ever served without one form of staple accompanying it. The reverse of course often happens, but in such cases excuses are always made for the deficiency. The ideal meal consists of one type of meat and one type of staple. I suspect that rather than search for common attributes, symbolic or natural or social, in the various types of foodstuffs, one should consider the possibility that, ideally speaking, no two foods of any kinds, beyond one of each of the complementary *ai* and *ratn*, should ever be cooked or eaten together. One might speculate that in the nomadic days, with only one, two, or three families travelling together, the chances of more than one animal being caught in any one day were fairly small. Certainly today it is rare for one man to shoot more than one animal during a day's hunting with the exception of several birds of the same species, or a mother and baby monkey or squirrel. Similarly, on most days not more than one staple will be collected, or, to judge from present-day practices, not more than one at any given outing. It must be remembered that whenever a hunter, fisherman, or tuber- or fruit-gatherer returns to the settlement, whatever is brought back is shared out and eaten immediately. It is not *punén* to fail to save food for anyone not yet back from the day's labour. So even if another hunter or gatherer should return with different food, the chances are that he would do so at a different time from anyone else and, consequently, whatever food which already had been brought home would have been consumed. It is therefore possible that the norm was to eat one type of *ai* with one type of *ratn* at any given meal, and that the rules of *talaiden* and *tika* originally included every kind of mixing beyond the one sample of *ai* and *ratn* respectively. The passage of time prescribed between the consumption of different types of food would also ensure a distribution of the food among all.

Such pseudo-historical reconstructions of origins of practices are of course to be avoided. Nevertheless, I think there is some justification in my doing so in the present context since there is empirical evidence of sorts. This is especially so since I was told that until recently fish had to be eaten and cooked separately. Similarly, the most commonly shot monkey, the banded leaf-monkey, *boweig*, is today eaten together with the wild pig, *gau*. Again I was told that it is only recently that one might do so without invoking *talaiden*, as is still the case if pig should be eaten together with any of the other monkeys. It seems to me therefore that there is a tendency towards a loosening of restrictions on the mixing of foods, and that for the sake of convenience, the ideal of keeping every species separate is being relaxed. When visiting the Chewong of the Dong area I found that nobody observed any restrictions of keeping different foods apart, an indication that these rules are abandoned upon contact with cultures who do not observe them.[1]

In view of what has already been discerned elsewhere in Chewong ideas and practices, this injunction upon keeping different kinds of food separate does not present a theoretical problem. Rather, it is consistent with the general stress upon separation already manifest in other areas of their ritual activities.

Another point to note in this connection, namely why the various foodstuffs must be kept separate, is that unlike the Batek who object to the simultaneous cooking of some meats because the mixing of smells of the different species is 'offensive to Gobar' (the 'thunder deity') (Endicott, 1979: 74), the Chewong make no such connection. To them the pertinent point is that no two different species of foodstuffs, beyond one example of *ai* and one of *ratn* should be together in the stomach at the same time. Nothing happens if the foods are just cooked together; it is when they are consumed together that it becomes significant. Therefore, everything must be cooked in different pots, over different fires, and consumed at different times. A prolonged period of time must be allowed to elapse before some other kind of food can be eaten. This is not all, however. The actual fire in which pork, for instance, has been roasted is said to contain pieces of pork meat, fat, or juices. So even if the pork was cooked several days previously, and no visible remnant is to be detected, there is nevertheless a lingering 'pigness' in that spot, and therefore no other meat may be cooked there. I have just mentioned that the banded leaf-monkey and pig can be eaten together. This means that the monkey may be cooked there; but the pig may not be cooked in the main house fire where the monkey is usually cooked, because all the other monkeys, etc., are also cooked there. The presence of pig in this fire would therefore lead to tiger *talaiden* when the pig was eaten. It would also invalidate the fire for other cooking purposes or rather, for the preparation of other food.

[1] When I returned in 1981, I found that the people living at Gandah had begun to buy and eat tinned food. As this became more common, the restriction upon heating it on the household fire began to be relaxed. Tinned pork, probably because wild pork was caught frequently, still had to be cooked separately.

All vegetables and fruit which are not *ratn* may not be cooked together with any meat, or with each other. I have watched people preparing to cook some animal make a fire in a spot different from where the same species had been cooked on previous occasions, for the reason that in the interim a lot of fruit had been eaten and that peel and stones had been discarded on the ground where the fire had been. To cook another category of food on the same spot would mean mixing. Similarly, I was told of a case when a woman died of *tika* after eating some hornbill from a plate on which papaya had been kept, and which apparently had not been properly washed. At Gambir, where I spent most of my time, we had two fires inside the house on which all *ratn* was cooked, all fish except those with red markings, and those animals permitted to be cooked together. There was one covered fire on the ground where we always cooked wild pig. This place was also used for baking the tapioca bread, as well as for cooking any other *ratn* when this was needed. There was one spot always used for building a fire to cook both species of porcupine: another for the two species of monitor lizard, and a third for all species of tortoise. Various species of common wild vegetables such as mushrooms, were cooked in their own separate spots. Whenever rarely caught animals or vegetables were brought back, a place was chosen to make the fire where no food had been cooked before. The same applied to food bought in shops, with the exception of rice, which is *ratn*. Tea or coffee could not be drunk together with anything except *ratn*. If it was raining very heavily, or if one just wanted to heat up a small piece of some food which could not be put in the household fire, one could build a small fire inside the house next to the main one and cook it on that. With regard to cooking, there is thus no ritual spatial divisions similar to that which Benjamin reports of the Temiar of off-the-ground, and on-the-ground cooking; nor is there one between house and field (or culture and nature). More difficult to understand is why there is no injunction on the mixing of firewood. Thus, a new fire may be lit by taking a burning log from the household fire. No one was able to explain this to me. The reason might be traced to the property of fire discussed in Chapter 7 whereby it is regarded as not only the destroyer, but also the transformer. Any 'mystical association' between what has been cooked on a spot is not seen to be lingering in a burning piece of wood.

So, the main principle of the Chewong food prohibitions is that no food except for one type of *ai* and one type of *ratn* can be mixed together at the same time in a person's stomach. If it is cooked, care must be taken that it is cooked in a different spot from all other foods.

The question of why there are different rules governing the mixing of foods not specifically allowed to be cooked and eaten together will now be discussed. The food itself is the carrier of the prohibition/repercussion. Some of the forbidden foods are said to be *tika*, others are *talaiden*. Of the *talaiden* ones there are some which are tiger *talaiden*, and others which are elephant *talaiden*, and this means that if the food in question is mixed with other forbidden foods, a tiger or an elephant will attack the eater. There seem to be no patterns regarding which foods are (elephant or tiger) *talaiden* and which are *tika*. All those foods not exempted and listed in Tables 9.3 and 9.4 are either *tika* or *talaiden*.

In addition to the prohibition on mixing in the stomach, we find that some animals and plants have special restrictions associated with them. These are set out in Table 9.5. I think that this is a far from complete list. Unless I happened to observe a certain food and someone thought of telling me that a specific rule was attached to it, or I actually noticed something unusual in the handling of it, I had no way of knowing. There would have been no systematic way of making this sort of enquiry. Nevertheless, enough instances of special rules regarding edible plants and animals came my way to establish the principle that idiosyncratic rules exist. Some of these rules exhibit sympathetic signatures. For instance oil,[1] which is slippery, is seen to have a mystical effect on the hunting procedure by making the darts also slippery. But one may ask why only squirrel and hornbill cannot be mixed with oil lest the darts become slippery, and not the monkeys. Some informants told me that siamang and gibbon could not be mixed with oil either, but the penalty in this case was tiger *talaiden*. Why only women can hunt the giant rat I do not know, and the Chewong could recount no myth to explain.

The *pantang* of throwing the washing-up water from all monkeys, apes, squirrels, and birds on the ground after dark, lest one's mother dies, is also difficult to explain. Here at any rate the Chewong are consistent in so far as the animals included are all those which may be

---

[1]Oil is extracted by the Chewong from one species of nut only (*hodj*), and they regard it as extremely delicious. Fat of all kinds is the best part of the meat. They do not buy commercial cooking oil, but when I brought some, the restriction was immediately extended to it.

Table 9.5
Animals and Plants with Special Prohibitions

Animal	Prohibition	Result
Binturong	Should not mix with siamang or *boweig* monkey.	Tiger *talaiden*.
Eggs	If found, must not eat.	Becomes snake.
Hornbill and squirrels	Bones must not be thrown on ground. Must place in the roof.	Poison loses its potency.
Kedogn (giant rat)	Only women can hunt. If no husband women cannot eat it.	?
Sipud (sp. water snail)	Must not be put on the ground alive.	Storm *talaiden*.
Pig and monitor lizard	Must not smoke after having eaten these.	*Tika*.
All monkeys	Cannot eat with oil.	Tiger *talaiden*.
Hornbill and squirrel	Cannot eat with oil.	Darts become slippery.
Hornbill and squirrel	Washing-up water must not be thrown on ground under house after dark.	One's mother will die.
Elephant and tapir	Cannot eat without special spells being said.	Body becomes heavy, unable to walk.
Siwai (lemon grass)	Cannot eat with any blowpiped animals not tortoise.	Tiger *talaiden*.
Kongrid root	Cannot eat with *boweig* monkey, hornbill, and siamang.	Tiger *talaiden*.
Klawògen leaf	Cannot wrap siamang, squirrel or binturong.	Tiger *talaiden*.
Yangler leaf	Cannot wrap any meat in it.	Spider *talaiden*. Itches in stomach.
Porau fruit	Cannot carry on shoulder.	*Yinlugen* binturong takes *ruwai*.
Tiri root	Cannot be put in bamboo.	Tiger *talaiden*.

Table 9.6
Prohibitions Explicitly Linked to
'Sympathetic Signature'

Name	Who	Reason
1. Animals		
Keo (flying lemur)	Women of child-bearing age	Red on ears: bleeding
Kinaw chinhai (red giant flying squirrel)	Women of child-bearing age	Red fur: bleeding
Bantoai (ant-eater)	Pregnant women and husbands	Strength in clasp: baby stuck
Pelig (horseshoe bat)	Pregnant women and husbands	Strength in clasp: baby stuck
Kawad (fruit bat)	Pregnant women and husbands	Strength in clasp: baby stuck
Rangsal (flying fox)	Pregnant women and husbands	Strength in clasp: baby stuck
Tuwò (slow loris)	Pregnant women and husbands	Slow movement: slow birth
Titchub (sp. bird)	Everybody	Red spots: blood in stomach
All fish with red spots	Everybody	Red spots: blood in stomach
Hornbill and squirrel	Everybody	If eaten with oil, darts become slippery
2. Plants and leaves		
Hali yangler (sp. stinging leaf)	Everybody	Tika to wrap meat: itchy stomach

cooked and eaten together, or if viewed differently, all those which are shot with the blowpipe and are not nocturnal. It is possible that we are here faced with an off-the-ground/on-the-ground dichotomy, such as is found among the Temiar and Semai (see Dentan, 1967), further reinforced by a dichotomization of daytime and nighttime as represented by the habits of the animals in question. But if this were so, one would immediately be puzzled by the rule that says that the bones of squirrels and hornbills, but not those of apes and monkeys, must not be thrown on the ground; they must be put in the thatch of the roof.

There are three alternative ways of accounting for the unusual composition of the foregoing rules. One alternative is that the Chewong do operate a symbolic categorization of the natural species, but that the principles have been virtually forgotten and that only a few remnants of what was previously an immense pattern has survived today. Another alternative is that they have adopted bits and pieces of symbolic practices from neighbouring tribes without understanding the underlying assumptions that governed these in their own setting. The third possibility, detailed later in this chapter, is that specific animals and plants are associated with specific rules due to contingent circumstances. In view of the rest of my data on Chewong modes of thought I would tend to favour the last two explanations. No conflict would arise at the inclusion of new items, since the principle of idiosyncratic rules is already in existence.

This summarizes my rather impressionistic attempt to identify underlying patterns in Chewong classification as manifested in those rules which govern behaviour, and which concern attitudes to animals and plants. In order to make my analysis more rigorous, and to ensure that there were no patterns which I overlooked, I also made use of a computer to test whether there existed any patterns more complex than I was able to ascertain by inspection.

THE COMPUTER ANALYSIS
AND IMPLICATIONS OF THE TABLES

In Appendix 4 the results of the computer analysis are summarized. Here I will simply describe what was done and draw certain conclusions from the results.

The variables under consideration consisted of selected animals and actual and possible attributes associated with them. The number of animals (elements) had to be restricted to forty, the maximum that the computer could accommodate. I included all those already singled out as vehicles for symbolic thought and used in my own tables, as well as others which in various ways were significant among the Chewong, as evidenced, for example, by inclusion in myths and songs. The attributes (constructs) were chosen partly according to indigenous concepts, such as *ruwai*, what rule might be applied, etc., as well as my own imposed ones, such as place of habitat, type of skin, etc., which although not mentioned spontaneously by the Chewong as significant might nevertheless reveal themselves as such. The total of twenty-five constructs were less than the computer could accommodate (the maximum would again have been forty), but as far as I could see there were no other possible significant attributes to be taken into consideration. The elements and the constructs are listed in Appendix 3.

The computer subjected these data to a 'principal components analysis'. This is a method commonly used in psychology to try to determine the underlying structure in the relations between elements and constructs (see Child, 1970). With certain limitations, this method of analysis can establish the existence of a 'structure' or 'pattern' in a set of data which cannot be readily discovered simply by looking at the data.

The results of this analysis (some of which are shown in Appendix 4) are consistent with the idea that there is a lack of structure, or at best a very loose structure, underlying the data. The method of analysis is such that it should be capable of discerning polythetic as well as monothetic principles, but none was found. It is possible that the relationship between the constructs is more complex than that considered in the computer analysis, or that I omitted one or more crucial attributes from the consideration. I do, however, regard this as unlikely for reasons already discussed.

My own attempts to establish underlying patterns I found unconvincing. As indicated in the previous pages, certain principles may be said to apply, but never in all cases, and the extent to which all attempted generalizations are vitiated by the facts is sufficient to condemn all but the most tautological statements. This view is supported by the computer analysis.

Having failed to establish overt and consistent principles upon which members are assigned to classes, two other alternatives may be considered. The first is based on the suggestion that the class is covert. The second is that the principles are not rigorously consistent.

Thus Whorf suggests an alternative way of establishing the existence of structural principles by what he calls a 'covert class' (1956: 69). What he means by this is a classification 'which has no overt mark actualised along with the words of the class but which operates through an invisible "central exchange" of linkage bonds in such a way as to determine certain other words which mark the class' (69). Thus 'a covert concept like a covert gender is as definable and in its way as definite as a verbal concept like "female" or feminine, but it is of a very different kind, it is not the analog of a word but of a rapport-system, and an awareness of it has an intuitive quality, we say that it is sensed rather than comprehended' (70). He then goes on to narrow down his discussion by saying that 'a covert linguistic class may not deal with any grand dichotomy of objects, it may have a very subtle meaning, and it may have no overt mark other than certain distinctive "reactances" with certain overtly marked forms. It is then what I call a CRYPTOTYPE' (70). In other words, a concept can exist as a covert category, so that the absence of an overt identification in the form of a word is no proof of its non-existence.

The value of Whorf's contribution is that he demonstrates that such 'cryptotypes' may be identifiable by means of linguistic analysis. Thus,

The Navaho so-called 'round' and 'long' nouns are not marked in themselves nor by any pronouns. They are marked only in the use of certain very important verb stems, in that a different stem is required for a 'round' or a 'long' subject or object. Many other verb stems are indifferent to the distinction. A new object, for which the Navaho has no name, will be put into one or the other class by analogy, not analogy as it would seem to me, but as guided by the contents of the two Navaho complexes.

(Whorf, 1956: 70)

Although I did not submit my data on Chewong language to a rigorous linguistic analysis, I certainly found no such patterning in their use of language. To establish a lack of pattern in language is similar to the problem which I have already been facing. Whereas I can assert that no evidence for the existence of any such 'cryptotypes' was found, the possibility cannot conclusively be ruled out. Indeed, it would be impossible to do so.

But may we not be confronted with what Wittgenstein called 'family resemblances' in his discussion on games (1953; sections 66–67), and which principle has proved so useful to some of the anthropologists discussed earlier in this chapter? This is an important alternative to be considered. Is it the case that the system underlying the apparently unpatterned classification is polythetic?

There are two objections to this suggestion. Firstly, the computer analysis fails to support such a claim. Secondly, the situation is, in the case of the Chewong, somewhat different. It is not that they always have clear-cut distinctions between groups of elements without any apparent features in common between the elements. In many cases they fail to make consistent distinctions between the groups (as for example in the case of superhuman beings discussed in Chapter 4). If there is not only an overlap in the defining features, but also an overlap between the classes which the features serve to distinguish, the situation is one of such complexity that alternative theories enter the realm of pure speculation. Ultimately, polythetic classification cannot be sharply contrasted with lack of principles in a class. One shades off into the other. No threshold can be identified beyond which it can be claimed without risk of contradiction that no underlying pattern of a polythetic nature exists. I believe that the Chewong represent a position very far along the spectrum from rigorous monothetic classification—but it is almost arbitrary whether this is called a very loose polythetic system or a simple enumerative system.

In the following section an alternative method for explaining the inclusion of a member in a class, namely the principle of contingency, will be considered.

LAUGHING AT ANIMALS

I begin with a question which has preoccupied anthropologists of Malay aboriginals since the days of Skeat, namely that laughing at certain animals leads to thunderstorms, since this can be seen to have particular relevance in the present context.

It appears from the literature that the various Orang Asli groups specify a finite number of animals which may not be laughed at or teased. So far the writers have concentrated upon the lists of animals included in what is assumed to be a special category of animals which are somehow linked according to some principle. Common features among the animals have therefore been searched for. Schebesta suggests that the animals thus singled out fall into two main groups. First, domestic or captive animals must not be ridiculed because they cannot defend themselves, whereas it 'is not a sin to laugh at a human being who can avenge himself' (1928: 190). Second, some of the animals are specifically said to be companions or servants of the 'thunder god', Karei (190).

Benjamin proposes that the 'ideal type of action' that leads to a state of *misik* (thunderstorms) is to mock those animals which are Karei's familiars (1967: 107), but there are several exceptions to this rule.

Endicott gives a list of nineteen animals which is the maximum that the Batek may not laugh at. These are both captive as well as free animals, thereby destroying Schebesta's thesis. He found that seven of the animals seem to form the 'core of the class', namely pig-tailed macaques, long-tailed macaques, land leeches, water leeches, dogs, cats, snakes (1979: 71). Furthermore, the Batek say that 'as a general rule one can laugh at any animal one can eat and cannot laugh at any animal one cannot eat' (71). His explanation of this statement is that all animals and plants were created by the superhuman beings. Some of them are useful to humans, others are not. Therefore to laugh at the useless ones would seem to be 'ridiculing the *hala*' themselves' and, 'what is prohibited then, is laughing at the very existence of the animal, at the order of things as established by the *hala*' (73). But, as Endicott points out, this rule is not clear cut since even in the core group we find animals which can be eaten, namely the two species of macaques. His justification for their inclusion, that they have an 'uncanny resemblance to human beings' (73) does not seem satisfactory. There are also several animals not eaten which may be laughed at, and others such as the tiger and the elephant which 'would not be laughed at anyway because, as the Batek say, people would be afraid to laugh at them' (73).

Other writers do not provide any detailed discussion on the subject of which animals may not be laughed at and why, beyond that of mentioning the prohibitions, and listing the animals prohibited.

The Chewong material will now be examined to see how it fits in with the previous hypotheses. Having read about and pondered upon the curious belief of the Orang Asli before going to the field, soon after my arrival I began to collect a list of those animals which the Chewong appeared to associate with laughter and thunderstorms, and which were said to be *talaiden*. The easiest way to do this was, in the first instance, to note whenever children were told off for laughing uproariously near animals by adults calling out '*talaiden*'. I would then follow this up by asking whether it was *talaiden* to laugh at a dog, leech, house-mouse, or whatever the animal in question was, and I always received an affirmative reply. As my list began to grow, and to include animals which none of the other writers had mentioned, I began to ask about all the animals whose names I knew. Much to my amazement I never once received a negative answer. It appeared that it was *talaiden* to laugh at all animals. But sometimes an informant would say that one particular animal was especially dangerous, or 'very much *talaiden*' (*talaiden lòi*). I also found that whenever I put my question differently and asked which are the *talaiden* animals, there was a noticeable correspondence between those spontaneously listed and those which in other contexts had been said to be *talaiden lòi*. For the record, the animals most frequently mentioned during my stay were: snake (*talòden*), poisonous millipedes (*keéb*), worms, and caterpillars (*komai* and *kaching*), leeches (*lawòi*), wild pig (*gau*), monitor lizard (*challag*), and the banded leaf-monkey (*boweig*).

When I enquired why the above-mentioned animals were *talaiden lòi*, they invariably said that someone had laughed at that particular animal in the recent past, or in a myth, and how a bad thunderstorm had ensued. In view of this, I would suggest that no logical links are to be sought when attempting to 'explain' the prohibition on certain animals and not on others. As far as the Chewong are concerned, the key concept is that no animal may be laughed at or teased. The prohibition applies also to meat being cooked, as well as to receptacles used for cooking meat and from which it is eaten.

A reconsideration of why a relatively small number of animals are said to be *talaiden lòi* is necessary. When the Chewong diagnose a particular disease, they examine the recent behaviour of the patient, or members of the community with whom he has recently had contact, in order to elicit any breach of a rule which might account for the disease. In just the same way they examine their own behaviour in relation to the animate non-human world whenever a severe thunderstorm is raging, in order to detect who amongst them has laughed at what animal. I have observed this attempt at diagnosis going on while the storm raged, and it was usually resolved by someone admitting to having laughed at an animal in the recent past. If no one is forthcoming, then it is assumed that one of the small children must have done so, and conciliatory actions are then entered into on behalf of all the children. Later the grown-ups will explain that children do not know what they are doing and that they are always laughing at one animal or other.

The animal most frequently mentioned as *talaiden lòi* is the worm (*kaching*). The reason they give for this is that about four or five years before my arrival, a sudden terrible storm arose during which a tree fell, killing three people and seriously injuring two others. In searching for the cause of the event, those who survived said that earth worms (*kaching*) had been laughed at by the people who were killed. Millipedes (*keéb*) are usually mentioned next, justified by a story about Jong who nearly died from a falling tree after having laughed at one, and so on.

What I suggest is that as each such event recedes into history and others occur, the actual species which are said to be *talaiden lòi* are gradually undergoing change. Each new event will tend to replace (or possibly, of course, reinforce) the association previously made, and the consequent identification of a specific animal as *talaiden lòi*.

This argument can also be applied to the earlier discussion regarding those species focused on for other special restrictions with regard to pregnancy, childhood, and so on. To seek resemblance is then, I would argue, futile. The selection of the actual species to which, at any given time, the rules apply is contingent upon events. It is the existence of different classes as named concepts which is important, not the members of each class. Thus we have the rules such as *pantang, tolæg, talaiden*, and even *tanko* which were all discussed in the last chapter; and the superhuman beings, such as *bi asal, bi inhar, bas*, discussed in Chapter 4. The labels exist, but the contents in many cases change, following particular circumstances and events.

A topical analogy will elucidate the point. The class of carcinogens contains all substances known to encourage the growth of cancer. Although events, under suitably rigorous experimental conditions, can identify some substance as a carcinogen, researchers have failed to find any underlying principle that unites the many different carcinogens. In effect, scientists are calling any cancer-causing agent a carcinogen, much as the Chewong say, for instance, that any animal known to have been eaten by a pregnant woman shortly before a miscarriage is henceforth *pantang* for pregnant women.

To conclude, I would maintain that certainly Chewong thoughts regarding their environment—both 'natural' and 'supernatural'— are ordered in a way which can justifiably be regarded as classification, but, as argued throughout this chapter, this concept does not necessarily imply either a hierarchical ordering or the existence of underlying structural principles.

10
Concluding Remarks

I began this study of the principles of Chewong thoughts by suggesting that in this case traditional anthropological methods did not provide one with useful tools for exploration and analysis, because Chewong society is marked by an absence of explicit and clear structures manifested in social and ritual organization. This meant that I was forced to search for a different method. I believed that this should be based on one or more perspectives which, as far as possible, were not imposed by myself but rather derived from what the Chewong themselves appeared to regard as particularly significant. Following this approach, I chose three main perspectives: principles of relationships, the indigenous concept of consciousness, and rules and classification; and presented each in a separate part. It now remains to sum up what has been established and, in so doing, to evaluate the method.

Before discussing the findings of each part, it must be said that I ultimately found that these three perspectives were in fact not so different from each other as was at first assumed. It was at times difficult to keep the issues separate, and, more importantly, similar underlying notions emerged as governing much of Chewong ideas and practices. It was, however, only at a fairly high level of abstraction that these principles could be discerned. They concern the principle of the essential unity perceived to permeate all areas of Chewong cosmology, and the principle of separation which must be adhered to in order to maintain and recreate this unity. They will be discussed below.

A further general point to have emerged is that Chewong social organization is in constant movement. There are no fixed groups— either empirically or conceptually. By contrast, their daily practices, or rather the meanings of these, offer a remarkable stability, ensuring the perpetuation in time of society as a whole, at the same time as they can accommodate new events, and alternative explanations. By treating the mundane tasks of cooking, eating, and the regular exploitation of the jungle as ritual acts, we are questioning the common anthropological definition of ritual as being an activity somehow set apart from the daily practical ones. Such a distinction is impossible to maintain with regard to the Chewong. There is no point where the 'ordinary' ends and the 'religious' begins. The superhuman beings are drawn directly into the mundane activities, and mundane activities constitute the major medium through which humans' relationships with the superhumans are expressed and maintained. It is food, and the handling of this, which is the chief vehicle of Chewong thought regarding their society.

An important point to arise from the discussion in Part I, is that in order to understand the underlying principles of Chewong ideas about themselves, one must extend one's view as to what constitutes their society to include all those beings in their universe who are attributed with consciousness (*ruwai*), whether these be human (i.e., Chewong), superhuman, animal, plant, or inanimate object. All take part in the working of the society, so that in this wider context society is coextensive with their cosmos.

I have argued that the relationship between each category of conscious being is governed by egalitarian values. By this is meant that nobody should use the manifest differences between them (such as male/female, parent/child, older/younger, *putao*/ordinary human, mortal/immortal) as levers for exerting power, or as a basis for expectations. Each has his own part to play, each of which is necessary, but none of which is generally, or overridingly, more highly valued than the rest.

Furthermore, everybody has something in common, namely *ruwai*. This means that they are all conscious beings who act according to rational principles, and this was explained in Part II. All those categories attributed with *ruwai* possess the same qualities, and the basic ingredients in the make-up of the person within each category are identical, as are their needs and desires; but the manifestations of these are often different. Thus the Chewong are able to reconcile their basic belief in the psychic unity of all personages with otherwise unacceptable behaviour. Each species is accorded its own worldview, often based on the notion that each species of personage has different eyes from the rest, resulting in a perception of reality different from humans. In this sense the Chewong are 'humancentric' in their attitude to other species. Cosmologically, the relativistic model of consciousness is thus encompassed by human values.

The various conscious beings have certain duties towards each other, and these are manifested in continuous processes of exchange, most of which emphasize not individuals (or corporate groups understood as individuals) in which reciprocity is the major concern, but rather the recreation of the total social universe. For the world order to continue and to reproduce itself, all the categories of beings actively involved in it have to fulfil their prescribed tasks. In this way, the survival of everyone depends not only on his or her own efforts, but also on those of everybody else. A *social* process of reproduction can therefore be seen to exist.

These concluding remarks began by stating that Chewong social organization is one of constant movement. This means that 'us' (*bi he*) constitute a definite number of people linked by kin-ties, common language, and common traditions. How and where any one sub-group of 'us' is constituted at any one time is unimportant, and in practice sub-groups are found to form and reform constantly. This flux is reflected in their classification system. Thus membership of any one class, be it that of superhuman beings or the various rules which govern individual or group behaviour, may change at any time depending upon contingent circumstances. What remains constant, however, is the concept that certain classes of beings or 'things' exist. But who or what constitutes a particular class at any one time may change. What also remains constant is the principle that continued order is dependent upon specified action. The issues are discussed in Part III.

Finally, despite my opening remarks about the absence of explicit and clear structures, I have nevertheless, throughout my study of the Chewong, discerned one principle which seems to underlie most of their ideas and actions. This is what I have named the principle of separation. In this book I have used the term very loosely to indicate many different things: the correct separation of child from mother; of placenta from child; of separation of food from the hunter to everybody in equal parts; of the need to keep specified things in specified places; of not mixing different kinds of the two main categories of food: *ai* and *ratn* (meat and staple); of not crossing the boundaries between the various parts of the cosmos; and of many other instances all of which can be seen to stipulate the necessity of keeping specified things, or acts, apart.

My study of the Chewong has focused on an approach which

interpreted the same ethnographic facts from three different perspectives. From these I intended to build up a composite picture of the principles guiding their ideas and practices, showing, as I did so, that although the Chewong lack structural principles commonly found elsewhere, they do not represent an example of a 'primitive mentality' somehow different in kind from the Western one. However, as the presentation developed, one single principle—that of separation—could be discerned throughout as an underlying theme.

Glossary

Abod:	Warm, hot.
Adi:	Younger sibling.
Ai:	Meat.
Asal:	Original.
Bajo:	(1) Shirt, blouse. (2) 'Body' as opposed to *ruwai*.
Bas:	General term for many harmful superhuman beings.
Batin:	J.O.A.-appointed headman.
Beri:	People, humanity as a whole.
Bi:	(1) People, usually as a sub-group of humanity. (2) Body, root, substance.
Bi asal:	Original people; superhuman beings who existed before human beings.
Bi hali:	Leaf people; superhuman beings who live in leaves and flowers.
Bi he:	Our people, as opposed to other species of humanity.
Bi inhar:	Hidden people; dead *putao*, superhuman beings who live on Earth Seven in waterfalls, rivers, large stones, mountains, and in the jungle.
Blau:	Blowpipe.
Bongso:	Youngest child of either sex. Usually *putao*.
Bremón:	Singing session on the occasion of the expulsion of the ghost of a newly dead person.
Chò:	(1) Name. (2) Interjection 'what?'
Chò lòi:	True (real) name.
Chò punlao:	Nickname.
Dödn:	Illness, to be ill.
Dòg:	(1) The poison used on the darts. (2) Name of the tree from which the sap is extracted. (3) Barkcloth which is taken from the same tree.
Gob:	Outsider (i.e., not *bi he*); usually refers to Malays only.
Hieng:	Spirit-guide who has become part of the personality

of the human being, its 'father'.

Jawab: Sexual intercourse, or marriage, between siblings.

Jeh: Wife.

Kòkn: Woman.

Lòi: True, real, very much.

Mali: Rule forbidding whistling, swinging one's feet, shouting in certain circumstances.

Maro: Rule insisting on the necessity of giving food to all visitors from other settlements, and on having to inform all settlements of a death.

Med: Eye.

Modn: Dew, more specifically the dew brought for healing purposes during a healing seance.

Moni: Odour, smell.

Njug: Breath.

Nöpoh: Singing seance, either for healing, or for contacting the superhuman beings.

Òz: Fire, firewood.

Òz taba: Scented woodchips from the agila tree placed in a special bowl and set alight—essential for contacting superhuman beings.

Pantang: Prohibitions mainly invoked during life crises.

Plò: Fruit.

Punén: (1) Rule which forbids unfulfilled desires, shouting at times of accidents, using certain words, anticipating pleasure, and insists upon a substitution language when collecting certain jungle produce. (2) State of vulnerability resulting from breaking the rule.

Putao: Shaman, healer, a person with esoteric knowledge and access to the superhuman beings.

Putao hain: Mouth shaman; one who heals through the invocation of spells only.

Putao modn: Dew *shaman*; one who has had his (her) blood exchanged with cool white blood; who has dew as his (her) spirit-guide.

Putao plò: Fruit *shaman*; one who is able to go to Earth Six and to bring fruit back to Earth Seven.

Putao salitn: Exchange (replace) *shaman*; one who can put on several different bodies and who upon death enters a new body and continues to live as a *bi inhar*.

Ratn: All kinds of staple vegetal foods.

Riding: A plaited loop made out of leaves and attached to the *shaman*'s headband and to the 'soul string' during a *nöpoh*.

Rus: Liver; seat of thought and emotion.

Ruwai: (1) Vital principle. (2) 'Soul' i.e., consciousness. (3) A certain type of spirit-guide.

Sanrugn: A hut built in the treetops in which the body of a *putao* is placed upon death.

Sedeig: Cool.

Talaiden: (1) The rule that forbids laughing at animals, as well as the mixing of certain types of meat. (2) The state of natural catastrophe that ensues.

Talòden asal: Original Snake; female being who lives below Earth Seven and causes flooding when someone has committed *talaiden*.

Tam: Water, juice, liquid, river.

Tankal: Spell, invocation.

Tanko: Sexual relation or marriage between categories of persons forbidden to do so. (2) The superhuman being who lives above and punishes transgressors of the *tanko* rule, makes thunder and lightning following a *talaiden* offence, and causes menstruation in women.

Teh: Husband.

Tika: Rule that forbids the mixing of specified foods.

Tòh: Older sibling.

Tokad: Cold.

Tolah: Rule that forbids showing disrespect to affines, and laughing at *ratn*.

Tolæg: (1) Rule that forbids small children to eat certain animals. (2) The name of the *yinlugen* of the animals in question who take the *ruwai* of offending children.

Wòng: Child.

Wòng hieng: Spirit-guide (see *hieng*).

Yinlugen: (1) 'Ghost', the aspect of a person which is activated upon death. (2) Certain harmful superhuman beings.

Yinlugen asal: Original ghosts; category of superhuman beings who existed before humanity.

Appendices

Appendix 1
Myths

MYTH 1

TA' TAHALA

Ta' Tahala, whose nickname was Ta' Totyor, wanted a wife. The problem was that his penis was extremely pointed and sharp, and there were thorns on it. He placed necklaces, sarongs, bracelets, and rings inside a very large cane fish-trap. After some days a bird spoke to him, 'Ta' Totyor, Ta' Totyor, there are fish corpses in your trap.' Ta' Totyor went with his dog (which was really a tiger) to investigate. Two young girls were inside the trap. He let them out and they went with him to his house where he cooked rice and gave it to them to eat. In the evening they slept next to each other, and the two girls became his wives, but they did not have sexual intercourse. After three or four nights the girls said to him, 'Ta' Totyor?' 'What?' he asked. 'Ta' Totyor, we want to have children.' So Ta' Totyor had intercourse with them by placing his penis between their toes.

After a while the girls became pregnant in their calves. Several months went by until one day the girls said, 'Ta' Totyor.' 'What is it?' he asked. 'Our children have grown large and the birth is close. It is time you went and found some bark so that we can make bark cloth for baby slings', they said. The following morning Ta' Totyor got out two large bags of rice and gave them to his wives, saying, 'This rice is good and you may eat it. This other bag of rice is poisonous and you must not eat it.' Having said this he and his dog set off. The two wives at home cooked some of the good rice which they ate. Then they decided to pretend to have eaten the poisonous rice and they cooked some of this as well but left it aside. They went to sleep to pretend that they had died. Meanwhile Ta' Totyor and his dog had arrived at the *dog* tree and started cutting off the bark, when a bird called, 'Ta' Totyor, Ta' Totyor, the two women at home have died.' 'Oh, but I told them that one bag of rice was poisonous and one was good', lamented Ta' Totyor. 'Come on, Master, we'll go home, the two women have died', said the dog. When they reached the house Ta' Totyor looked at his two wives. They were asleep, but he thought they were dead. He saw the rice in the saucepan and tried a little. It tasted very bad and he vomited. He looked at his wives' swollen calves and said sadly, 'They were so pregnant too.' 'What shall we do, Master, shall we bury them?' asked the dog. 'No', said Ta' Totyor, 'we'll make a bamboo raft and send them down the river to where they came from.' So they carried the two corpses and put them on some leaves while they built the raft. When it was ready Ta' Totyor went up to the two women and looked at them. Yes, they were truly dead he decided, and he put them on the raft together with all the things he had given them, and went home. After a while the girls arrived at their own settlement and they told everybody what they had done. The people there said they had been very clever.

Ta' Totyor built another large fish-trap and put sarongs, necklaces, rings, and bracelets inside. Two other girls wanted the things and they entered the fish-trap. 'Ta' Totyor, Ta' Totyor, there are fish corpses in your trap', called out the bird. 'Come let us go and have a look', said Ta' Totyor to his dog. When he saw the two girls inside he asked his dog—who was really a tiger—'What do you say? Is that meat for you?' 'No', said the dog, so Ta' Totyor let the girls out and they went home with him. After a few days they said, 'Ta' Totyor, we want to make children.' So Ta' Totyor had sexual intercourse with them, but this time he did it properly in their vaginas. But the thorns on his penis scraped their vaginas, and they cried out with pain. After a while they got pregnant. This time the wives were properly (lòi) pregnant, in their stomachs. As the time for delivery drew near, they said to their husband, 'Ta' Totyor, our babies are getting large. You must go and get some bark so that we can make bark cloth for baby slings.' The next morning, Ta' Totyor showed his wives two bags of rice. 'This rice is sweet and you may eat it. This rice is poisonous and you must not eat it.' Having said this, he and the dog set off to find the bark. The girls cooked the good rice and ate. Then they cooked the poisonous one and left it so that Ta' Totyor would think they had eaten it and died. They then lay down to sleep.

Ta' Totyor was busily hacking at the bark of a *dog* tree. The bird called out to him, 'Ta' Totyor, Ta' Totyor', but he did not hear. The bird called again, this time louder, 'Ta' Totyor, Ta' Totyor.' 'What?' said he. 'The two women at home have died', said the bird. 'Oh but I told them which rice was good and which was poisonous', exclaimed Ta' Totyor. So he and the dog went home. Ta' Totyor was very sad. He looked at his two wives and their big stomachs. 'And they were so close to giving birth', he lamented. 'Well, what shall we do?' he asked the dog. 'Are they meat for you?' 'No, no', said the dog, 'we'll build a raft as we did the last time.' They carried the girls to the river and put them on some leaves together with the things they had been given. Ta' Totyor kept looking at them. They were truly dead. 'We'll leave them here to be eaten by wild animals.' He then said to the dog, 'Let us go home.' When the girls heard this they were frightened, 'No, no', they cried, 'we have lied and pretended to be dead.' When Ta' Totyor heard this he told his dog to bite them. 'They lied to me', he said. The dog (which was really a tiger) bit them and this time they died properly. Their corpses fell into the river and drifted down to the settlement. When the people there saw them they said that they had been less clever than the other two. No more girls dared go to Ta' Totyor's fish-trap, and he went up to Earth Six.

MYTH 2

THE PANDANUS WOMAN

Once there was a pandanus woman. She very much wanted a baby, but no man would sleep with her for her vagina was full of thorns. So one day, she slept with her legs wide open so that the wind could enter her vagina. After about one year she became pregnant and in due course she gave birth to a girl. The pandanus woman wanted more children. Many men came to have sexual intercourse with her, but the sharp thorns in her vagina cut off their penes and they died.

After a while Bòngso went to have a look at the pandanus woman. All his elder brothers had died from having slept with her and Bòngso was curious. He saw all the thorns and made himself into a tiny being so that he could enter the woman's stomach without being torn to shreds by the thorns. He wanted to enter her, but not to die in the process. The woman thought she was pregnant when Bòngso was inside her. He grew inside her stomach until the day came when she started her labour pains. The woman told her daughter by the wind, 'Take great care at this birth of your younger sibling. It is a boy.' Bòngso was born and the pandanus woman thought that he was a real baby. She would chew the tapioca herself before putting it inside his mouth as one does to babies, but he spat it out. He was no baby, but a man who had made himself very small and entered her stomach. So the woman gave him proper rice and tapioca and this he ate. He grew very fast. After seven days he could walk. When he was a little bigger the mother told her 'wind daughter' to take him with her into the forest to search for edible roots. She gave them a knife each, but Bòngso hid his knife and when he returned home he told the pandanus woman that he had lost it. 'Never mind', said she, 'I have lots of knives.' The next day they went into the forest again, and when they had finished digging, Bòngso hid his knife on the ground telling his mother that he had lost it. 'Oh never mind, there is no shortage of knives', she replied. The same thing happened each time Bòngso went into the forest, but the woman did not mind losing all the knives. Bòngso kept the knives for use later.

Time passed and Bòngso grew up. When his sister was quite big, she had grown breasts, Bòngso said to her one day, 'I am not really your brother. I made myself very small in order to enter your mother's stomach. I knew how many men had died from having their penes cut off while having intercourse with her. All my elder brothers were also killed in this way. Are you very fond of your mother?' he asked her. 'No', she said. 'No, I am not very fond of her.' 'Truly?' he insisted. 'No, truly I am not fond of her', she replied. 'Well if you are not, then I will destroy her', said Bòngso. The girl again affirmed that she was not fond of her mother. Then Bòngso went to the pandanus woman's house. He took the bones of his brothers which she kept inside. He set light to her house and shouted out, 'Become pandanus leaf. Become a true pandanus plant.' From then on she was never able to be human. Bòngso took all the bones of his brothers and laid them out on the ground. He washed them and placed them in the right order. Then he blew magical smoke (òz taba) over them. They became alive again. 'Oh, what happened?' they exclaimed upon awakening. 'Your penes got cut off by the pandanus woman and you died', said Bòngso. 'Oh, where is she now?' they wanted to know. 'I have destroyed her with fire', he told them. Then the brothers saw the 'wind girl' and asked who she was. 'That is my wife', said Bòngso. So Bòngso blew more magical smoke over his brothers and in the night he and the 'wind girl' slept together. After a few days the brothers were strong enough to walk, so Bòngso collected all the knives he had been hiding and they set off to their mother's house. 'Is that your wife, Bòngso?' the mother asked when she saw them. 'It is my wife', he replied. 'Where have you all been for so long?' the mother further enquired. 'Oh, my brothers had their penes cut off by the pandanus woman's vagina and died', said Bòngso. 'Oh, and where is she now?' she asked. 'I destroyed her with fire. She has become a true pandanus plant', said Bòngso.

MYTH 3

BÒNGSO WHO WENT TO EARTH SIX FOR FRUIT

Once upon a time people were very hungry. They did not yet know how to make swiddens and grow tapioca. They only went digging wild roots and tubers. There was one family consisting of mother, father, and two brothers. The younger, Bòngso, was not very strong. His mother scolded him for not being any good at digging and carrying roots. They all wanted to eat fruit very much, but there was none on Earth Seven. There was fruit on Earth Six only. They became more and more hungry as they could not find enough to eat. They decided to nöpoh. They made riding (headbands) and ruwai string, and they built a special house in the jungle for them to nöpoh in. First the older brother sang. But he was not putao and he could not travel up to Earth Six. Then Bòngso began to sing. His ruwai became a large bumble-bee and it flew up to Pinto Lancob. This is the entrance to Earth Six and only big putao—dew putao—can enter for the door consists of several huge stones that roll to and fro. When the people saw Bóngso they asked, 'Who are you? Are you dew putao?' 'No', replied Bòngso, but as he said that he became a dew putao and was able to enter Pinto Lancob. The people up there looked at him as he flew from flower to flower. They did not want him to take any fruit down with him. They ran after him trying to push him off. He flew hither and thither, but they pursued him until they managed to expel him. It is very hot on Earth Seven, but Earth Six is cool, which is why the fruit trees bear all the year round, and the people who live there are very frightened of the heat, and will under no circumstances let any of their fruit be taken away. But Bòngso managed to bring with him one piece of durian skin. This he put over magical smoke, and then he gave his mother to eat. When she was full, she passed it on to her husband to eat. When he had eaten his fill he gave it to his older son who also ate and then passed it to his wife, and so on. Everyone could eat from the same piece of fruit and be satisfied.

The next night they *nöpoh* again and Bòngso flew up through Pinto Lancob with no difficulty this time. He had become dew *putao* as well as fruit *putao*. He could bring fruit. This time he took one durian fruit down with him, and after having put it over magical smoke, everybody ate until they were satisfied from that one fruit. He then dug a hole in the ground and planted the durian skin. It grew into a huge tree with lots of fruit. Everybody climbed up and picked as much fruit as they wanted. 'Don't eat it all, keep some', Bòngso told them. The people did not listen to him. They picked all the fruit and filled their houses with it. They smoked it so that it would not go rotten. Then they just ate and ate. They no longer bothered to go searching for roots and wild tubers. When Bòngso saw this he moved all the fruit up to Earth Six. Then in the evening they *nöpoh*, and Bòngso carried his parents and his brother and sister-in-law up to Earth Six with him. They still live up there eating fruit. The rest of the people down on Earth Seven had no more fruit. If they had not given up digging, then they would still have some fruit. But they became lazy and depended on Bòngso to feed them.

MYTH 4

THE BATS

Bòngso was out hunting one day. He came across a binturong which he shot. The corpse fell, but the *ruwai* of the binturong did not die, it became *pongkal* (a species of *bas* which eat human being) and entered the body of the binturong. Bòngso did not know this. He went to gather firewood so that he could cook the binturong. When he returned he saw a slight movement of the body. He realized that it had become *pongkal* and he decided to run away, but he pretended that he was going for water. He met a flying lemur. 'I shot at a binturong, but did not hit it', lied Bòngso. 'Now I want to go home. Will you help me get to my house by the sea?' The flying lemur agreed, and Bòngso climbed on to its back. The flying lemur climbed up to the top of a tree, then it jumped and glided to the ground. Again it climbed up another tree, jumped and glided to the ground. Meanwhile the *pongkal* was waiting for Bòngso to return. When he did not do so, the *pongkal* said to himself, 'Where is my meat? He must have known.' So he set off in pursuit of

Bòngso. He saw Bòngso being carried off by the flying lemur. The binturong *pongkal* climbed up a tree, but since it could not glide it had to jump to a tree very close by and work its way along the branches. Meanwhile the flying lemur continued to climb, jump, and glide. The binturong never lost sight of it, but could not catch up with it either. After a while the flying lemur became very tired. He took Bòngso to the house of the flying squirrel. Bòngso told the squirrel that he was fleeing from the binturong *pongkal*. The flying squirrel told him to sit on his back, and he climbed up to the very top of a tree, then jumped off and glided to another tree some distance away. Then he climbed up to the top again, jumped, and glided. The binturong *pongkal* saw Bòngso being carried by a flying squirrel. 'Oh, my food, my meat', he exclaimed. 'There are two of them.' He climbed up a tree and tried to jump off and glide the way the flying squirrel did, but he did not know how, and fell to the ground. Still he continued to pursue as hard as he could. He tried to hit out at them, but he could not reach them. The flying squirrel came to a tree full of sleeping fruit bats. They were all hanging upside down asleep. The whole tree was covered with bats. The flying squirrel moved towards the tree. Bòngso told him that he wanted to sit on a bat and be flown by him, so the flying squirrel looked at the tree that was full of bats. Only one bat was awake. All the others were fast alseep. Bòngso asked the bat if he would carry him to his house by the sea. The bat looked at him. 'Well, Bòngso,' he said, 'do you happen to have any fishing hooks?' 'I do', replied Bòngso, 'I do have fishing hooks.' 'I will carry you if you give them to me', said the bat. Bòngso agreed, and he climbed up on the bat's back. The binturong *pongkal* watched from a distance. The bat took off. He circled around the tree several times. Up and down he went all around the tree. This woke up the other bats, and they all flew up, covering the whole sky. The *pongkal* could not see where the bat carrying Bòngso went, there were so many bats flying hither and thither. So the *pongkal* had to give up his pursuit of Bòngso. The bat carried Bòngso for a long time towards the coast. When they caught sight of Bòngso's house by the sea the bat flew there and landed next to the house. Then Bòngso gave him the fishing hooks. That was how the bats came to have claws that look just like fishing hooks.

MYTH 5

THE MANGO MAN

Once there was a young woman, Bòngso, who lived alone with her pet squirrel in a house on its own. One day she and the squirrel went out into the jungle. She found one mango fruit lying on the ground by itself. 'Oh, look, a mango', she said, and bent down to pick it up and put it in her sling. When she got home she placed the mango in a basket for it was not yet ripe enough to be eaten. She then cooked some rice and some vegetables and ate. There was still some left in the saucepan. After eating she went to sleep. In the night the mango, which was really a man who had put on a mango 'cloak', got out of the basket. He took off the mango cloak and put it aside. He proceeded to finish up the rice and the vegetables that the girl had left in the saucepan. Having eaten, he smoked her tobacco and ate her betel nuts. Then he lay down next to the girl and went to sleep. In the early morning before the sun was up, the man arose and after putting on his mango cloak he returned to the basket. When she woke, the girl thought she would finish off the left-overs from the night before. She went to get them but when she opened the lid they had all gone. She could not understand what had happened, but she cooked herself some more before going out fishing.

In the evening she returned and having prepared and cooked the fish and some rice she went to sleep. There were left-overs of her meal which she planned to eat the following morning. When he saw that she was fast asleep, the mango man came out of his basket, took off his mango cloak and ate, smoked, and ate betel nuts as he had done the night before. Then he lay down next to the girl and went to sleep until just before daybreak, when he put on the mango cloak and returned to the basket. In the morning the girl found the empty saucepans. 'Are people about?' she asked herself when she saw this. She was baffled, but cooked some more and went out fishing again. She remembered the mango she had found and said to her squirrel, 'I have forgotten about the mango we found. I must remember to eat it. It should be ripe by now.' But when she got home in the evening with her day's catch she forgot all about the mango. She cooked and ate as she had on the previous nights, and when she was asleep the mango man emerged from his basket and ate the rest of the food. The same thing happened the following day and the day after. Then the girl decided to find out who was eating her food in the night. She went into the jungle and found *pangogn* leaves which resemble the *sirih* leaves eaten with betel nuts, but are poisonous. She then found some *hibol* fruit which look just like the betel nuts, but are also poisonous. She substituted these for the *sirih* leaves and betel nuts in the pouch in which she kept them, and having eaten she lay down pretending to go to sleep. After a while, the mango man emerged from the basket. He took off his mango cloak and placed it on the floor, then he went over to the saucepans. The girl watched what he was doing. 'The mango I forgot all about!' she said to herself. Then she crept up and took the mango cloak and destroyed it. When the man had eaten and smoked he took the betel nut pouch and ate the leaves and the fruit inside. No sooner did he chew it than he yelled out in pain, 'I have been poisoned!' He ran over to get his mango cloak, but could find it nowhere. 'My cloak, where is my cloak?' he exclaimed. Then the girl stood up and said, 'I have taken it. I don't want a mango man.' Then she blew magical smoke (*òz taba*) over him and said spells so that the effect of the poison was neutralized. The man became well again, and Bòngso gave him a real shirt instead of the mango one that she had destroyed. Then they slept together and became husband and wife.

MYTH 6

THE SPIDER MAN

A spider man (a man who had a spider 'cloak') lived with his aunt (older than his parents). One day he gave his aunt some bracelets, earrings, and sarongs saying that he wanted a wife. 'Aunt, take these things over to the house there and offer them to the unmarried girls.' The aunt went. She arrived at the house and the people were at home. 'Step inside, auntie', they told her. She was given tobacco and betel nut. Then the wife of the house cooked rice. When they had eaten the aunt extended her hand to the mother of the girls. 'What is it, auntie?' the mother wanted to know. The aunt gave her the things and said that her spider nephew wanted a wife. The girls did not want to marry a spider so the aunt went home. 'Well, aunt?' enquired the nephew. 'They did not want to marry a spider', said the aunt. So they went to sleep. The spider slept on the ladder which led from the cooking platform to the main part of the house.

The next morning the spider told his aunt, 'Aunt, take these things and go to the house over there.' 'I don't think that they will want to marry you', said the aunt. 'Go, aunt!' commanded the spider, so the aunt went. She entered the house and sat down. The people there gave her tobacco and betel nut. Then they cooked rice. When they had finished eating the aunt extended her hand to the old woman. 'What is it, auntie?' she wanted to know. The aunt gave the things and said that her nephew wanted a wife. 'We don't want to, we don't want to', said the girls, 'it will be so difficult to sleep together.' So the aunt went home. 'Well, aunt?' the nephew asked. 'They did not want to. Said it would be difficult to sleep together', said the aunt. They then went to sleep.

The next morning the nephew said to the aunt, 'Take these things and go over to the house over there.' 'No, I don't want to go. The girls do not want a spider for a husband', the aunt replied. 'Go, aunt!' the spider insisted. So the aunt went. When the aunt arrived at the house she was given tobacco and betel nut and then a meal of rice. After the meal the aunt extended her hand to the mother. 'What is it, aunt?' asked the mother. The aunt explained how her nephew wanted a wife. 'There are lots of male dogs on the ground underneath the house if that is what we are after', the girls replied. The aunt returned and told her nephew. They went to sleep. The nephew never ate rice or tapioca in his aunt's house. If he had she would have realized that he could become a human being.

The next day the same thing happened again. While the aunt was away the young girls from the houses she had already been to came to have a look at the spider. He sat on the ladder and looked back at them. None of them wanted him as husband.

The following day the aunt was sent on her errand again. When she arrived at the swidden, they had just finished making tapioca 'bread'. The mother was a very old woman and she had two unmarried daughters. They were sitting picking lice out of each other's hair when the aunt arrived. 'Enter the house, aunt', the old woman insisted. The aunt was given tobacco and betel nut and a meal of freshly baked tapioca 'bread'. When they had eaten, the aunt extended her hand to the mother and laid out the things explaining that her nephew wanted a wife. The two girls looked at the things. They wanted them and told the aunt that they would go back to the house with her. When they arrived the nephew said, 'Well, aunt?' And the aunt replied, 'These two girls have come to be your wives.' The women cooked rice and soup, and then ate betel nut. The spider did not eat. When the women had finished eating there was still some food left in the saucepans. The wives went to sleep on their mat, the spider sat on the ladder leading up to the next level. When the girls were fast asleep, the spider took off his spider 'cloak' and became a real man. He ate the rest of the rice and vegetable stew. Then he smoked tobacco and ate betel nut. He looked at his two wives. They were fast asleep. He lay down between them and made love to each one in turn. Then he went to sleep. When it began to get light he put on his spider cloak and settled down on the ladder. The wives woke up. 'There is still some food left over from last night', they said. They went over to look. 'No, it is finished. Who has eaten it?' they exclaimed. The aunt said she did not know as she had been asleep all night.

The wives wanted to go for a swim. The spider went as well. He walked between them. When the girls had finished bathing, the husband said that he wanted to bathe as well, but that he wanted to do so alone, and he told the wives to go home on their own. When they had disappeared he took off his spider cloak and put it on a stone. Then he went fishing. He caught lots and lots of fish and left it all by the riverside. Then he bathed, put on his spider cloak and returned home telling his wives that a friend of his had given him much fish and left it by the river. 'Go and fetch it', he told them. They did and cooked a large fish stew which they ate, leaving some in the pan, and then went to sleep. The spider waited until they were fast asleep. Then he took off his spider cloak and ate the rest of the fish stew, smoked tobacco and ate betel nut. Then, as he had done the night before, he lay down between the two wives, made love to them, and fell asleep. In the morning before it was light he put on his spider cloak again and settled on the ladder. In the morning the wives wanted to finish the stew from the evening before. They went to get it. 'Oh, it is finished', they exclaimed; 'who has eaten it?' The aunt did not know.

Later that day people came to have a look at the spider and his wives. 'Has he slept with you yet?' they wanted to know. 'No, we sleep separately', the wives replied. The wives cooked rice and the rest of the fish caught the day before and when the visitors had eaten they went home. The wives wanted to go bathing again so the husband went with them. When they had finished the spider told his wives to go home for he wanted to bathe on his own. He took off his cloak, went fishing, left the fish on the bank, put his spider cloak back on again, and went home to tell his wives that a friend had given him lots of fish for them to fetch. This they did. They then cooked a stew, ate, and went to sleep. The spider took off his cloak, finished off the meal, slept with his wives, and returned to his spider cloak in time not to be discovered. This happened every night until one day all the fish had been eaten. The wives said to their husband, 'There is no more fish.' They all went to the river to bathe, and as he had done before, the spider told his wives to go home on their own as he wanted to bathe alone. But instead of going home as they had been told to do, the wives hid behind a tree and watched the spider. They saw how he took off his spider cloak and became a real man. When he went to the river to fish they ran forward and took the spider cloak between their fingers and crumpled it up and scattered the pieces. When the husband returned after having placed a lot of fish on the river bank he could not find his spider cloak anywhere. 'Where is my cloak. My original spider's cloak?' he cried out. On hearing this the two wives leaped out from behind the tree and grabbed hold of his arms. They held one arm each. 'I want my cloak, where have you put it?' he demanded. 'No, we cannot sleep together when you have your spider cloak', the wives said. So the husband went back to the house as a real man and they all sat down together to have a big meal. After they had eaten they smoked tobacco and ate betel nut. At nightfall the husband lay down between his two wives.

MYTH 7

THE BAYÆZ* WOMAN

Once Bòngso went hunting. He caught a monitor lizard. He also found some *bayæz* fruit. He returned home with his catch and cooked the monitor lizard. The *bayæz* fruit, however, he placed on the shelf above the fire on the ground. He ate the monitor lizard but forgot all about the fruit. The next day he went hunting again. Suddenly he remembered the *bayæz* fruit he had found the day before. 'What did I do with the *bayæz* fruit?' he asked himself. 'Oh yes, I remember, I put it on the shelf above the fire.' But he was going on a long hunting trip and he did not return home to his house for more than a month. On his return, he cooked the meat he had caught and then lay down and went to sleep. When he woke the next morning he saw a woman lying next to him on the mat. 'Who are you?' he asked her. 'I am the *bayæz* fruit you left on the shelf above the fire some time ago', she replied. Bòngso and the *bayæz* woman became husband and wife and lived together.

Bòngso lived alone some distance from his parents. One day his mother decided to visit him. She walked to his house, but Bòngso had gone hunting. She sat on the ladder leading up to the house and looked inside. Then she

---

*Bayæz is a form of palm heart.

returned to her own house and told her husband, 'Our child has got a wife.'
She had seen a woman's loincloth inside Bòngso's house. The next day she
returned to Bòngso's house. She went very early in the morning and Bòngso
and his wife were still asleep when she arrived. She placed herself on the
ladder and asked her son, 'You have a wife, Bòngso?' 'No, I live on my
own,' lied Bòngso. 'I came here yesterday and saw a woman's loincloth
inside your house', insisted the mother. So Bòngso admitted that he did in
fact have a wife. 'Where did you meet her?' the mother wanted to know.
'Oh, I just met her in the jungle', replied Bòngso. He did not want his
mother to know that his wife was a *bayæz* fruit woman. The mother
returned to her husband, but after a while she went to live with Bòngso and
her daughter-in-law.

One day Bòngso was out hunting. The daughter-in-law was picking lice
out of her mother-in-law's hair. When she had finished, the mother-in-law
wanted to pick the lice out of the daughter-in-law's hair. 'I don't want you
to', she said. However, the mother-in-law insisted, 'You have picked my
lice, now it is my turn to pick yours.' So the girl let her do it. While she was
doing it she came across several thorns at the back of the girl's neck. 'You
have some thorns on your neck', she said to her daughter-in-law, 'I'll pull
them out.' The girl protested and said, 'No, no, don't do it.' But the
mother-in-law took no notice of the girl's protestations and pulled them out.
Immediately her daughter-in-law turned into a true *bayæz* fruit. She could
no longer be a woman.

When Bòngso returned that evening he had not caught any game. 'Where
is my wife?' he asked his mother. She told him, 'When I was picking lice out
of her hair I came across some thorns which I wanted to pull out. She would
not let me do it, but I did it anyway, and then she turned into that *bayæz* tree
over there.' When Bòngso heard this he turned into a *jòg* tree (another fruit
tree).

The mother returned to her husband. If she had not gone against her
daughter-in-law's wishes her son would not have turned into a *jòg* tree nor
her daughter-in-law into a *bayæz* tree.

MYTH 8

THE MAN WHO ATE TIGER-HOWAW

A man went hunting. He saw a *tobowad* monkey and shot it. It fell to the
ground. As it fell a fruit, *howaw*, also fell down. It did not have any thorns
however. The man put the *tobowad* and the *howaw* in his backbasket and
went home. When he reached home he handed the meat over to his wife and
told her how the fruit had also fallen from the tree. The wife cooked the
tobowad and they ate it. When they had finished eating, the man offered the
howaw to his youngest brother, Bòngso. Bòngso did not want it so the man
ate it himself. His body became very hot. He went down on the ground and
ran around to try to cool off. The wife became very annoyed with him and

hit him with some cooking tongs. The husband turned into a tiger and ran into the jungle. A tiger *ruwai* had entered the *howaw* fruit and this was why the fruit had no thorns.

They all went to sleep. In the middle of the night a *sinjae* (a species of cricket) spoke to Bòngso in his dream: 'The tiger, the tiger. It is coming, but it is still far away.' The next day they all left the house and ran away. In the evening they built a lean-to on the ground and ate the food they had brought with them. After they had eaten they went to sleep. In the night the *sinjae* again spoke to Bòngso; 'The tiger, the tiger. It is coming, but it is still far away.' Later in the night the *sinjae* said, 'It is near, it is near.' Bòngso woke the others who got up, wrapped a burning log in leaves so that they could see in the dark and started running. When it became day they stopped and built another lean-to (the tiger sleeps in the day-time). They went digging for various edible roots and after having eaten these they went to sleep. In the middle of the night the *sinjae* spoke again to Bòngso, 'The tiger, the tiger. It is still far away'. So they continued their sleep. But later it spoke urgently, 'It is near, it is near.' They got up quickly, wrapped a burning log in leaves as well as pieces of resin they had found, and started running. They arrived at the house of the mother and father of the man who had eaten the *howaw*. Here they stopped and told them what had happened.

They were given meat and cassava to eat and then everyone went to sleep. In the night the *sinjae* said to Bòngso, 'The tiger is still far away.' Later in the night it said, 'It is near, it is near', so Bòngso woke everyone, and they made torches and started to run into the jungle. When it became day they stopped and built lean-tos. They dug roots in the forest, ate, and in the evening they went to sleep. In the night the *sinjae* again warned Bòngso in his dreams; 'The tiger, the tiger, it is still far away', but later it told him 'It is near, it is near.' Everyone got up, made torches and ran. In the morning they arrived at the swidden of some friends. They were given meat and cassava to eat and they then told their friends what had happened. They slept at the house of the friends and in the night the *sinjae* said, 'The tiger is still far away.' Later in the night he spoke again saying, 'It is near, it is near.' Everybody got up, made torches, and ran away into the jungle. When it became day they stopped, built lean-tos, went searching for jungle roots which they ate together with the cassava they had brought with them, and in the evening they went to sleep. In the night the *sinjae* spoke to Bòngso, 'The tiger is still far away.' Later it spoke again, 'It is near, it is near.' They got up, made torches, and ran. The same thing happened the next day and the day after.

Eventually Bòngso returned to the place where they had last slept. Here he built a trap with double sets of spears on each side. The tiger came and went straight into the trap. All the four spears hit him and he died. Bòngso turned himself into a gibbon and carried the tiger back to the swidden. Then he returned to the others. They did not know that Bòngso had been away. In the early part of the night they heard the *sinjae* saying that the tiger was still far off, but after that they heard nothing. In the morning they said that since they had heard no warning from the *sinjae* that the tiger was near, they would return home. They were hungry and it was difficult to find wild roots. Bòngso did not tell them what he had done in the night. When they arrived at the swidden they saw the corpse of the tiger. They all sat down around the corpse and looked at it. Bòngso took some incense and blew the smoke at the head of the tiger. The head lifted slightly. Bòngso asked why he had wanted to eat them. 'I don't remember', said the tiger, 'all I wanted was meat. When I looked at you I only saw meat.' Then the head fell back. Bòngso blew once more. The head lifted. 'Why did you want to eat us?' asked Bòngso. 'I don't remember', answered the tiger, 'all I wanted was meat. When I looked at you I only saw meat.' Then the head fell down and he was dead.

The people all returned to their own swiddens where they ate a lot of cassava, plantains, and hill rice.

MYTH 9

TA' TATRAHOI

Once there was a child who wanted the moon to play with. The father cut a long bamboo and dug it into the ground. Then he started to climb. He climbed for three months, but was still a long way away from the moon. He climbed for six months then seven, but was still far away from the sky. It is very far away, our sky. After one year he finally reached the sky. He waited for the evening. It became dark and a full moon arrived. She saw the man. 'What do you want?' she asked him. 'Oh, I want you', said the man, 'my child wants you for a pet.' 'Disrespect!' (*tolah*) exclaimed the moon and she kicked at the bamboo stalk so that it and the man fell to the ground. He fell down into a land far away. As he fell on soil which had been newly turned over, for the people who lived there had just been digging tapioca, he was not killed. The people were 'original people' (*bi asal*). They looked at him. 'What has happened?' they enquired. 'Oh, I fell from the sky. My child wanted the moon for a pet and the moon kicked me', he said. The people gave him meat and tapioca to eat and when he had finished eating they asked, 'So, you have a child?' He replied, 'Yes, I have children and I have a wife.' He wanted to start for home and decided to follow the bamboo. The people tied a long string to one of his ankles so that he could return to them should he want to. They also gave him a basket full of meat. When he had finished all the meat he became very hungry and so he had to return to the people by following the string tied to his ankle. 'What do you want?' they asked when they saw him. 'My meat is all eaten', he said. 'What have you been eating since?' they wanted to know. 'I have been licking at my knife', he replied. They gave him more meat and he set off again. He had become, however, a *keòi* (*bas* that eat peoples' bodies). If he had not licked at his knife he would not have become a *keòi*.

As he came close to his own settlement, his meat again was finished, so he was hungry. When he reached his own house, his wife was cooking plantains. He wanted to put a plantain inside his wife's vagina and eat it from there. 'No, that is dirty,' (*kama*) objected his wife angrily. He really wanted to eat his wife's vulva. His eyes had become different. When he looked at human beings he only saw them as potential food.

They went to sleep and in the morning he told his wife that he wanted to go into the jungle to dig for *takad* (an edible tuber) and that he wanted his oldest child to accompany him. The two set off and when they reached a spot where he knew there was *takad*, he stopped and told his daughter to make a big fire so that they could cook the *takad* after he had dug it up. 'Bring lots of water also', he told her, 'I shall be very thirsty when I have finished digging.' She did as he told her and he went looking for *takad*. When he had collected enough, he cooked it and gave some to his daughter to eat. 'Eat well, I want to eat lots of stomach content later', he told her. 'What did you say, Father?' she asked. 'No, no, I said that you must eat fast and well. I want to go home to fondle your mother', he quickly corrected himself. When she had finished eating, he looked over her shoulder into the distance behind her. 'What are you looking at, Father?' she asked. 'I think there are some people coming', he replied. As she turned round to have a look, he pushed her over and stabbed her with the digging stick used for digging out the *takad*. 'Ouch, ouch, ouch, Father!' she cried, but she soon died and he drank all her blood. He took off her *sega* (waist-band) and necklace and hung them up on a branch a little way off. Then he cut her open and ate the content of her stomach and her intestines. The flesh he cut into small pieces and boiled in bamboo. When he had finished eating he plaited *riding* and hung them on branches nearby. Towards evening he wrapped the rest of the flesh in leaves and put it in his backbasket. He also wrapped the rest of the *takad* separately, put them in his basket as well, and set off for home. 'Where is the child?' asked his wife when he came home alone. 'We met grandmother in the forest and the girl went home with her to spend a few days in her settlement', he lied. He then gave her the wrapped *takad* telling her to eat it all saying that he had already eaten a lot and was full. 'This', he said indicating the wrapped flesh, 'is some herbal roots which I am going to take for my toothache.' After the wife had eaten they went to bed, and as soon as the wife was fast asleep he got up and ate the rest of the flesh.

The next morning he told his wife that he wanted to go and dig for more *takad*. He took with him another of his children. When they reached the spot where he had eaten his daughter the day before, he pointed to the *riding* and told the child, 'These your grandmother and aunt made yesterday. They said they might return today, so you had better go and make a big fire and collect a lot of water so that we can give them cooked *takad* to eat and water to drink when they arrive.' She did as he told her and he brought a lot of *takad* which he gave her to cook. After a while she said, 'The *takad* is cooked, Father.

When is Grandmother coming?' He looked behind her. 'What are you looking at, Father? Is that Grandmother coming?' She turned round to have a look. He pushed her over and stabbed her with the digging stick. He drank the blood. Then he took her *sega* and necklace and hung them up with those of the other daughter. He cut her up and ate the stomach and the intestines raw. The rest of the body he cooked in bamboo. Then he plaited *riding* as he had the previous day and threw away the old ones which were beginning to wither, and hung the newly-made ones up instead. He wrapped the flesh and the *takad* as he had the day before and set off for home. 'Where is the child?' asked his wife when she saw him returning without her. 'Oh, we met Aunt in the forest and the girl wanted to go back with her as her sister had done', he again lied. He gave her the *takad* saying that his parcel contained medicine for toothache, and after the wife had gone to sleep he ate the rest of his daughter.

On the following days he killed all his remaining children, each night telling his wife that they had gone after their brothers and sisters to the grandmother's settlement. When he came home after the seventh and last child had been consumed, his wife gave birth in the night. He took the afterbirth with the navel string attached and told his wife he would wrap it in a mat and leave it out in a tree as is the practice, but instead he took it outside and ate it all. Then he went to the area underneath the house and licked all the blood which had fallen down through the split bamboo floor. The next day the wife said she wanted to go to her mother's and see all her children. Her husband pretended to want to do the same. 'You go on ahead', he told her. 'No, I don't know the way', she objected. 'Yes you do, just follow the path over there', he insisted. So she started off. When she reached the spot where he had killed and eaten all their children, she discovered the *sega* and necklaces of her daughters, and she knew that he had eaten them. She ran and hid in a tree, but in her hurry she forgot her baby. When the husband arrived and saw the baby abandoned he realized that his wife had guessed. He took the baby, put it on a skewer and roasted it in the fire. After having eaten it he went looking for his wife. He discovered her sitting up in a tree. 'Ah, I'll go and fetch my blowpipe', he said to himself. He brought the blowpipe and shot at his wife, but he did not hit her. Then he made a large fire at the stem of the tree in order to smoke her out. He climbed up to get her, but as he was very near she threw her knife at him and he lost his balance and fell into the fire where he was burned to death. The wife called out, 'Become flying lemur! You who eat humans!' He became a flying lemur ghost (*yinlugen*).

MYTH 10

BÒNGSO AND THE ELEPHANT WOMAN

Once an elephant arrived at Bòngso's fields. The elephant ate his bananas. When Bòngso saw him he threw his spear at him and it hit him in the flank.

The elephant ran away with the spear still stuck in his body. Bòngso did not want to lose his spear so he ran after the elephant. He followed the trail of blood that the elephant left behind. He went for several days, walking during the day and sleeping in the jungle at night. In those days there was still a path to the land of the elephants. Their land is called Moöden. After three days and nights he arrived at Moöden. He came to a house which he entered. It was not the house of the elephant which he had speared, but that of other elephants. In their own land the elephants take off their elephant 'cloaks' and become people. The elephants gave Bòngso food, and in the evening they sat about chatting. The elephants told Bòngso about Ta', an old man, who was very sick. He just wanted to die, but no one could understand what was the matter with him. The elephants wanted to go to Ta's house to see how he was getting on. Bòngso also went. He saw his spear in the old man's flank and there was a deep wound. The elephants could not see the spear, the wound, or the blood. Only Bòngso saw it. It is the same way with us when a *bas* has thrown its spear at us. We cannot see it, we only feel very ill. Bòngso said healing spells and threw away the poison from the wound. The next day he went and found a long piece of bamboo, the same length as the spear in the elephant's side. In the evening he returned to Ta's house bringing the bamboo with him. He entered the house and said his spells. Then he placed the bamboo over the spear and pulled it out keeping it inside the bamboo so that nobody could see it. He took the spear in the bamboo and put it on the ground hidden in the undergrowth. For Bòngso just to look at the wound was sufficient for it to start to heal. Ta' quickly recovered. When the three days of *pantang* following the healing rite was over, he asked what had happened. The people told him that Bòngso had cured him. When he heard that, Ta' wanted to meet Bòngso, and the people went to collect him from the house where he was staying. Bòngso told Ta' how he had thrown a spear at him, and how he had taken it out again. 'You are a good man', said Ta', 'I want to give you my two daughters for wives.' Bòngso accepted and there was a big wedding feast. After a while, however, Bòngso became homesick, and he set out for his own settlement. His two wives accompanied him. On the way they slept in the jungle underneath a very large tree. The wives were frightened that it might break and fall on them. 'No, no, it won't fall', said Bòngso, but the wives would not listen. They gathered together their belongings, put on their elephant cloaks and returned to their own land. Bòngso went to his mother's house, 'I have got wives, mother', he told her, 'but they have returned home.' 'Oh!' exclaimed his mother.

When the two girls reached their father's house, their father was very angry with them for leaving their husband. 'But we were frightened that the tree would break', they told him.

After a while Bòngso missed his wives very much and he set out with his mother to go to Moöden. When he arrived back, the wives were glad to see him and they gave him an elephant cloak for wearing outside. Whenever we meet an elephant that is not frightened of humans, it is Bòngso we have met.

MYTH 11

TIGER TALAIDEN
A man went hunting with his blowpipe. He shot a *boweig* monkey, a siamang, and a binturong. He put all three animals in his backbasket and went home. On the way home he saw a tiger. When he arrived at the swidden he gave the meat to his wife to cook. They ate all the three meats, but his uncle (older than parent) who was a *putao* would not eat the binturong together with the siamang. He was afraid of tiger *talaiden*. In the night they all climbed trees to sleep. They were frightened that the tiger might come.

The nephew brought his blowpipe with him up into his tree. During the night he kicked it and it fell to the ground. 'I am going down for my blowpipe', he told his wife. 'Oh, but what about the tiger?' said she. He took no notice of this and climbed down. Just before he reached the ground he felt something scratch his legs. 'Hey, there are lots of thorns here', he shouted to his wife, but it was the claws of the tiger waiting for him at the bottom of the tree. The tiger bit the man in the throat and he died. 'I'll sleep in the house over there for the rest of the night', called out the tiger to the wife, pretending to be the husband. The tiger ate the body and the blood of the man, but he did not eat the head. He then tried to climb the tree in which the uncle was sleeping, but he could not do so for the uncle had placed a knife in the trunk, and said spells over it so that the tiger could not pass.

The next day the uncle went hunting. He shot *boweig* monkey, *tayog* monkey, and squirrel. The head of his nephew's ghost followed him all the way. It wanted to seize his uncle's *ruwai*, but he could not take it for the uncle had said spells.

In the evening the uncle went home. The head of his nephew's ghost followed him. The uncle plaited headbands and *riding*. They made *nöpoh* for seven nights because they wanted to expel the ghost. After seven nights the ghost vanished.

MYTH 12

TIGER TALAIDEN
Two sisters went to catch long-tailed giant rats in the jungle. (Only women can catch these.) The younger sister caught one. She wrapped it in *klawògen* leaf. To do so is tiger *talaiden*. Having done this they returned to their house in the hollow of a tall tree. The younger girl cut long strips of rattan and built spear-traps around the tree and carried the extension of each trap into the house. They waited. In the evening a tiger came. They waited until it came very close and was underneath one of the traps when the younger sister cut

the rattan and the spear fell down piercing the tiger. The girls climbed down and they looked at the corpse. Then they cut off the tail; this they would eat. In those days people still ate tigers. Then they went to sleep. The next morning they went to their mother's house. 'There is some "binturong" meat', they told her. The mother knew that they meant tiger, and as she liked eating tiger very much she went off with her backbasket to collect the carcass. The girls only wanted the tail, the rest of the body they left for their mother.

The two sisters went hunting for long-tailed giant rats again. Having caught one they wrapped it in *klawògen* leaf and went home to their tree house. They collected rattan and made traps all around the tree. This time they did not use spears, but made loop traps. In the evening the tiger came. They waited until it was right underneath one of the traps, then they cut the line and the loop fell over the tiger's head and strangled it. They climbed down and cut off the tail which was all they wanted to have. They cooked the tail, ate it and went to sleep. The next morning they went to their mother's house. 'There is "binturong" meat today also', they told her. The mother was very pleased. She went to collect the carcass.

The next day they went to collect *tiri*, a root which if applied to the body makes one itch very badly. They found some and put it in a bamboo. To do so is also tiger *talaiden*. Then they went home to their real house, not the one in the tree. They made traps all around the house and another one just by the ladder to the house. The ends of all the traps they brought into the house. Then they waited. In the evening the tiger came. By chance it avoided all the outlying traps and it reached the house. It put its front paws on the ladder and was about to enter the house when the girls cut the rattan for the trap by the ladder, and the loop fell over the tiger's front legs. The girls then took the *tiri* and wiped it thickly over the tiger's hind parts. The older sister rubbed *tiri* and the younger sister rubbed *tiri*, and finally the tiger died from itching. The girls cut off the tail for themselves and gave the rest to their mother.

The next day after having told their mother about the meat they said to everybody, 'We are going "binturong" hunting today.' They set off and gathered some more *tiri* which again they put in the bamboo. This time they went to the tree house, but the younger sister was feeling lazy about making rattan traps and instead made a hole in the door to the entrance of the tree house. This they suspended above the entrance, then they climbed higher and sat waiting on a branch. In the evening the tiger came. He climbed up to their house and entered. They let the door fall down and the tiger was caught inside with its tail protruding through the hole. The girls pulled at the tail and rubbed it with *tiri*. The older sister took *tiri* out of the bamboo and rubbed it along the whole length of the tail, and the younger sister did the same. Finally the tiger died from the itching. They then cut off the tail and ate it.

(The rest of the story was not known.)

MYTH 13

TIGER PUNÉN

A man went hunting with his blowpipe. He shot a *tobowad* monkey which he placed in his backbasket. Then he found some *pre* fruit. These he put in his tobacco pouch which he pushed down the front of his loincloth. He returned home to the swidden where he gave the *tobowad* to his two wives (sisters) and his parents-in-law, but he did not tell them that he had found any *pre* fruit. They all ate the meat with tapioca and rice and the parents-in-law went to sleep immediately afterwards. The man shared his fruit with his wives and only the three of them ate it. Not to share fruit is tiger *punén*.

The next day he went hunting again. He returned to the same spot where he had shot the *tobowad* monkey the day before. Here he shot another one. Then he went to the *pre* fruit tree and knocked a lot down with a long stick. Again he put the fruit in his tobacco pouch which he put down the front of his loincloth. He went home, gave the *tobowad* to his wives and mother-in-law and told them 'I cannot find any *pre* fruit.' The women cooked the meat which they all ate. The parents-in-law went to sleep and the man shared his *pre* fruit with his wives only.

A few days later the man and his two wives went on a hunting expedition. They made a lean-to on the ground, and were going to spend a few nights in the jungle. The husband went off with his blowpipe while the wives stayed behind. He shot a squirrel. It fell to the ground and he wrapped it with leaves, *hali klawògen* (to wrap a squirrel in *hali klawògen* is tiger *talaiden*). As he bent over to place the wrapped meat in his backbasket a tiger came upon him from behind and bit him in the neck.

The tiger took the man's tobacco pouch and went to the lean-to where the wives were waiting for their husband to return. The tiger threw the tobacco pouch from a distance. There was some blood on it. 'What is this blood?' asked the wives. 'It is some blood from a *boweig* monkey', replied the tiger. The wives could not see the tiger, they thought it was their husband speaking. Then the tiger went and collected the man's blowpipe and quiver. He threw the blowpipe to the wives. It broke. He also threw the quiver which split open. There was some blood on the quiver. 'What is this blood?' asked the wives. 'That is blood from a *boweig* monkey', replied the tiger. The tiger went to the dead man and bit off his penis, brought it back to the wives and threw it to them from a distance. 'Whose penis is that?' the wives wanted to know. 'That is the *boweig* monkey's penis', replied the tiger. He went and tore out the man's stomach and threw that as well. The wives now realized that a tiger had killed their husband and they ran over to a tall tree and climbed up it.

In the morning the wives heard siamang chatter in the distance. They also heard gibbons and *boweig* monkeys. 'I am going hunting', said the tiger, 'I'll be back in the evening.' The tiger went off in the direction of where they heard the siamang, gibbon, and *boweig* monkey. The wives climbed down from the tree and ran as fast as they could towards the swidden. They stumbled and fell. When the older sister fell the younger one stepped over her, and when the younger sister fell the elder stepped over her. When they reached the swidden they told their mother 'A tiger has killed our husband.' They explained how they had committed *punén* by not sharing the *pre* fruit. They all ate and then went to sleep.

The next day the father-in-law built a spear-trap on the path to the swidden. In the night the tiger came but the spears did not hit him. He killed a domestic pig, but he only ate the blood. The following day the father-in-law built a trap right next to the ladder leading up to the house. He dug a hole in the ground and placed many spears at the bottom of the pit with the pointed ends upwards. He covered it with leaves. In the night the tiger came carrying the corpse of the husband in his mouth. He carried him by the neck where he had first bitten him. The tiger fell into the prepared trap, on top of all the spears, and the father-in-law came out of the house where he had been waiting, and finished him off.

The next day they buried the two corpses. The tiger was buried on one side of a tree and the husband on the other. (There must be a division between the two graves.)

MYTH 14

TIGER PUNÉN

A man went hunting with his son, Hadd, while the people in the settlement were preparing *payòng* nuts. They came across a *tobowad* monkey and the father shot at it. It fell to the ground. Later he shot two more. Hadd meanwhile was digging for *takad* tubers. When he saw the *tobowad* he said to his father, 'We'll be eating meat with *payòng* this evening.' 'Watch what you are saying', said the father angrily, 'it is tiger *punén* to say that. It is to speak badly.' The father then climbed a tree to get firewood so that they could burn off the *tobowad*'s fur before bringing it home. There was lots of firewood on the ground, but he wanted to collect it from the tree tops. Hadd saw something move in the undergrowth. 'There is something moving over there!' he shouted to his father who climbed down to have a look. It was a tiger, but when it saw the father it moved away and he could not see anything. 'Maybe it is a tiger', he said to Hadd. 'Oh, no', said Hadd, so the father climbed up again for more firewood. The tiger moved closer. 'Father, there is something moving around here!' shouted Hadd, and the father climbed down to have a look, but he could see nothing. After they had burned off the three monkeys they set off for home. The father walked in front carrying the *tobowad* in his backbasket, and Hadd followed carrying the *takad* roots in his basket. A bird spoke in the distance. 'Maybe that is a tiger', said the father as a joke. The tiger, however, was following behind Hadd.

They reached a river. The father crossed it, but as Hadd was about to do so, the tiger leaped out and bit him at the back of the neck. The father turned back quickly and caught Hadd as he was falling, and when the tiger saw this it ran away. The father carried Hadd on his back and the tiger followed the trail of blood. They came to another river. When he had crossed it, the father hid behind some bushes and waited. When the tiger arrived, the father shot ten poisoned darts at it, then he picked up Hadd and ran home. He did not wait to see if the tiger was killed by the poison. When he reached home, Hadd's sisters who had been preparing the *payòng* nuts asked what had happened. 'Oh, he spoke badly', said the father, 'and the tiger came and bit him.' In the evening Hadd died. A man from the settlement went to see if the darts that the father had shot had hit the tiger. When he came to the river he found the corpse of the tiger lying there.

MYTH 15

THE GOLL-TREE GHOST (PUNÉN)

A man made a small clearing in the jungle in order to plant tobacco there. To do so he had to burn down a very large *goll*-tree. This tobacco field was some distance from his own settlement. After some days he told everyone 'I am going to get some of the tobacco leaves from my new field.' To say that one is going to collect tobacco from a distant field is *punén*.

When he reached the field he saw that the *goll*-tree was still smouldering. He looked closely and in the smoke he saw the ghost of the *goll*-tree. This ghost became a deer. The man took to his heels. After he had run for a while he came to a different settlement. The people there were clearing a new field. 'What's up?' they enquired when they saw him. 'I am running away from the *goll*-tree ghost which has turned itself into a deer', he told them. He sat down to rest a little when the deer came after him. The people tried to kill it with their bush-knives, but although they cut at it this did not hurt it, so the man got up and ran away. After a while he came to another settlement. Here the people were clearing an old field in order to plant afresh. 'What's the matter?' they asked when they saw him. 'I am running away from the *goll*-tree ghost. I spoke badly and said I was going to get tobacco, and now the *goll*-tree ghost which has become a deer is after me,' explained the man. The people there gave him a loincloth for the old one had been torn off in his flight. They also gave him some food. While they were eating, the deer arrived. The people tried to kill it with spears, but it had no effect, and the man ran on. After a while he came to yet another settlement. The people were burning off a new field. 'What's up?' they asked when they saw him. 'Oh, I am running away from the *goll*-tree ghost which is after me. There is *punén*. The ghost has turned itself into a deer', he said. The people gave him a pair of shorts, for the loincloth he had been given earlier had been torn into shreds during his flight. They all sat down to smoke when the deer arrived. The people tried to kill it with their knives and spears, but it did not die and the man ran on. After a while he arrived at Bòngso's settlement. 'What is the matter with you?' asked Bòngso when he saw him. The man told him what had happened; and when the deer arrived, Bòngso poured water over it and extinguished it. Bòngso knew that the only way to kill the *goll*-tree ghost was to pour water over it.

MYTH 16

YA' POPAG

Ya' Popag, who was a *nlab* (*bas* who eat people's bodies as opposed to their *ruwai*) lived alone in her house in a large field where she had planted lots of rice. A man from another settlement went out hunting one day when he passed Ya' Popag's house. 'Come over here, grandchild, rest a little', she called out to him. He entered her house. Ya' Popag gave him some betel nut to eat. These betel nuts, however, were poisonous and the man fell asleep. He lay flat out on his back. Ya' Popag went up to him and asked, 'Are you asleep, grandchild?' He did not reply. She then took her knife and slit his throat. She drank his blood and ate his body. Then she took his blowpipe, his quiver, and the bones, and brought them over to the house of a young girl nearby. Ya' Popag had already eaten the girl's mother, but the girl herself—she was Bòngso (and therefore *putao*)—made herself very, very small so that Ya' Popag did not want to eat her. She thought there would be no blood in her and no meat on her bones. The girl was tiny only in the daytime when she might be visited by Ya' Popag. In the evening she became normal again.

The man's brother went hunting as well. He also came across Ya' Popag's house, and she called out to him to enter her house and have a rest. When they had eaten she gave him some of the poisonous betel nut, and when he fell asleep, she cut his throat, drank his blood and ate his body. Then she placed his blowpipe, quiver, and bones in the young girl's house. After a few days yet another brother came to Ya' Popag's house, and the same thing happened. The following day Bòngso went out looking for his brothers. He arrived at the house of the young girl. There he saw his brothers' blowpipes and quivers. 'Ya' Popag has eaten all your brothers', the girl told him. He then walked over to Ya' Popag's house. 'Is that you, my grandchild?' she called out when she saw him. 'It is I, Granny', he replied. 'Come in and rest a little and have something to eat', she said. 'No, I am staying over there', he replied, pointing towards the girl's house. He did not want to eat human flesh. To do so would be dirty (*kama*). The following morning he returned to Ya' Popag's house. 'Let us go and harvest your rice, Granny', he said, 'I can see that it is ripe.' 'Not today, grandchild, it is too hot. Come inside the house for a bit', she answered. 'No, come on', he insisted, 'grandmother and grandchild working together won't notice the heat.' So they went. As the sun got higher in the sky, Ya' Popag complained of the heat. 'Let us go home, grandchild', she said. 'No, no, Granny, when grandmother and her grandchild work together they don't notice the heat', he replied. They worked on and it was very hot. Every so often Ya' Popag wanted to go home, but Bòngso would not let her. She did not want to oppose him as she intended to kill and eat him later. When the sun began to set, Bòngso said, 'Let us go bathing, Granny.' They went to the river, but by this time it was almost evening, and Ya' Popag said, 'It is too cold to bathe now, grandchild.' 'No, it is not. In you go', he told her. She jumped in. 'Oh, it is cold', she exclaimed and wanted to get out straight away. 'No, not yet Granny,' said Bòngso, 'stay in a bit longer. You will feel very good afterwards.' When Ya' Popag finally was allowed to get out of the water she was shivering with cold. 'I'll run on ahead and build you a fire so that you can warm yourself', Bòngso told her. He made a large fire on the ground underneath the ladder leading up to Ya' Popag's house, and when she arrived she leant against the ladder to warm herself. She was shivering. After a while Bòngso told her to enter the house. She started climbing up the ladder. She had to do it on all fours. She was so exhausted after the day's work and her trials. When she was halfway up, the ladder collapsed into the fire and Ya' Popag was burned to death. (The only way to kill *nlab* is to use fire.)

Bòngso then went over to the girl's house. He took the bones of his three brothers and washed them. Then he laid them out on the ground and blew magical smoke over them and on top of their heads. Three times he did this and they became alive again. 'Oh, dear, we have been sleeping in the day time', they exclaimed, 'it was very nice.' 'Nice indeed!' replied Bòngso, 'you have been killed and eaten by Ya' Popag.' He then told them all that had happened. In the night Bòngso and the girl slept together and they became husband and wife. The next day they all returned to their mother's house. 'You have been out hunting for a long time', said she when she saw them. 'No, they were killed and eaten by Ya' Popag', said Bòngso, 'I took their bones and made them alive again.' 'Oh', said the mother, 'where is Ya' Popag now?' 'I have killed her with fire', Bòngso told her. After a few days, when the three brothers were strong again, they all returned to Ya' Popag's field. They did not want the rice that was still there. They threw away the roof, floor, and beams of her house and built a new one for themselves to live in.

MYTH 17

THE DOG MAN

A long, long time ago there were still dog people. A man (dog man) and his brother-in-law went hunting with their blowpipes. They came across a *boweig* monkey and shot it. It fell dead to the ground. They left it on a stone and went further. They found a *tobowad* monkey which they also shot. This they took back to the place where they had left the *boweig* monkey, and they made a fire in order to cook some of the meat. The man took out the stomachs of the animals and placed them on a leaf. He then wiped the meat with some leaves. 'Do you want to eat it, brother-in-law?' asked the man. 'No, that's dirty', replied the brother-in-law. They cooked and ate a little of the meat, put the rest in their backbaskets and set off for home. Half way, the man exclaimed, 'Oh, brother-in-law.' 'What, brother-in-law?' asked the other. 'I have forgotten my knife', said the man. Before he said this he had hidden the knife in his loincloth. 'Go back and get it, brother-in-law', said the other. Meanwhile he brought the monkeys home and gave them to his wife to cook. She cooked the meat and she cooked tapioca. 'Brother-in-law is very late', she said. Finally the man turned up saying that he had not found his knife at first as it was lying underneath some leaves. Everybody ate and then went to sleep.

For the next four days the same thing happened except that each time the man gave a different reason for being late back. He said that his knife had fallen underneath a stone, that there were lots of mosquitoes which made searching very difficult, that the stone had fallen into the river, and that he had forgotten where he had left it.

On the seventh day the younger brother of the brother-in-law joined the two men on the hunt. When the man said that he had forgotten his knife and went back to look for it, the other man told his brother, 'You go home with the meat. I want to follow brother-in-law to see what he does.' He went after the man and saw that he returned to where they had gutted the animals. Here he ate the stomachs and licked the blood off the leaves. The other man went home and told everyone what he had seen. When the man arrived home his wife was angry with him for being late. 'I met a tiger which was eating a pig it had killed, and it followed after me', lied the man. The wife told him what her brother had seen. The husband and wife quarrelled. The man hit his wife and killed her. He then bit off a piece of her flesh and ate it.

The next day the wife's father came to the house. He knew what had happened. He was a great *putao*. He took the corpse of his daughter and touched her on the shin, toes, and head. Then he blew 'magical' smoke (*öz taba*) through his right hand onto the corpse seven times. She became alive. He then took his spear and hit his son-in-law in the chest. The son-in-law died. The father placed the corpse inside the house and set fire to it. The corpse of the son-in-law burned up and became ashes. This was the end of dog people. From now on they were true dogs only.

MYTH 18

THE STAR THAT MARRIED BÒNGSO

Once a star came down from the sky. She went to Bòngso's house. They slept together and became man and wife. The next day Bòngso went hunting. His wife wanted binturong. He shot one and brought it home, where the wife cooked and ate it. The following day he went hunting again and this time his wife accompanied him. They passed a rotten tree full of maggots. The wife asked Bòngso to kill the maggots, but he said that to eat maggots is dirty (*kama*) and he would not touch them. The wife caught the maggots, built a fire, and roasted them. Then she ate the maggot fat. Bòngso would not eat any. In the evening they returned home, and went to sleep. In the night the wife became very hot. She went to sit in the doorway. 'Oh my body is so hot', she complained. She went down on the ground and ran around. Bòngso followed her. 'You must burn down the house', she told Bòngso. Since he wanted to help her, he set fire to his house. The wife went into the smoke. He could see her above the house in the smoke. 'I do not want you, and you do not want me', she said to Bòngso, and then she returned home to the sky using the smoke as her path.

Appendix 2
Funeral Song

Raw raw, di raw
Chabogn di chabogn
Kisare, berelig, kisare
Kisare nilagen chabogn
Berelig, chib daí, kisare
Pampong blihai laga pampòng laga
Laga bayang
Laga di mandi
Laga di ranchogn
Bukan saja di mayin
Kisare di la rugn la bajo
Kisare di la rugn la porung
Linga di bowang
Kawan ramai
Ohalowai!
Rioh, rioh
Sama rioh rinchaw, niniow
Di balai niniow di ninen
Ninen a balai

Hoawhowai!
Le bog morelogn
Saja bremon, saja kawan
Kawan guru kenell buwang la bajo
Kisare la bajo la rung
Hankad

Translation
Pull hard, pull hard
(at the) *chabogn* tree
Shake, turn over
Shake one side of the *chabogn* tree
Turn over, come here, shake
Pampong fruit split open, water
Water shadow
Water bathing
Water splash about
Not just make a noise
Shake the body, the cloak
Shake the body, the frame
Linger (in the house) the throwing off[1]
Ramai fruit friends[2]
Hey, ho!
Noise, noise
Together noise of much talking
In the house much talking, rowdiness
Rowdiness in the house[3]
Hey, ho!
The (small) container is full (but it is nice to bathe)[4]
Just drum and say the expelling spells, just friend
Friend teacher,[5] watch the throwing off of the cloak
Shake the body, shake the cloak
Move.

[1] This refers to the *putao* sending out his *ruwai* and 'throwing off' his body when he goes in a trance to accompany the *yinlugen* to Pulao Klam.

[2] One type of *bi hali* who have come to witness and help.

[3] The rowdiness of dancing and shaking. This is unusual Chewong behaviour, in fact only indulged in at times of funerals to frighten the *yinlugen* to abandon the living.

[4] This refers to the *putao*'s container of dew obtained from his spirit-guides.

[5] The dead *putao* of the past (*bi inhar*) also come to watch the event. They are often referred to in the songs as *guru*, Malay for teacher (from the Sanskrit).

Appendix 3
Computer Analysis

LIST OF FORTY ELEMENTS USED IN THE COMPUTER ANALYSIS

1	Horseshoe bat	21	Bamboo rat
2	Flying fox	22	Frog
3	Fruit bat	23	Wild fowl
4	Scaly ant-eater	24	Long-tailed porcupine
5	Binturong	25	Common porcupine
6	Squirrel	26	Dusty leaf-monkey
7	Banded leaf-monkey	27	Long-tailed macaque
8	Monitor lizard (water)	28	Flying squirrel
9	Monitor lizard (land)	29	Slow loris
10	Pig	30	Small mousedeer
11	Tortoise	31	Barking deer
12	Mountain tortoise	32	Sambar deer
13	Gibbon	33	*Tichub* bird
14	Hornbill	34	Tiger
15	River turtle	35	Mouse
16	Fish	36	Toad
17	Siamang	37	Elephant
18	Flying lemur	38	Shrews
19	Otter	39	Leech
20	Pig-tailed macaque	40	Worms

LIST OF TWENTY-FIVE CONSTRUCTS USED IN THE COMPUTER ANALYSIS

1	*Ruwai*	14	Habitat: land
2	People in the past	15	Habitat: water
3	*Yinlugen*	16	Habitat: mixed
4	Domestic fire	17	Blowpiped
5	*Tika*	18	Fur
6	*Talaiden* (tiger)	19	Feather
7	*Talaiden* (elephant)	20	Scales
8	*Tolæg*	21	Other
9	*Pantang* (pregnancy)	22	'Mammals'
10	Idiosyncratic rules	23	Nocturnal
11	Sympathetic signatures	24	Edible
12	Habitat: trees	25	Day and night movement
13	Habitat: air		

Appendix 4
Percentage of Total Variance Accounted for by Principal Components

Component	Root	As Per Cent
1	5.2552	21.02
2	3.9719	15.89
3	2.9257	11.70
4	2.2645	9.06
5	1.9063	7.63
6	1.5467	6.19
7	1.2575	5.03
8	1.0655	4.26
9	0.9014	3.61
10	0.7226	2.89
11	0.7082	2.83
12	0.5440	2.18
13	0.4637	1.85
14	0.3318	1.33
15	0.2592	1.04
16	0.2408	0.96
17	0.1853	0.74
18	0.1428	0.57
19	0.1038	0.42
20	0.0757	0.30
21	0.0574	0.23
22	0.0384	0.15
23	0.0264	0.11
24	0.0052	0.02
25	0.0000	0.00

The component space is limited to twenty-five dimensions.

CONCLUSIONS FROM THE ANALYSIS

1. Of the twenty-five components, no fewer than twenty-three were identified as significant on the basis of the Bartlett test.

2. The first principal component accounted for only 21.02 per cent of the total variance, and the first three principal components for only 58.61 per cent.

Child (1970), one of the authorities of principal components analysis and factor analysis, would regard this figure of 58 per cent as being rather low. Typically in an analysis of the kind we have performed one would expect a greater proportion of percentage of the variance to be explained by the first three components and, correspondingly, one would expect fewer significant components. The fact that in this analysis we find both a low percentage variance accounted for by the first three components, as well as a large number of significant components, shows that the correlations—in other words, the relationships—between the attributes is extremely weak, from which we may conclude either (1) that there is no overall structure in the domain (2) that there is overall structure but not in relation to these attributes (3) there is a structure within sub-sets of the domain, but not overall. We may dismiss the second of these conclusions on the basis of there being no other attributes to consider, and the third conclusion because my own analysis by hand showed this not to be the case.

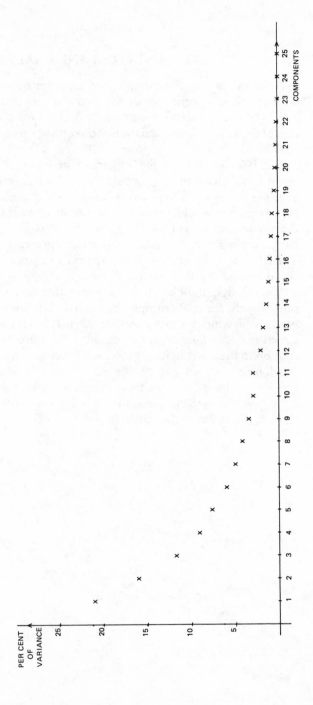

Graph 1
Percentage of Total Variance Accounted for by
Principal Components

Graph 2
Loadings of Elements (Animals) and Constructs (Attributes): Components 1 and 2

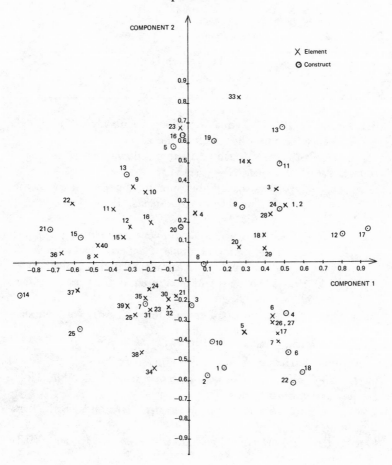

Bibliography

BENJAMIN, G. (1967), 'Temiar Religion', Cambridge, Cambridge University. Unpublished doctoral thesis.

―――― (1968), 'Temiar Personal Names', *Bijdragen Tot de Taal-, Land-, en Volkenkunde*, 124: 99–134.

―――― (1976), 'Austroasiatic Subgroupings and Prehistory in the Malay Peninsula', in *Austroasiatic Studies*, P. N. Jenner (ed.), Hawaii, University of Hawaii Press.

―――― (1980), *Semang, Senoi, Malay: Culture, History, Kinship and Consciousness in the Malay Peninsula*, Canberra, Department of Prehistory and Anthropology, Australian National University.

BLOCH, M. (1977), 'The Past and the Present in the Present', *Man*, 12: 278–92.

BLUNT, R. (1981), 'Linguistic Evidence for some early Austronesian Taboos', *American Anthropologist*, 83: 285–319.

CAREY, I. (1976), *Orang Asli; the Aboriginal Tribes of Peninsular Malaysia*, Kuala Lumpur, Oxford University Press.

CHILD, D. (1970), *The Essentials of Factor Analysis*, London, Holt, Rinehart and Winston.

COON, C. S. (1976), *The Hunting Peoples*, Harmondsworth, Penguin Books.

COOTE, E. (1976), *Malay–English, English–Malay Dictionary*, Kuala Lumpur, Macmillan.

COUILLARD, M. A. (1977), *A Jah Hut Community and its Wood Carvings*, Kuala Lumpur, Conference on Orang Asli.

―――― (1980), *Tradition in Tension: Carvings in a Jah Hut Community*, Penang, Penerbit Universiti Sains Malaysia.

DE COPPET, D. (1981), 'The Life-giving Death', in *Mortality and Immortality*, F. C. Humphreys and H. King (eds.), London, Academic Press.

DENTAN, R. K. (1967), 'The Mammalian Taxonomy of the Sen'oi

Semai', *Malayan Nature Journal*, 20: 100—6.

_____ (1968), *The Semai: a non-violent people of Malaya*, New York, Holt, Rinehart and Winston.

_____ (1978), 'Notes on Childhood in a Nonviolent Context: The Semai Case (Malaysia)', in *Learning Non-Aggression*, A. Montagu (ed.), Oxford, Oxford University Press.

DIFFLOTH, C. F. (1974), 'Austroasiatic Languages', in *Encyclopedia Britannica Macropedia*, Chicago, Encyclopedia Britannica, Inc.

_____ (1977), *Aslian Languages and Southeast Asian Prehistory*, Kuala Lumpur, Conference on Orang Asli.

DOUGLAS, M. T. (1966), *Purity and Danger, an analysis of the concept of pollution and taboo*, London, Routledge and Kegan Paul.

DURKHEIM, E. (1915), *The Elementary Forms of the Religious Life: A Study in Religious Sociology*, London, Allen and Unwin.

_____ AND MAUSS, M. (1963), *Primitive Classification*, London, Cohen-West. Translated by R. Needham.

ELLEN, R. F. (1979), 'Omniscience and Ignorance: Variation in Nuaulu Knowledge, Identification and Classification of Animals', *Language and Society*, 8: 337—64.

ENDICOTT, K. L. (1979), 'Batek Negrito Sex Roles', Canberra, Australian National University. Unpublished M.A. thesis.

ENDICOTT, K. M. (1974), 'Batek Negrito Economy and Social Organization', Cambridge, Mass., Harvard University. Unpublished doctoral thesis.

_____ (1976), 'Batek Negrito Religion', Oxford, Oxford University. Unpublished doctoral thesis.

_____ (1979), *Batek Negrito Religion*, Oxford, Clarendon Press.

EVANS, I. H. N. (1923), *Studies in Religion, Folk-Lore, and Custom in British North Borneo and the Malay Peninsula*, Cambridge, Cambridge University Press.

_____ (1927), *Papers on·the Ethnology and Archaeology of the Malay Peninsula*, Cambridge, Cambridge University Press.

_____ (1937), *The Negritos of Malaya*, Cambridge, Cambridge University Press.

FRIEDL, E. (1975), *Women and Men: An Anthropological View*, New York, Holt, Rinehart and Winston.

GIMLETTE, J. D. (1971), *A Dictionary of Malayan Medicine*, Kuala Lumpur, Oxford University Press.

HARRISON, J. (1974), *An Introduction to Mammals of Singapore and Malaya*, Singapore, Malayan Nature Society.

HOCART, A. M. (1954), *Social Origins*, London, Watts and Co.

HOOD, M. S. (1974), 'An Ethnographic Investigation of the Semelai of Malaysia', Oxford, Oxford University. Unpublished B.Litt. thesis.

———— (1978), 'Semelai Rituals of Curing', Oxford, Oxford University. Unpublished doctoral thesis.

HOWELL, S. (1977), 'Some Issues in the Study of Malay Aboriginal Ethnography', Oxford, Oxford University. Unpublished M.Litt. thesis.

———— (1981a), 'Rules not Words', in Indigenous Psychologies, P. Heelas and A. Lock (eds.), London, Academic Press.

———— (1981b), 'The "Che Wông" Revisited', Journal of the Malaysian Branch of the Royal Asiatic Society, LIV, Part 3: 57–69.

———— (1982), Chewong Myths and Legends, Kuala Lumpur, Malaysian Branch of the Royal Asiatic Society, Monograph No. 11.

LEENHARDT, M. (1979), Do Kamo, Chicago, The University of Chicago Press.

LÉVI-STRAUSS, C. (1966), The Savage Mind, London, Weidenfeld and Nicholson.

MEDWAY, LORD (1978), The Wild Mammals of Malaysia (Peninsular Malaysia) and Singapore, Kuala Lumpur, Oxford University Press.

MORRIS, B. (1976), 'Whither the Savage Mind? Notes on the natural Taxonomies of a Hunting and Gathering People', Man, 11: 542–57.

NEEDHAM, R. (1956), 'Ethnographic Notes on the Siwang of Central Malaya', Journal of the Malayan Branch of the Royal Asiatic Society, XXIX: 49–69.

———— (1963), 'Primitive Classification' by E. Durkheim and M. Mauss, London, Cohen-West.

———— (1974), 'Age, Category, and Descent', in Remarks and Inventions, London, Tavistock Publications.

———— (1975), 'Polythetic Classification: Convergence and Consequences', Man, 10: 349–69.

———— (1978), Primordial Characters, Charlottesville, Va., University Press of Virginia.

OGILVIE, C. S. (1940), 'The "Che Wông". A Little Known Primitive People', Malayan Nature Journal, 1: 23–5.

———— (1948), 'More of the Che Wông', Malayan Nature Journal, III: 15–27.

———— (1949), 'Che Wông Word List and Notes', Bulletin of the Raffles Museum, Series B, No. 4: 11–39.

Rivière, P. G. (1975), 'The Couvade: a Problem Reborn', *Man*, 9: 423–35.

Robarcheck, C. A. (1978), 'Frustration, Aggression, and the nonviolent Semai', *American Ethnologist*, 4: 762–79.

Schebesta, P. (1928), *Among the Forest Dwarfs of Malaya*, London, Hutchinson. Reissued, 1974, Kuala Lumpur, Oxford University Press.

Skeat, W. W. and Blagden, C. O. (1906), *Pagan Races of the Malay Peninsula*, London, Macmillan, 2 volumes.

Stewart, K. R. (1949), 'Magico-religious Beliefs and Practices in Primitive Society—a sociological interpretation of their therapeutic aspects', London, London School of Economics. Unpublished doctoral thesis.

Van Gennep, A. (1960), *The Rites of Passage*, London, Routledge and Kegan Paul. Translated from the French by M. B. Vizadren and G. I. Caffee.

Wazir-Jahan, A. K. (1981), *Ma' Bétisek Concepts of Living Things*, London, The Athlone Press, London School of Economics, Monographs on Social Sciences.

Whorf, B. L. (1956), *Language, Thought, and Reality*, Cambridge, Mass., The M.I.T. Press.

Wilkinson, R. J. (1910), *The Aboriginal Tribes*, Papers on Malay Subjects, Supplement, Kuala Lumpur, F.M.S. Government Press.

Williams-Hunt, P. D. R. (1952), *An Introduction to the Malayan Aborigines*, Kuala Lumpur, The Government Press.

Wittgenstein, L. (1953), *Philosophical Investigations*, Oxford, Basil Blackwell.

Index